PREHISTORY AND HUMAN ECOLOGY
OF THE VALLEY OF OAXACA

Kent V. Flannery and Joyce Marcus
General Editors

Volume 1   *The Use of Land and Water Resources in the Past and Present Valley of Oaxaca, Mexico*, by Anne V.T. Kirkby. Memoirs of the Museum of Anthropology, University of Michigan, No. 5. 1973.
Volume 2   *Sociopolitical Aspects of Canal Irrigation in the Valley of Oaxaca*, by Susan H. Lees. Memoirs of the Museum of Anthropology, University of Michigan, No. 6. 1973.
Volume 3   *Formative Mesoamerican Exchange Networks with Special Reference to the Valley of Oaxaca*, by Jane W. Pires-Ferreira. Memoirs of the Museum of Anthropology, University of Michigan, No. 7. 1975.
Volume 4   *Fábrica San José and Middle Formative Society in the Valley of Oaxaca*, by Robert D. Drennan. Memoirs of the Museum of Anthropology, University of Michigan, No. 8. 1976.
Volume 5   Part 1. *The Vegetational History of the Oaxaca Valley*, by C. Earle Smith, Jr. Part 2. *Zapotec Plant Knowledge: Classification, Uses and Communication*, by Ellen Messer. Memoirs of the Museum of Anthropology, University of Michigan, No. 10. 1978.
Volume 6   *Excavations at Santo Domingo Tomaltepec: Evolution of a Formative Community in the Valley of Oaxaca, Mexico*, by Michael E. Whalen. Memoirs of the Museum of Anthropology, University of Michigan, No. 12. 1981.
Volume 7   *Monte Albán's Hinterland, Part 1: The Prehispanic Settlement Patterns of the Central and Southern Parts of the Valley of Oaxaca, Mexico*, by Richard E. Blanton, Stephen Kowalewski, Gary Feinman, and Jill Appel. Memoirs of the Museum of Anthropology, University of Michigan, No. 15. 1982.
Volume 8   *Chipped Stone Tools in Formative Oaxaca, Mexico: Their Procurement, Production and Use*, by William J. Parry. Memoirs of the Museum of Anthropology, University of Michigan, No. 20. 1987.
Volume 9   *Agricultural Intensification and Prehistoric Health in the Valley of Oaxaca, Mexico*, by Denise C. Hodges. Memoirs of the Museum of Anthropology, University of Michigan, No. 22. 1989.
Volume 10 *Early Formative Pottery of the Valley of Oaxaca*, by Kent V. Flannery and Joyce Marcus, with ceramic analysis by William O. Payne. Memoirs of the Museum of Anthropology, University of Michigan, No. 27. 1994.
Volume 11 *Women's Ritual in Formative Oaxaca: Figurine-Making, Divination, Death and the Ancestors*, by Joyce Marcus. Memoirs of the Museum of Anthropology, University of Michigan, No. 33. 1998.
Volume 12 *The Sola Valley and the Monte Albán State: A Study of Zapotec Imperial Expansion*, by Andrew K. Balkansky. Memoirs of the Museum of Anthropology, University of Michigan, No. 36. 2002.
Volume 13 *Excavations at San José Mogote 1: The Household Archaeology*, by Kent V. Flannery and Joyce Marcus. Memoirs of the Museum of Anthropology, University of Michigan, No. 40. 2005.
Volume 14 *Excavations at Cerro Tilcajete: A Monte Albán II Administrative Center in the Valley of Oaxaca*, by Christina Elson. Memoirs of the Museum of Anthropology, University of Michigan, No. 42. 2007.

Related Volumes

Flannery, Kent V.
1986   *Guilá Naquitz: Archaic Foraging and Early Agriculture in Oaxaca, Mexico*. New York: Academic Press.

Flannery, Kent V., and Joyce Marcus
2003   *The Cloud People: Divergent Evolution of the Zapotec and Mixtec Civilizations*. Clinton Corners, NY: Percheron Press.

Marcus, Joyce, and Kent V. Flannery
1996   *Zapotec Civilization: How Urban Society Evolved in Mexico's Oaxaca Valley*. London: Thames and Hudson.

Frontispiece. Monte Albán, as viewed from the west side of Cerro Tilcajete's Plaza II.

Museum of Anthropology, University of Michigan
Memoirs, Number 42

PREHISTORY AND HUMAN ECOLOGY
OF THE VALLEY OF OAXACA

Kent V. Flannery and Joyce Marcus
General Editors
Volume 14

Excavations at Cerro Tilcajete
A Monte Albán II Administrative Center
in the Valley of Oaxaca

by Christina Elson

Ann Arbor, Michigan
2007

©2007 by the Regents of the University of Michigan
The Museum of Anthropology
All rights reserved

Printed in the United States of America
ISBN 978-0-915703-66-1

Cover design by Katherine Clahassey

The University of Michigan Museum of Anthropology currently publishes two monograph series: Anthropological Papers and Memoirs, as well as an electronic series in CD-ROM form. For a complete catalog, write to Museum of Anthropology Publications, 4009 Museums Building, Ann Arbor, MI 48109-1079, or see www.lsa.umich.edu/umma/

Library of Congress Cataloging-in-Publication Data

Elson, Christina M., 1969-
  Excavations at Cerro Tilcajete : a Monte Albán II administrative center in the Valley of Oaxaca / by Christina Elson.
     p. cm. -- (Prehistory and human ecology of the Valley of Oaxaca ; v. 14) (Memoirs ; no. 42)
  Includes bibliographical references.
  ISBN 978-0-915703-66-1 (alk. paper)
  1. Cerro Tilcajete Site (Mexico) 2. Monte Albán Site (Mexico) 3. Zapotec Indians--Kings and rulers. 4. Zapotec Indians--Politics and government. 5. Zapotec Indians--Antiquities. 6. Elite (Social sciences)--Mexico--Oaxaca Valley. 7. Power (Social sciences)--Mexico--Oaxaca Valley. 8. Excavations (Archaeology)--Mexico--Oaxaca Valley. 9. Social archaeology--Mexico--Oaxaca Valley. 10. Oaxaca Valley (Mexico)--Antiquities. 11. Oaxaca Valley (Mexico)--Social life and customs. I. University of Michigan. Museum of Anthropology. II. Title. III. Series.

  F1219.8.Z37E57 2007
  972'.7401--dc22

                              2007025257

The paper used in this publication meets the requirements of the ANSI Standard Z39.48-1984 (Permanence of Paper)

Contents

LIST OF TABLES, *vii*
LIST OF ILLUSTRATIONS, *viii*
INTRODUCTION TO VOLUME 14, *x*
ACKNOWLEDGMENTS, *xv*

CHAPTER 1.   AN INTRODUCTION TO ELITES AT SECONDARY CENTERS IN THE ZAPOTEC STATE, *1*
    An Overview of Cerro Tilcajete and the Early Zapotec State, *2*
    Anthropological Approaches to Defining Zapotec Elites, *5*
        Zapotec Elites As Members of Socioeconomic Groups, *5*
        Zapotec Elites as Administrators, *6*
        Zapotec Elites, Power Sharing, and Conflict, *7*
    Summary, *8*

CHAPTER 2.   ELITE BEHAVIOR IN THE EARLY ZAPOTEC STATE, *9*
    Zapotec Polities in the Sixteenth Century, *9*
        Zapotec Nobles, *10*
        Zapotec Policy-Makers, *11*
        Zapotec Priests, *13*
        Zapotec Warriors, *13*
        Zapotec Merchants, *14*
    Summary, *14*

CHAPTER 3.   THE OAXACA VALLEY IN MONTE ALBÁN II (100 B.C.–A.D. 200), *15*
    Archaeological Indicators of Elite Behavior, *15*
    The Regional Picture, *16*
        The Settlement Hierarchy, *16*
        I-Shaped Ballcourts, *20*
        Pottery Production Network, *21*
    Monte Albán, *22*
        The North Platform Governmental Palace, *22*
        The Main Plaza, *22*
        The Mound of the Carved Stone, *23*
        The Northeast Zone, *28*
        Zone East of Building P, *28*
        The El Pitahayo Mounds, *28*
        Mounds and Terraces on the North Slope, *31*
        Summary, *31*
    San José Mogote, *32*
    Dainzú, *33*
    Regions Outside the Valley, *33*
        The Cuicatlán Cañada, *33*
        Ejutla, *35*
    Summary, *35*

CHAPTER 4. CERRO TILCAJETE DURING MONTE ALBÁN II (100 B.C.–A.D. 200), *37*
    The Surface Data, *37*
        Site Layout and Occupational History, *37*
        Surface Ceramics as Possible Clues to Status, *45*
        Other Materials from the Surface, *47*
        Summary, *47*
    Excavation Data, *47*
    Temples and Civic-Ceremonial Buildings, *47*
        Structure 2, *47*
        Mound E, *49*
    Residential Excavations, *51*
        Structure 1, *51*
        Structure 3, *51*
        Structure 4, *56*
    Pottery Types Believed to Reflect Status, *61*
        Ceramic Types and Forms Found in Residences, *65*
        Ceramic Types and Forms Found in Middens, *66*
        Subsistence Activities, *66*
    Household Ritual, *75*
        Figurines and Urns, *75*
        Incense Burners, *76*
        Mortuary Ritual, *78*
    Obsidian, *78*
    Shell, *79*
    Summary, *79*

CHAPTER 5. CERRO TILCAJETE AND THE DECLINE OF THE ZAPOTEC STATE, *81*
    Monte Albán, *81*
    The Oaxaca Valley in the Classic Period, *83*
    The Chronology of the Late Classic and Epiclassic, *83*
    Jalieza, *84*
    Cerro Tilcajete, *86*
        The Adoratory and Mound F at Cerro Tilcajete, *86*
        The North Mound Complex, *88*
        Structure 5 Ceramics, *92*
    Summary, *92*

CHAPTER 6. CONCLUSIONS, *95*

APPENDIX A. CERAMIC TERMS, ANALYSIS, AND ILLUSTRATIONS, *99*
APPENDIX B. HUMAN REMAINS FROM SURFACE COLLECTIONS AND FEATURES IN STRUCTURES AT CERRO TILCAJETE, *by William Duncan, 119*
APPENDIX C. THE SHELL ASSEMBLAGE FROM CERRO TILCAJETE, *by Gary M. Feinman and Linda M. Nicholas, 121*
APPENDIX D. RESUMEN EN CASTELLANO, *by Christina Elson, 125*

BIBLIOGRAPHY, *131*

Tables

3.1. Settlement hierarchy and population ranges for Late Monte Albán I and Monte Albán II sites in the Valle Grande-Ocotlán, *18*

4.1. Mound and plaza dimensions at Cerro Tilcajete, *40*
4.2a. Surface data from Cerro Tilcajete by collection unit: units 130-148, *41*
4.2b. Surface data from Cerro Tilcajete by collection unit: units 149-166, *42*
4.2c. Surface data from Cerro Tilcajete by collection unit: units 167-176, *43*
4.3. Surface data by collection unit (non-vessels), *44*
4.4. Surface ceramic categories by zone at Cerro Tilcajete, *45*
4.5. Ceramics coded in Test Pit 1, Mound E, Cerro Tilcajete, *51*
4.6. Offerings with Structure 4 burials at Cerro Tilcajete, *59*
4.7. Ceramics in residential structures by paste, diagnostic form, and type, *66*
4.8. Ceramics in residential structures, by vessel form, *67*
4.9. Minimum number of vessels in Feature 1, Structure 3, Cerro Tilcajete, *71*
4.10. Minimum number of vessels in Feature 6, Structure 4, Cerro Tilcajete, *73*
4.11. Minimum number of vessels in Feature 2, Structure 4, Cerro Tilcajete, *74*
4.12. Ceramics by weight and number in Feature 2, Structure 4, Cerro Tilcajete, *75*
4.13. Figurines and urns in residential excavations at Cerro Tilcajete, *77*
4.14. Obsidian in Structures 1-4, Cerro Tilcajete, *78*

5.1. Paste and weight of sherds in Feature 2, Mound E, Cerro Tilcajete, *92*
5.2. Diagnostic rim and bowl base sherds in Feature 2, Mound E (by type), *93*

A1. Data on G.12 motifs and rim forms from residential structures at Cerro Tilcajete, *108*
A2. Diagnostic elements of G.29 vessels in residential structures, *109*
A3. Diagnostic aspects of orange-paste ceramics, *111*
A4. All cream-paste rim forms coded in Structures 1, 3, and 4, *115*
A5. Motifs on C.11 and C.12 vessels, *115*
A6. The frequency of cream-paste types of all decorated cream vessels coded, *115*

C1. Shell found in surface collection units at Cerro Tilcajete, *122*
C2. Shell in excavations by excavation area and genus, *123*
C3. Shell in excavations by excavation area and ornament class, *123*
C4. Shell in excavations at Cerro Tilcajete by object and genus, *123*
C5. Shell in excavations at Cerro Tilcajete by ornament type and genus, *124*

Illustrations

Frontispiece. Monte Albán, as viewed from the west side of Cerro Tilcajete's Plaza II.

1.1. Central Mexico, showing location of Oaxaca Valley, Sola de Vega, and Cuicatlán Cañada, *2*
1.2. The Oaxaca Valley, showing classes of agricultural land and places mentioned in text, *3*
1.3. Photo of Cerro Tilcajete as viewed from an adjoining hilltop to the south, *5*

2.1. Formative Period gray-paste ceramic bottle depicting *Cociyo*, *10*
2.2. Plan of Yagul's ceremonial core, *12*

3.1. Plan of Cerro Tilcajete showing residential terraces and mound groups, *17*
3.2. The Monte Albán II settlement hierarchy in the Oaxaca Valley, *19*
3.3. The I-shaped ballcourt at Monte Albán, *20*
3.4. Cream-paste bowl with bulbous supports found in Tomb 77 at Monte Albán, *21*
3.5. Orange-paste bowl with red-painted designs; found at Cerro Tilcajete, *21*
3.6. Plan of Monte Albán's ceremonial core, *24*
3.7. A detailed view of buildings on the North Platform at Monte Albán, *25*
3.8. Three ceramic statues from Tomb 113, a Monte Albán II tomb at Monte Albán, *26*
3.9. An urn, showing a noble lord, from the antechamber of Tomb 104 at Monte Albán, *27*
3.10. Plan of the El Pitahayo mound group at Monte Albán, *29*
3.11. Plan of Tombs 77 and 78 in the El Pitahayo mound group at Monte Albán, *29*
3.12. Plan of Tombs 95 and 96 in the El Pitahayo mound group at Monte Albán, *30*
3.13. Map of San José Mogote, *32*
3.14. Map of Dainzú's ceremonial core, *34*

4.1. Topographic map of a section of the Ocotlán subregion showing the relationship between the subregional capitals, *38*
4.2. Plan of Cerro Tilcajete showing the location of surface collections, *39*
4.3. Map showing the frequency of cream-paste ceramics across the surface of Cerro Tilcajete, *46*
4.4. Plan of Structure 2, Mound B, a two-room temple, *48*
4.5. Profile of the east wall of Mound B, supporting Structure 2, a two-room temple, *49*
4.6. Profile of the west wall of Mound B, supporting Structure 2, a two-room temple, *50*
4.7. Plan of the Monte Albán II phase structures on Mound E, *50*
4.8. Plan of Structure 1, Mound A, a residential palace, *52*
4.9. Plan of the south wall of Structure 1, *53*
4.10. Photo of the south wall of Structure 1, showing plastered adobe pedestal, *53*
4.11. Photo of the southeast corner of Structure 1, showing plastered adobe, *54*
4.12. Modeled gray-paste ceramic ornament showing a deceased individual, *54*
4.13. Plan of Structure 3, Area C, a residential palace, *55*
4.14. North profile of Structure 3, Area C, *56*
4.15. West profile of Structure 3, Area C, *57*
4.16. West profile of Feature 1, Structure 3, *57*
4.17. Plan of Feature 1, Structure 3, Area C, *57*
4.18. Plan of Structure 4, a lower-status residence, *58*

4.19. Photo of Burial 2, Structure 4, *59*
4.20. Gray-paste turkey figurine, Burial 1, Structure 4, *60*
4.21. Orange-paste figurine of a person with an elaborate headdress, *60*
4.22. Orange-paste figure of a man with an elaborate headdress and walking stick, *61*
4.23. Photo of Burial 4, Structure 4, *62*
4.24. Gray-paste figure, Burial 4, Structure 4, *62*
4.25. Café-paste bowl with a pinched ovate rim and incised step-fret motif, *63*
4.26. Photo of Feature 2, Structure 4, a storage room, *63*
4.27. Photo of Feature 4, a hearth in Structure 4, *64*
4.28. Fragments from stuccoed and painted vessels, *65*
4.29. Rim forms of vases with lids recovered at Cerro Tilcajete, *67*
4.30a. Rim forms of serving bowls recovered at Cerro Tilcajete, *68*
4.30b. Rim forms of serving vessels recovered at Cerro Tilcajete, *69*
4.31. Rim forms of cooking/storage wares recovered at Cerro Tilcajete, *70*
4.32. Examples of figurines found in residential excavations at Cerro Tilcajete, *76*
4.33. Incense burner fragments from Cerro Tilcajete, *77*

5.1. The Tomb 105 residence at Monte Albán, *82*
5.2. The Oaxaca Valley showing major Classic and Epiclassic sites, *84*
5.3. Photo of the Early Classic Jalieza site, *85*
5.4. Photo looking west along the ridge line supporting the ceremonial core of the Late Classic-Epiclassic Jalieza site, *86*
5.5. Schematic plan of the post A.D. 500 layout of Plaza I, *87*
5.6. The Plaza I adoratory platform associated with Mound H, Plaza I's eastern mound, *87*
5.7. A bifacially flaked chert knife found on the adoratory, Plaza I, *88*
5.8. Photo of Structure 5, Mound E, a civic-ceremonial structure, *89*
5.9. Plan of Structure 5, Mound E, a civic-ceremonial structure, *90*
5.10. Plan of the looted Monte Albán IIIb-IV tomb in Mound F, Plaza I, *91*
5.11. Stylized G.35 vessel forms found in Feature 2, Mound E, *94*

A1. Examples of G.12 bowl base decoration found on vessels at Cerro Tilcajete, *101*
A2. Examples of G.12 rim forms and rim decoration, *102*
A3. Examples of G.21 bowl base decoration found on vessels at Cerro Tilcajete, *102*
A4. G.12 bowl base motifs, *103*
A5. G.12 rim motifs, *104*
A6. Examples of G.15, G.16, G.25, and G.26 rim forms and vessel decoration, *105*
A7. Examples of G.34 jars from Cerro Tilcajete, *106*
A8. Examples of G.29 rim and base forms and vessel decoration, *107*
A9. Examples of A.9 rim form and vessel decoration from Cerro Tilcajete, *110*
A10. Examples of A.11 rim form and vessel decoration from Cerro Tilcajete, *111*
A11. K.17 vessels with incised motifs, *112*
A12. Motifs found on C.11, C.12, and K.17 vessels, *113*
A13. Photo of C.7 and C.11 sherds found at Cerro Tilcajete, *114*
A14. Examples of C.7 and C.11 rim form and vessel decoration, *116*
A15. Examples of C.12 and C.20 rim form and vessel decoration, *117*

An Introduction to Volume 14 of the Series

by Kent V. Flannery and Joyce Marcus

This volume—the fourteenth in our series of monographs on the prehistory and human ecology of the Valley of Oaxaca—deals with Cerro Tilcajete, a secondary administrative center below Monte Albán, the capital of the prehispanic Zapotec state.

To put Christina Elson's excavations at this secondary center into perspective, let us review what we have recently learned about Monte Albán and its relationships with other sites in the Valley of Oaxaca. To be sure, our knowledge of Monte Albán's relations with areas *outside* the Valley of Oaxaca has also expanded during the last decade, and interested readers will want to consult those contributions as well (e.g., Balkansky 1998, 2002; Feinman and Nicholas 1990, 1993; Spencer 1998, 2006; Spencer and Redmond 1997, 2001a).

The Valley of Oaxaca has been the scene of extensive archaeological fieldwork throughout the twentieth century and into the twenty-first. Impressive early excavations were conducted at the city of Monte Albán, situated on the top of a mountain 400 meters above the valley floor (e.g., Caso 1932, 1933, 1935, 1938, 1942; Bernal 1946, 1949; Acosta 1958-1959, 1965, 1974). The excavation team of Alfonso Caso, Ignacio Bernal, and Jorge Acosta worked there throughout the 1930s and 1940s, expanding on the pioneering work of Leopoldo Batres (1902) at the beginning of the twentieth century.

These excavations laid the foundation for all the work that has followed. We owe a major debt to Caso, Bernal, and Acosta (1967) because their deep stratigraphic excavations established a well-defined ceramic chronology of five periods—Monte Albán I, II, IIIa, IIIb/IV, and V—which allowed subsequent generations of archaeologists to focus on questions of social and political change.

Three of the major questions were—How did Monte Albán gain control over the Valley of Oaxaca? When did each part of the Valley of Oaxaca come under the sway of the capital? Did Monte Albán establish new centers, or take over extant centers, to administer the various regions of the valley?

Current evidence suggests that Monte Albán was founded mainly by the former inhabitants of San José Mogote and its satellite communities in the northern (Etla) subvalley (Marcus and Flannery 1996). It is no surprise, therefore, that when it came time for Monte Albán to establish a regional administrative center for the Etla subvalley during Monte Albán II, it chose to put that center atop the earlier site of San José Mogote (Flannery and Marcus 1983:111-13; Marcus 1999; Marcus and Flannery 2004). Comparable Period II centers are known from other subvalleys, but until recently their history was not known in the detail of San José Mogote.

The Oaxaca Settlement Pattern Project (Blanton et al. 1982; Kowalewski et al. 1989) identified San Martín Tilcajete in the southern (Zimatlán-Ocotlán) subvalley as the second largest pre-Monte Albán site in the valley (San José Mogote being the largest). In 1993, Charles Spencer and Elsa Redmond began intensive surface pickup and mapping at three related archaeological sites near San Martín Tilcajete—SMT-11a, SMT-11b, and SMT-23. In subsequent seasons, Spencer and Redmond excavated extensively at two of these three sites, SMT-11a ("El Mogote") and SMT-11b ("El Palenque") (Spencer and Redmond 2001b, 2003, 2004a, 2004b, 2004c, 2005, 2006). Christina Elson took on the task of excavating the third site, SMT-23 or "Cerro Tilcajete" (Elson 2003).

Spencer and Redmond's excavations indicated that the El Mogote site (SMT-11a) had not participated in the founding of Monte Albán, but instead had behaved like a political rival. Instead of losing population during Early Monte Albán I (= Period Ia), as San José Mogote had, El Mogote doubled its size to 52.8 hectares, and created a ceremonial plaza oriented 25° east of true north, providing a defiant contrast to the true north-south orientation of Monte Albán's main plaza. At the end of Period Ia, El Mogote's main plaza was abandoned in a conflagration, almost certainly the result of a raid by Monte Albán (see Beckmann et al. 2002; Redmond and Spencer 2006; Spencer in press *a*, in press *b*; Spencer and Redmond 2001b, 2003, 2004a-c, 2005, 2006).

Spencer and Redmond's research has further documented the Tilcajete polity's resistance to Monte Albán's attempt to take over its region. During Late Monte Albán I (= Period Ic), El Mogote's population moved uphill to a more defensible location at the El Palenque site (SMT-11b) and built a new ceremonial plaza with the same orientation as El Mogote's. It also added defensive walls. Throughout Period Ic, Monte Albán seems to have denied El Palenque full access to the luxury pottery and imported obsidian that it made available to other communities that were its allies.

The rivalry between Monte Albán and the Tilcajete polity continued for centuries until a final attack by Monte Albán, during the first century B.C., left the palace and major temples at El Palenque destroyed by fire (Spencer 1999, 2003; Spencer and Redmond 2001b). This time, Tilcajete did not recover. Victorious Monte Albán then turned to a mountain overlooking the burned El Palenque site and created an administrative center for the Ocotlán region.

This new Monte Albán II mountaintop administrative center, Cerro Tilcajete (SMT-23), is the subject of this Memoir. Elson excavated there for three seasons (1999-2001) and showed that, in contrast to San José Mogote (Marcus and Flannery 1996), Cerro Tilcajete was a newly created regional center rather than a reoccupied earlier site.

One goal of Elson's excavations was to document the nature of Cerro Tilcajete's ties to Monte Albán, especially the links between the elite families at the capital and those at Cerro Tilcajete. By Period II, the site of Monte Albán had become the capital of a fully developed state and had begun to solidify its core region, investing in the administration of the area within one to two days' travel of the capital (Marcus 1992; Spencer 1998).

Elson's work moves us away from our usual top-down, capital-centric Monte Albán focus, and in so doing, gives us new insights into secondary administrative centers in a pristine state. For more than 100 years, archaeologists have speculated about Monte Albán's impact on the rest of its valley (Bernal 1967, 1989; Bernal and Oliveros 1988; Marcus and Flannery 1996; Marcus 1983:113-15; Paddock 1966, 1983), and with this study some of their questions are answered. We can now see that Monte Albán brought different subvalleys under its control gradually, using a variety of strategies. We believe that the future excavation of second-tier centers in other parts of the valley would continue to open up new avenues for understanding first-generation states.

Bibliography

Acosta, Jorge R.
1958-59   Exploraciones arqueológicas en Monte Albán, XVIII temporada. *Revista Mexicana de Estudios Antropológicos* 15:7-50.
1965   Preclassic and classic architecture of Oaxaca. In *Handbook of Middle American Indians*, vol. 3, edited by Robert Wauchope and Gordon R. Willey, pp. 814-36. Austin: University of Texas Press.
1974   Informe de la XIV temporada de exploraciones en la zona arqueológica de Monte Albán, 1945-1946. *Cultura y Sociedad* 1(2):69-82.

Balkansky, Andrew K.
1998   Urbanism and early state formation in the Huamelulpan Valley of southern Mexico. *Latin American Antiquity* 9:37-67.
2002   *The Sola Valley and the Monte Albán State: A study of Zapotec Imperial Expansion*. Memoirs, no. 36. Museum of Anthropology, University of Michigan. Ann Arbor.

Batres, Leopoldo
1902   *Exploraciones en Monte Albán*. México: Inspección y Conservación de la República Mexicana, Calle Gante.

Beckmann, Jennifer, Charles S. Spencer, and Elsa M. Redmond
2002   *Early State Development at San Martín Tilcajete*. New York: American Museum of Natural History. http://anthro.amnh.org.

Bernal, Ignacio
1946   *La cerámica preclásica de Monte Albán*. Master's thesis, Escuela Nacional de Antropología e Historia, México.
1949   *La cerámica de Monte Albán IIIa*. Doctoral dissertation, Universidad Nacional Autónoma de México, México.
1967   *Excavaciones en Dainzú*. Boletín del Instituto Nacional de Antropología e Historia 27, pp. 7-13. México.
1989   *Official Guide. Oaxaca Valley*. Instituto Nacional de Antropología e Historia. México: Salvat.

Bernal, Ignacio, and Arturo Oliveros
1988   *Excavaciones Arqueológicas en Dainzú, Oaxaca*. México: Instituto Nacional de Antropología e Historia.

Blanton, Richard E., Stephen A. Kowalewski, Gary M. Feinman, and Jill Appel
1982   *Monte Albán's Hinterland, Part I: Prehispanic Settlement Patterns of the Central and Southern Parts of the Valley of Oaxaca, Mexico*. Memoirs, no. 15. Museum of Anthropology, University of Michigan. Ann Arbor.

Caso, Alfonso
1932   *Las exploraciones en Monte Albán, temporada 1931-1932*. Instituto Panamericano de Geografía e Historia, Publicación 7. México.
1933   *Las tumbas de Monte Albán*. Anales del Museo Nacional de Arqueología, Historia y Etnografía, Tomo VIII, pp. 641-47. México.
1935   *Las exploraciones en Monte Albán, temporada 1934-1935*. Instituto Panamericano de Geografía e Historia, Publicación 18. México.
1938   *Las exploraciones en Oaxaca, quinta y sexta temporadas, 1936-1937*. Instituto Panamericano de Geografía e Historia, Publicación 34. México.
1942   *Resumen del informe de las exploraciones en Oaxaca, durante la 7^a y la 8ª temporadas 1937-1938 y 1938-1939*. Vigesimoséptimo Congreso Internacional de Americanistas, Actas de la Primera Sesión, Celebrada en La Ciudad de México en 1939, tomo 2, pp. 159-87. México: Secretaria de Educación Pública, Instituto Nacional de Antropología e Historia.

Caso, Alfonso, Ignacio Bernal, and Jorge R. Acosta
1967 *La Cerámica de Monte Albán*. Memorias del Instituto Nacional de Antropología e Historia, no. 13. México, D.F.

Elson, Christina M.
2003 Cerro Tilcajete: un centro secundario del estado zapoteco temprano (100 a.C.-200 d.C.). *Arqueología* 31:5-24.

Feinman, Gary M., and Linda M. Nicholas
1990 At the margins of the Monte Albán state: settlement patterns in the Ejutla Valley, Oaxaca, Mexico. *Latin American Antiquity* 1:216-46.
1993 Shell ornament production in Ejutla: implications for highland-coastal interaction in ancient Oaxaca. *Ancient Mesoamerica* 4:103-19.

Flannery, Kent V., and Joyce Marcus
1983 San José Mogote in Monte Albán II: a secondary administrative center. In *The Cloud People: Divergent Evolution of the Zapotec and Mixtec Civilizations*, edited by Kent V. Flannery and Joyce Marcus, pp. 111-13. New York: Academic Press.

Kowalewski, Stephen A., Gary M. Feinman, Laura Finsten, Richard E. Blanton, and Linda M. Nicholas
1989 *Monte Albán's Hinterland, Part II: Prehispanic Settlement Patterns in Tlacolula, Etla, and Ocotlán, the Valley of Oaxaca*. Memoirs, no. 23. Museum of Anthropology, University of Michigan. Ann Arbor.

Marcus, Joyce
1983 Monte Albán II in the Macuilxochitl area. In *The Cloud People: Divergent Evolution of the Zapotec and Mixtec Civilizations*, edited by Kent V. Flannery and Joyce Marcus, pp. 113-15. New York: Academic Press.
1992 Dynamic cycles of Mesoamerican states. *National Geographic Research and Exploration* 8:392-411.
1999 Early architecture in the Valley of Oaxaca: 1350 B.C.-A.D. 500. In *Mesoamerican Architecture as a Cultural Symbol*, edited by Jeff Karl Kowalski, pp. 58-75. Oxford: Oxford University Press.

Marcus, Joyce, and Kent V. Flannery
1996 *Zapotec Civilization: How Urban Society Evolved in Mexico's Oaxaca Valley*. New York and London: Thames and Hudson.
2004 The coevolution of ritual and society: new ^{14}C dates from ancient Mexico. *Proceedings of the National Academy of Sciences* 101:18257-61.

Paddock, John
1966 *Ancient Oaxaca*. Stanford, CA: Stanford University Press.
1983 Monte Albán II in the Yagul-Caballito Blanco area. In *The Cloud People: Divergent Evolution of the Zapotec and Mixtec Civilizations*, edited by Kent V. Flannery and Joyce Marcus, pp. 115-17. New York: Academic Press.

Redmond, Elsa M., and Charles S. Spencer
2006 From raiding to conquest: warfare strategies and early state development in Oaxaca, Mexico. In *The Archaeology of Warfare: Prehistories of Raiding and Conquest*, edited by Elizabeth N. Arkush and Mark W. Allen, pp. 336-93. Gainesville: University of Florida Press.

Spencer, Charles S.
1998 A mathematical model of primary state formation. *Cultural Dynamics* 10:5-20.
1999 Palatial digs. *Natural History* 108(2):94-95.
2003 War and early state formation in Oaxaca, Mexico. *Proceedings of the National Academy of Sciences* 100(20):11185-87.

2006   Modeling (and measuring) expansionism and resistance: state formation in ancient Oaxaca, Mexico. In *History and Mathematics: Historical Dynamics and Development of Complex Societies*, edited by Peter Turchin, Leonid Grinin, Andrey Korotayev, and Victor C. de Munck, pp. 170-92. Moscow: Russian State University for the Humanities.

in press *a*   Territorial expansion and primary state formation in Oaxaca, Mexico. In *Latin American Indigenous Warfare and Ritual Violence*, edited by Richard Chacon and Ruben Mendoza. Tucson: University of Arizona Press.

in press *b*   Testing the morphogenesist model of primary state formation: the Zapotec case. In *Macroevolution in Human Prehistory*, edited by Anna Prentiss, Ian Kuijt, and James C. Chatters. Salt Lake City: University of Utah Press.

Spencer, Charles S., and Elsa M. Redmond

1997   *Archaeology of the Cañada de Cuicatlán, Oaxaca*. American Museum of Natural History, Anthropological Papers 80. New York.

2001a   The chronology of conquest: implications of new radiocarbon analyses from the Cañada de Cuicatlán, Oaxaca. *Latin American Antiquity* 12:182-202.

2001b   Multilevel selection and political evolution in the Valley of Oaxaca, 500-100 B.C. *Journal of Anthropological Archaeology* 20:195-229.

2003   Militarism, resistance, and early state development in Oaxaca, Mexico. *Social Evolution and History* 2(1):25-70.

2004a   Conquest warfare, strategies of resistance, and the rise of the Zapotec early state. In *The Early State: Its Alternatives and Analogues*, edited by Leonid E. Grinin, Robert L. Carneiro, Dmitri M. Bondarenko, Nikolai N. Kradin, and Andrey V. Korotayev, pp. 220-61. Moscow: Uchitel Publishing House.

2004b   Primary state formation in Mesoamerica. *Annual Review of Anthropology* 33:173-99.

2004c   A Late Monte Albán I phase (300-100 B.C.) palace in the Valley of Oaxaca. *Latin American Antiquity* 15:441-55.

2005   Institutional development in Late Formative Oaxaca: the view from San Martín Tilcajete. In *New Perspectives on Formative Mesoamerican Cultures*, edited by Terry G. Powis, pp. 171-82. British Archaeological Reports, International Series 1377. Oxford, UK: Archaeopress.

2006   Resistance strategies and early state formation in Oaxaca, Mexico. In *Intermediate Elites in Precolumbian States and Empires*, edited by Christina Elson and R. Alan Covey, pp. 21-43. Tucson: University of Arizona Press.

Acknowledgments

My excavations at Cerro Tilcajete began in 1999. Several years earlier, in 1994, Charles Spencer and Elsa Redmond had mapped the site and made intensive surface collections. I am indebted to them not only for encouraging me to work at Cerro Tilcajete, but also for graciously providing me with their site map and surface collections to analyze. In all, I excavated for three seasons and conducted two seasons of analysis. Although the analysis continues, this Memoir seeks to provide the most important results of my research thus far, in terms of the site's chronology, architecture, and material remains.

The National Science Foundation, the Foundation for the Advancement of Mesoamerican Research, Inc., the University of Michigan, and the American Museum of Natural History funded the project. In Oaxaca, I thank the National Institute of Anthropology, its director Eduardo López Calzada, and its representatives Marcus Winter and Cira Martínez López for assistance. At Cerro Tilcajete, Luca Casparis and Michelle Crossier expertly directed some excavation units. Many skilled workmen from the municipality of San Martín Tilcajete climbed more than 100 m to the site each day and worked carefully to uncover the structures and features.

Since completing work at Cerro Tilcajete, Luca Casparis and I have gone on to work at Jalieza, the successor to the Tilcajete site. In Luca I am lucky to have a great co-director with whom I can plan to work for the many years it will take to sort out the long-term processes affecting Ocotlán after 100 B.C.

Heartfelt acknowledgments must go to the many people who helped me get to, and get through, graduate school. I consider myself lucky to have had a series of committed professors, including Gabriela Uruñuela, Patricia Plunket, William Parry, Gregory Johnson, Jeffrey Parsons, Robert Whallon, John O'Shea, Conrad Kottak, and David Frye. Graduate school was made less of an ordeal by studying with an amazing cohort made up of Kamyar Abdi, Alan Covey, Patrick Livingood, and Jason Sherman. Alan Covey worked with me at Cerro Tilcajete, helped me code thousands of sherds, and listened patiently and supportively to a million little complaints all while completing his own dissertation work in Peru. Alan and I defended our dissertations on the same day and I am as proud of his work and accomplishments as he is of mine. While being a young academic can be hard, having four truly outstanding advisors—Charles Spencer, Elsa Redmond, Kent Flannery, and Joyce Marcus—who time and time again offered enthusiastic support and encouragement made the work more worthwhile.

The realm of moral support belongs to my family—James, Sue, Elizabeth, and Scott Elson—who think archaeology and archaeologists are pretty odd but are firm believers in doing what one likes. Finally, I want to thank my husband Kevin, who has kept me grounded and my priorities in order while somehow managing to get me to focus all my efforts on writing this monograph.

Chapter 1

An Introduction to Elites at Secondary Centers in the Zapotec State

Just over 2000 years ago, the first states formed in Mexico. One of those polities, the Zapotec state, emerged in the modern state of Oaxaca and was centered in the Valley of Oaxaca (Figs. 1.1-1.2). The valley, almost completely enclosed by mountain ranges, has roughly 1400 km² of bottom land, and its three subregions form a distinctive Y-shape. The valley sits at an elevation of about 1500 m above sea level (masl) and receives 600-800 mm of rain a year, creating a generally warm, almost frost-free climate with little seasonal variation. Because of Oaxaca's marked topographical variation, however, small nearby valleys can have elevations of 500 masl and hot, tropical climates, or elevations of over 2000 masl and cold, mountainous climates (Kowalewski et al. 1989:8).

The Zapotec capital, Monte Albán, was founded circa 500 B.C. Archaeologists still debate whether state-level society emerged during the Middle Formative or Early Monte Albán I period (500-300 B.C.) or not until the Late Formative or Late Monte Albán I period (300-100 B.C.), when the first palace and two-room state temple appeared. Notwithstanding this debate, it is increasingly clear that the process of state formation in Oaxaca fits general patterns noted worldwide regarding the dynamics of state formation and expansion (e.g., Marcus 1998; Spencer 1998). These dynamics include (1) the use of warfare and coercion, and (2) the fact that early in their territorial expansion, states may campaign against weaker polities located farther from the core if there are polities nearby initially able to withstand aggression (Flannery and Marcus 2003; Marcus 1992a; see also Carneiro 1970, 1981; Covey 2006; Fash 1991; Flannery 1999; Hodge 1996; Scullard 1980; Spencer 1998).

During its early expansion, Monte Albán conquered and incorporated the ethnically and geographically distinct Cuicatlán Cañada at roughly 300 B.C., but was not able to defeat a rival polity, El Palenque (SMT-11b), located at Tilcajete *within* the Valley of Oaxaca, until circa 100 B.C. (Redmond 1983; Spencer 1982; Spencer and Redmond 1997, 2001a, 2001b, 2004). More research needs to be done in the eastern or Tlacolula subregion to examine when it was brought under Monte Albán's control, but it is likely that it also occurred by 100 B.C. (Marcus 1983a). These recent data suggest that the valley was not unified into one overarching political system until some 200 to 400 years after Monte Albán was initially founded.

The present study presents detailed information on excavations at Cerro Tilcajete (SMT-23), a secondary administrative center founded in Ocotlán after its incorporation into the Monte Albán state circa 100 B.C. Cerro Tilcajete was founded at the onset of Monte Albán II (100 B.C.-A.D. 200). Research at Cerro Tilcajete, in conjunction with work at Monte Albán and the valley's other subregional centers, allows for the creation of a more nuanced picture of Monte Albán II. Given that Zapotec state formation was at least initially somewhat *ad hoc*, we should consider whether or not its political expansion was regular or standardized. If, as Marcus (1992a) has suggested, after an initial period of outward growth, states tend to invest in more intensive administrative strategies for the core region near the capital, then they may also invest in standardizing their administrative structure. One goal of this monograph is to show that during Monte Albán II we find not only territorial growth, but also growth in the hierarchical organization of the state. Initially, Monte Albán's governmental policies probably were opportunistic and developed out of interactions between the capital and compliant and non-compliant subregional populations. During Monte Albán II, we see an attempt by Monte Albán's rulers, as evidenced in

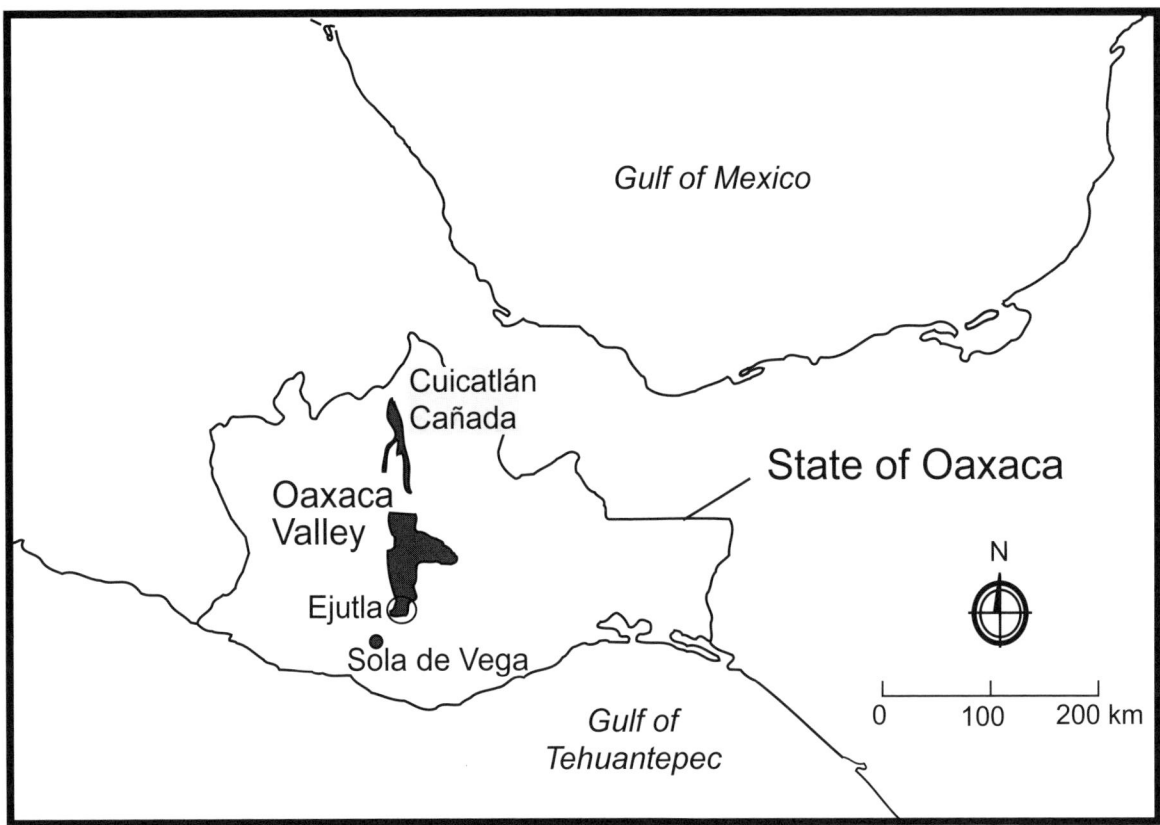

Figure 1.1. Central Mexico, showing the location of the Oaxaca Valley. Sola de Vega, and the Cuicatlán Cañada were controlled by the Zapotec during Monte Albán II.

the built environment of secondary centers, to create particular kinds of ceremonial environments that mirror the relationships between the local and the capital elite.

To examine the social and political dynamics of the Zapotec state as it existed during Monte Albán II, I will both look at regional and site-specific data and call upon ethnohistoric data collected by the Catholic priests and Spanish officials who documented sixteenth-century Zapotec society. This strategy follows suggestions by Marcus and Flannery (1996:158, 208) who have proposed that after 100 B.C., Zapotec culture shows strong cultural continuity in language, religion, and social structure, as indicated by material culture, writing systems, and architecture. This allows archaeologists to use the direct historical approach (see Ritchie 1938; Strong 1933; Wedel 1938) and consider historic data in interpreting many aspects of prehistoric Zapotec culture.

However, because the sixteenth-century Oaxaca Valley was composed of many small, balkanized polities that were not necessarily united into a valley-wide state, ethnohistoric approaches may provide less success at describing the kinds of hierarchical relationships that developed between elite families at the capital and those at second-order centers. Therefore, I will consider more general social and anthropological theory that sheds light on intra-elite relationships in pre-modern states.

An Overview of Cerro Tilcajete and the Early Zapotec State

The Valley of Oaxaca has been the focus of many research projects. Systematic archaeological excavation at Monte Albán began in the 1930s under the direction of Alfonso Caso. The early phases of this work uncovered the remains of many buildings ringing the Main Plaza, defined key traits of Zapotec culture, and produced a ceramic chronology (Acosta n.d., 1958, 1965, 1974, 1976; Bernal 1949; Caso 1932, 1933, 1935, 1938, 1942, 1947, 1967; Caso and Bernal 1952; Caso et al. 1967). Caso and his colleagues proposed that the city was founded about 500 B.C. (Caso et al. 1967:267).

A second major research project conducted at Monte Albán was "The Monte Albán Settlement Pattern Project" directed by

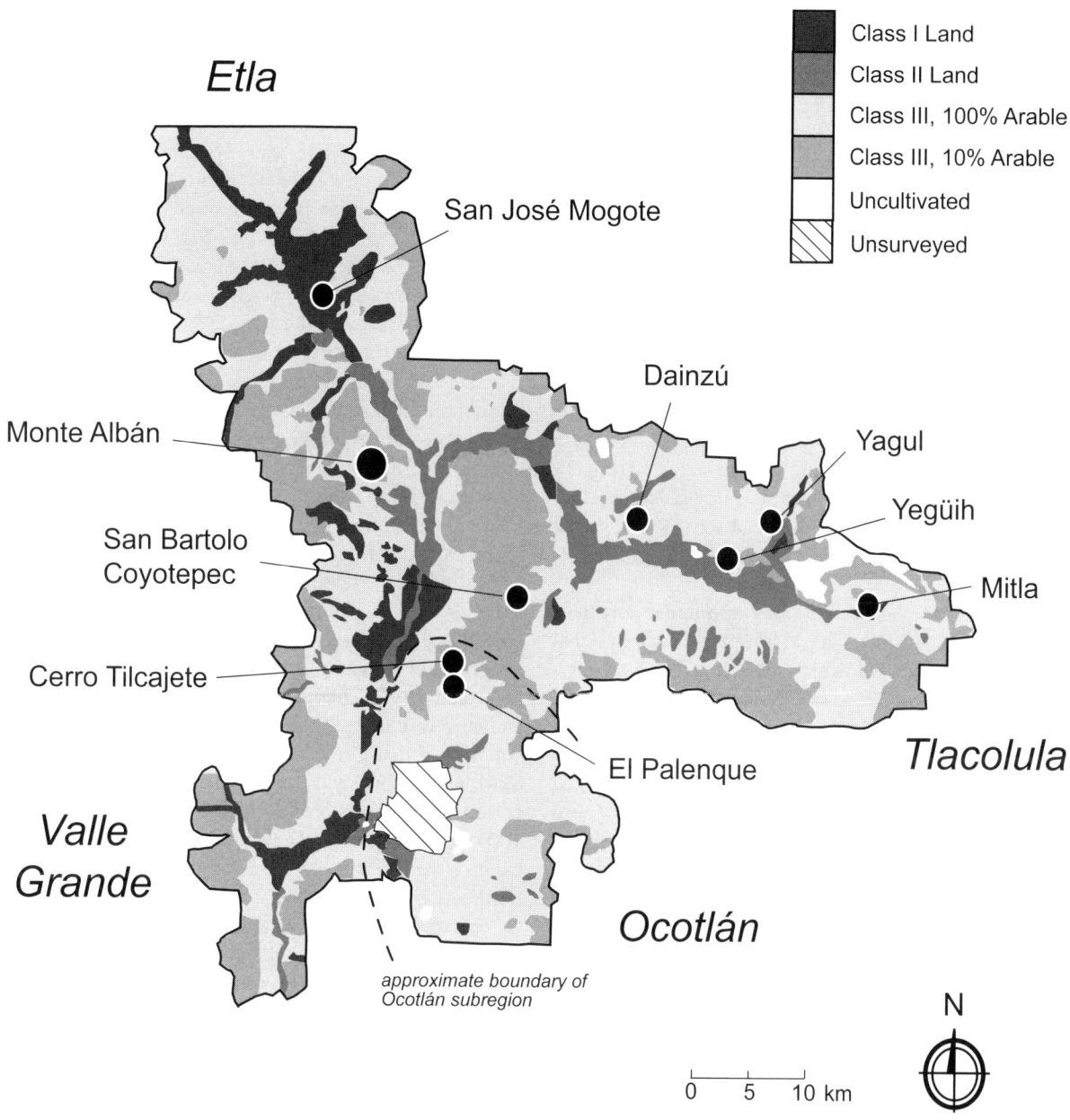

Figure 1.2. The Oaxaca Valley, showing classes of agricultural land and places mentioned in the text (agricultural land-use map adapted from Marcus and Flannery 1996).

Richard Blanton (1978). The goal of this project was to map and surface collect the city completely. Blanton's work defined the spatial extent of the city during different time periods. Most recently, Marcus Winter has directed archaeological investigations at Monte Albán as part of the "Proyecto Especial Monte Albán," funded by the Mexican government. This project has provided new data on architecture and material culture (Martínez López 1998; Martínez López et al. 2000; Martínez López and Winter 1994; Winter 1994a, 1994b, 1995).

Blanton suggests that during its initial occupation, the Early Monte Albán I period (500-300 B.C.), Monte Albán had a population of approximately 5000. At the onset of Monte Albán II, the capital was a city of more than 14,000 people. During Monte Albán IIIa (A.D. 200-500), the population might have reached 16,500 and by Monte Albán IIIb (A.D. 500-700), perhaps 24,000. Around this time, however, the centralized Zapotec state began to collapse and the valley broke apart into a number of smaller political entities.

Outside the city of Monte Albán, the best data available for the majority of Zapotec towns, villages, and hamlets are those gathered by the "Valley of Oaxaca Prehispanic Settlement Pattern Project," whose members located and surface collected roughly 2700 archaeological sites in the Oaxaca Valley (Blanton et al. 1982; Kowalewski et al. 1989). These data provide a regional picture upon which we can overlay data from site-specific excavations.

While the first palaces and two-room state temples may have occurred by Late Monte Albán I, it is during Monte Albán II that all indicators of state-level political organization are clearly evident in the archaeological record (see Balkansky 1998; Blanton et al. 1999; Flannery 1995, 1999; Marcus and Flannery 1996; Spencer 1990, 1998; Wright 1977, 1986). First, there is a four-tiered settlement hierarchy. Monte Albán is the largest site and the state capital, while Dainzú, San José Mogote, and Cerro Tilcajete serve as secondary centers, spaced roughly equidistant from Monte Albán. Each of these secondary centers is, in turn, surrounded by a ring of tertiary centers (Marcus and Flannery 1996:174-75). Functionally distinct public buildings, including colonnaded two-room temples, ballcourts, and palaces, appear at Monte Albán and its subordinate centers (Flannery 1983a, 1983b; Marcus and Flannery 1994; Robertson 1983a, 1983b). Elaborate tombs associated with palaces and other elite residences express the symbolism and ideology of the ruling class of a socially stratified society (Flannery 1998; Joyce and Winter 1996). Monte Albán controlled not only the Valley of Oaxaca, but also strategic or productive regions outside the valley such as the Cuicatlán Cañada (Redmond 1983; Redmond and Spencer 1982; Spencer 1982; Spencer and Redmond 2000), Ejutla (Feinman and Nicholas 1990), and Sola de Vega (Balkansky 2002).

For the purposes of this study, we also can draw on previous research at the secondary centers of Dainzú (Bernal 1967, 1968, 1973, 1981; Bernal and Oliveros 1988) and San José Mogote (Flannery and Marcus 1976a, 1976b, 1983a, 1983b, 1994, 2005; Marcus and Flannery 1996). With the excavation of Cerro Tilcajete, reported in this volume, we now have sufficient data to compare Monte Albán II secondary centers in all three branches of the valley to each other and to the capital. We can also describe how the administration of the Valle Grande-Ocotlán subregion was similar to, or different from, that of other subregions. These data are presented in detail in Chapters 4 and 5.

Cerro Tilcajete, located 18.5 km southeast of Monte Albán, is in the Ocotlán section of the Valle Grande-Ocotlán subregion (Fig. 1.3). The site was first recorded as OC-SMT-SMT-23 by the Valley of Oaxaca Settlement Pattern Project in 1974. The Ocotlán subregion covers approximately 280 km^2 and includes the modern towns of San Martín Tilcajete, Santo Tomás Jalieza, Santa Ana Zegache, and Ocotlán (Blanton et al. 1982). It is bounded on the east by a chain of mountains that separates this part of the valley from the Tlacolula region; on the south by a topographically differentiated but contiguous region called the Valley of Ejutla; on the west by the Atoyac River; and on the north by a chain of three ridges rising to about 1800 masl. Cerro Tilcajete is located on relatively poor farmland atop the northernmost of these three ridges. The site is extensively terraced, but there is no evidence of irrigation canals, which leads us to believe that much of the inhabitants' food would have been grown several kilometers away on the valley bottom. The site affords good views of the central valley (including Monte Albán) and portions of the Ocotlán alluvium.

Preliminary research suggested that Cerro Tilcajete was an ideal place to investigate the relationship between elites at the capital and elites at second-tier sites because—unlike San José Mogote and Dainzú—it is largely a single component site. In 1993 and 1994, Charles Spencer and Elsa Redmond mapped and surface collected the site. My analysis of their collections determined that Cerro Tilcajete was first occupied at the onset of Monte Albán II and was largely abandoned at the end of this period. It was reoccupied during Monte Albán IIIb-IV (A.D. 500-1000); however, this reoccupation was limited to the northernmost of the site's two civic-ceremonial plazas and the terraces north and east of this plaza.

The surface collections aided us in choosing areas for horizontal excavations. Over the course of three field seasons, our excavations recovered (1) complete building plans (and associated materials) from one two-room temple, one civic-ceremonial building, and three residences dating to the Monte Albán II occupation, and (2) the plan of a temple, looted tomb, and low platform dating to Monte Albán IIIb-IV. The analysis of ceramics and other artifacts from these structures provides data on domestic and ritual activities.

The material remains suggest the presence of state administrators; however, as noted above, any hypothesis suggesting who these people were, what kinds of policy decisions they made, and what kinds of directives they received from the capital must rely on a larger theoretical framework for the nature of Monte Albán II state administration.

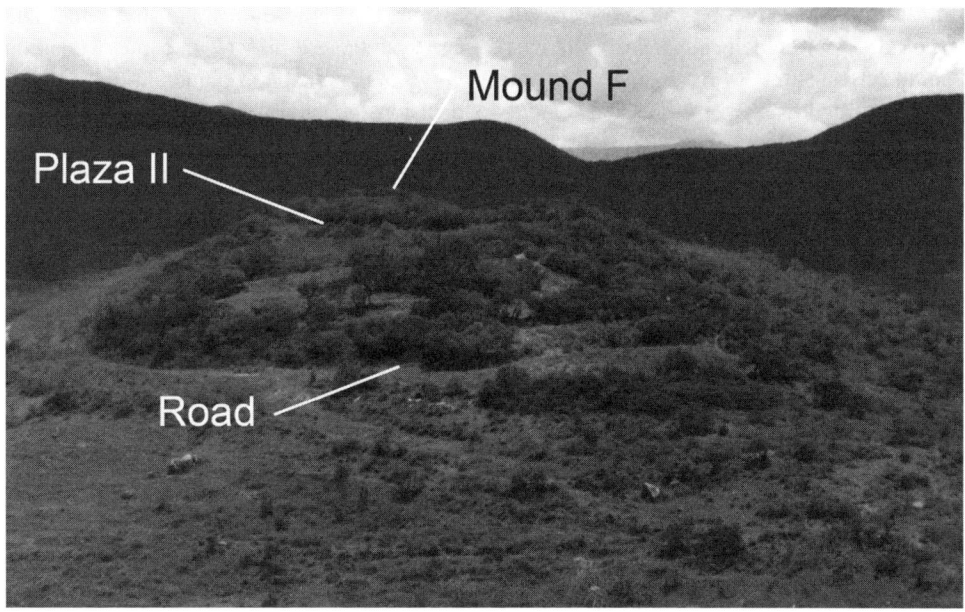

Figure 1.3. Photo of Cerro Tilcajete as viewed from an adjoining hilltop to the south.

Anthropological Approaches to Defining Zapotec Elites

Zapotec Elites As Members of Socioeconomic Groups

Many modern states comprise millions of citizens, but the populations of the smallest pre-Hispanic Mesoamerican states may have numbered only in the tens of thousands (Feinman 1998:97; Sanders and Price 1968:85; Upham 1987:355-56). The population of the Valley of Oaxaca may have been in the range of 25,000 to 50,000 during Monte Albán II (Kowalewski et al. 1989: Fig. 1.19). States have been distinguished from other kinds of sociopolitical organizations as they are administered through a "central decision-making process which is both externally specialized with regard to the local processes which it regulates, and internally specialized in that the central process is divisible into separate activities which can be performed at different places at different times" (Wright 1977:383).

Decision-makers are organized hierarchically (Eisenstadt 1969:13-22). Those in higher echelons "tend to be concerned with policy, while those in the lower echelons are ordinarily involved with more specific decision-making activities" (Spencer 1990:10-12). In pre-modern states, policy-makers usually belong to the "elite," a vague term that can incorporate groups defined by class, social stratum, or kin-based organization. Here, I will define the elite as persons in decision-making roles who maintain their dominant position by controlling access to material resources as well as to esoteric information or knowledge (Eisenstadt 1969:6; Giddens 1984:91, 373; G. Marcus 1992:296; see also Cohen 1981; Chase and Chase 1992; Stanworth and Giddens 1974).

In Oaxaca, the process of state formation is intertwined with the emergence of social stratification, and by Monte Albán II, archaeological data are used to posit that Zapotec society was divided into noble and commoner classes (Blanton et al. 1999:87-88; Marcus and Flannery 1996:170-71, 180-81; see also Whalen 1981; Winter 1974; Winter et al. 1995). As the state grew, rulers had to find ways to expand their control over conquered populations and maintain their position at the top of the social hierarchy.

Anthropologists have shown that the rulers or ruling families of most historically documented pre-modern states employ many strategies to maintain political control over their realm and to solidify their social position at the head of an elite class. For example, rulers may spur the creation of irrigation facilities, and then decide both when they are used and the content of the ceremonies related to their use (Sidky 1996). In other cases, rulers act as military leaders or fund expeditions that acquire land, access to exotic goods, or knowledge of the non-local world (Akinjogbin 1976:400-402). Many ruling elite craft a state religion, appoint themselves as its head, and create physical temple spaces and ceremonies that are carried out exclusively by state religious practitioners (Obayemi 1976:236-37). The tangible and non-tangible assets these policies produce are used to foment or reinforce the perception that rulers (and their families) are all-powerful, have close ties with the supernatural, and can influence the course of nature—in essence, demonstrate control over material resources and esoteric information or knowledge.

Although rulers promote the perception of omnipotence, they must rely on others to carry out and enforce policy. The persons they call upon to fulfill these duties can be called lower-order elite or "intermediate elites." More specifically, I will call lower-order elites at the capital "urban elites" to distinguish them from "the ruling elite," while calling lower-order elites at secondary centers "local elites."

In pre-modern states, most intermediate elites were drawn from the noble social strata; however, some rulers are known to have selectively chosen commoners to fill certain positions of authority (Flannery 1999). In some instances—often in cases where emerging nobles seek to consolidate power—they employ a strategy called "linearization" where, as representatives of the central government, commoners (and even some slaves and eunuchs) wield power over members of the noble class. Promoting commoners to positions of importance may be particularly useful in the creation of administrative hierarchies put into place at the capital because in stratified societies, commoners are less likely to be able to legitimize political aspirations through the dominant religious and social ideology—they are political or economic, but *not* social, elites. Several social scientists have pointed out that ideally, administrators should be servants of the ruler, but not representatives of any particular group or stratum (Eisenstadt 1969:14; Hansen and Parish 1983:274; G. Marcus 1983:10-11). Essentially, elevating commoners to high-ranking administrators can initially function to isolate them socially and divorce them from the bonds of kinship.

Zapotec Elites as Administrators

In the previous section I stated that Monte Albán II society was divided into noble and commoner social strata. The ruling elites were nobles based at Monte Albán. At the time of European contact, roughly 10% of pre-Hispanic society belonged to the noble social stratum and marriage was class-endogamous, with limited opportunity for social advancement (Marcus and Flannery 1996; Smith 1996; Whitecotton 1977; Webster 2002:96). A very rough estimate would suggest that in Monte Albán II society, 2500-5000 people were nobles, and about half these people might have lived at Monte Albán; I emphasize, however, that this estimate seeks only to illustrate the relatively small number of people who likely belonged to this social stratum.

I pointed out that while, in principle, rulers promote an ideology claiming ultimate authority over resources, in reality successful rulers cannot function as despots. As states become more populous and incorporate more territory, rulers either rely on few people to do more work or further diversify the administration and employ more people, and possibly a wider range of people (family members, nobles drawn from lower-ranking families and, on certain occasions, non-noble individuals), to function as administrators or bureaucrats.

Functionally, the roles of bureaucrats and the intermediate elites can overlap, but these are not necessarily interchangeable terms. Theoretically, the model of bureaucracy advanced by Max Weber defines a bureaucrat as a person who (1) holds an office that exists independently from a particular officeholder; (2) is assigned specific duties and given the authority necessary to carry out those duties; (3) occupies a position (and its associated goods or benefits) that cannot be sold or inherited; and (4) makes decisions guided by a particular law or code, and keeps records of state business (Weber 1976; see also Albrow 1990; Mommsen 1974, 1989; Roth and Wittich 1968:956-1005).

Weber's model implies a dichotomy between public and private action, but this is not always the case in pre-modern states. Postclassic Mesoamerican states are usually considered second or third generation states, in the sense that they grew out of prior state level organizations. In two Postclassic states, the Texcocan and Tarascan states, urban bureaucrats usually were nobles appointed by the ruler. At the same time, their administrative powers were compartmentalized. In both states, rulers allocated offices along similar lines: legal/political, military, religious/artistic, and economic. Individual administrators were supported by resources attached to their office. In some instances, functionaries from the capital were appointed to administer places outside the capital directly or to oversee local elites. If local elites were left in place, usually they were required to maintain personal contact with the king through regular visits or reports to the capital, and often the local elite ruler or a member of his family was required to reside in the capital. Usually, urban and local elite "bureaucrats" could be dismissed, demoted, or put to death at any time by the king (Offner 1983; Pollard 1993).

For a ruler, this is an ideal way to occupy lesser nobles as administrators and keep their decision-making power in check. At the same time, several studies of pre-modern states show that bureaucratic offices could be inherited as long as the ruler approved of the new officeholder (Bossler 1998; D'Altroy 2002; Herskovits 1938; McCaskie 1995:12-23). Even in capitalist societies with "modern" bureaucracies, studies suggest that these elite organizations are strongly influenced by kin and family connections (even more than by state, political party, and corporate membership) (Hansen and Parish 1983:260; Mosca 1939; Pareto 1935, 1950, 1968). No matter the position of rulers, kinship exerts a powerful influence on state administration and is one way that lesser elites (as an organizational unit) can negotiate power over the long term.

Archaeology has the potential to become adept at examining these long-term processes. One goal of the present study is to examine how social class and administrative position intersected in the first-generation Zapotec state. Intermediate elites commonly are thought of as simply lower-ranking nobles, but this kind of generalization does not encourage a dynamic examination of how primary states worked. In early or primary states, do we find evidence of legal/political, military, religious/artistic, and economic "arms" of the state administration? What were the social positions of the individuals who occupied these positions? Once Monte Albán's rulers had subjugated the entire valley, they were faced with setting up a valley-wide administration, and how they did this had long-term consequences. At Tilcajete, ruling elites may have relied on or co-opted the existing local hereditary leader or, if he (or she) was deposed, may have come to terms with a more compliant offspring or close relative. Such newly minted local administrators might have retained their noble status, though at times local elites were placed under someone (whether noble or commoner) sent from the capital, or were required to live in or make frequent visits to the capital (Eisenstadt 1963:15-17; Flannery 1972, 1999; Kottak 1980; Marcus 2006a). In the next section, I examine how the interplay between rulers and lesser elites relates to concepts of power sharing and conflict.

Zapotec Elites, Power Sharing, and Conflict

Certainly, over time, the hierarchical organization of agents can and does vary (see Brumfiel and Fox 1994). Subordinate elites are subject to policy decisions by the ruling elite, but they are not passive, powerless groups (Giddens 1984:14-16). As stated above, ruling elites aim to convince others that they control material resources and esoteric information or knowledge. Ideally, these abilities support their exclusive hierarchical position and decision-making power, but in reality, intra-elite struggles are common.

In a general sense, power is "the relative ability of a person or group to cause another person or group to obey, or conversely, the ability 'not to have to give in'" (Service 1975:11). From one point of view, elites perform a necessary "labor" in societal maintenance and are invested with their position through *social consensus* (for example, Durkheim 1933). From another point of view, groups establish dominance over one another through *social conflict*, not social consensus (for example, Marx and Engels 1848, 1884). In one of the few anthropological studies of elite power and culture, Cohen (1981:7-8) pointed out that "consensus" and "conflict" are, in reality, extremes of one continuum:

> Elitists would concede that, while serving the general interests of society, elites develop organizational mechanisms to advance their sectional interests. The conflict theorists, on the other hand, would concede that, while serving their own sectional interests dominant groups develop ideologies purporting to articulate the general interests of society.

As an ideal, power is the natural order of hierarchy expressed through the customary ways of doing things (Arendt 1961:92-93; Eisenstadt 1969:27, 365-68; Giddens 1984:23-25, 185; McCall 1999:17-18; Service 1975:11-12). Many have noted that the nobility are united in their desire to project an ideology supporting their position of dominance. At the same time, ruling elites seek to limit access by intermediate elites (and non-elites) to resources that can be used to affect or direct social reproduction. Yet, by virtue of their social class, many subordinate elites do have access to some of the same material resources and knowledge as the ruling elite. Coercion or conflict may be more likely to occur among social elites (nobles) who have more contact with one another (Eisenstadt 1995:241; Giddens 1984:317).

As a state matures, the royal family grows and intermarries with local elite families and urban bureaucrats. Many rulers have multiple wives and concubines and scores of offspring, all competing for positions of power. Bonds of kinship can reinforce loyalty; however, disaffected nobles can use their knowledge to legitimize power struggles with rulers. In organizations where social status and political position are closely intertwined, it may be more likely that rulers will have to work to find ways to negotiate power with lesser elites. For example, ideology dictated that the Inca king ruled by divine mandate; however, in practice, he had to work closely with families that claimed descent from previous Inca rulers in order to accede to and retain the throne (D'Altroy 2002:89-91).

In primary states, finding ways to identify how rulers employed nobles and non-nobles as administrators is the first step in examining how these groups may have functioned as self-perpetuating members of potentially powerful kin-based organizations. A recent study by Bossler (1998) provides an interesting case study documenting the development of a hereditary urban bureaucracy in the Sung Dynasty, China (A.D. 960-1000). Bossler found that during the first forty years of the dynasty, the highest-ranking officials (the Grand Councilors) of the Sung court were drawn from high-ranking officials of the previous dynasty and persons who had achieved military success in the creation of the new dynasty. The next generation of officials included sons or near relatives of these men. About A.D. 1100, noble factionalism within the Sung rulership brought new rulers to the throne. The new rulers employed bureaucrats who were from established local elite families, but who were not kin of the previous urban bureaucracy (Bossler 1998:35-39).

In this case urban bureaucrats who successfully institutionalize their positions may become a threat to their patrons. In addition, the creation of imbalance between the urban bureaucracy and local elites may lead to a political crisis, a point illustrated with an example from the eastern Han dynasty of China (A.D. 25-220) (Hsu 1995; Paludan 1998). In order to consolidate political power, the first Han emperor harshly suppressed local nobles and confiscated their lands. The Han rulers then turned to a group of urban intellectuals (both commoner and noble) whom they employed to oversee the state system of imperial bureaucrats. Hsu (1995:187) notes that as this class of intellectual bureaucrats prospered they gained "intellectual autonomy by systematizing knowledge, which gave them the power to legitimize the regime." The self-regeneration of knowledge instilled in this highly organized bureaucracy made the intellectuals indispensable to the state. At the same time, as their members developed a shared sense of social solidarity and began to accumulate economic resources (land taken from suppressed local elites), their power intimidated and alienated the rulers, who began to surround themselves with (and rely on) eunuchs and personal retainers (Hsu 1995:185, 187).

Power struggles between the intellectuals and the rulers in the last centuries of the dynasty came to a head when the ruler tried to bypass the bureaucrats and instead promoted eunuchs to positions of importance. The eunuchs were given hereditary titles that were then passed on to adopted sons. Subsequent rulers tried to massacre the eunuchs, but the former had become so politically weak that the eunuchs seized control of the government in A.D. 168. However, over the course of the next two decades, natural disasters (floods and famine) and bureaucratic corruption (including the open selling of offices) created an atmosphere of political and ideological unrest. In A.D. 189, the system was so decayed that a western warlord was able to invade and burn the capital, effectively usurp all political power, and order the massacre of 2000 eunuchs. The fall of the Han dynasty was followed by three and a half centuries of political decentralization and warfare (Paludan 1998:44-55).

This example reiterates the points that (1) the proliferation of one elite faction at the expense of another (for example, the urban bureaucracy versus the local elite) is potentially dangerous for a ruler, and (2) the institutionalization of an administrative system can limit the potential a ruler has to develop new resources. As states form, dynamic rulers create novel social and behavioral frameworks, but over the course of time these structures become institutionalized in society as custom or tradition. If power sharing with a self-legitimizing bureaucracy becomes institutionalized, it may hinder the future success of the ruling elite to maintain power. In both the cases described above, the point came when rulers needed to reestablish relationships of authority over the lower echelons of the administration. In the first case, the ruler managed to purge the individuals without modifying the system. In the second case, the bureaucracy was so entrenched that the ruler tried to resort to a radical new policy, which eventually failed.

Summary

This chapter has outlined key issues regarding the organization of pre-modern states. One goal of this study is to consider how these ideas may shed light on early state administration in Oaxaca. Recent research suggests that although Monte Albán was founded around 500 B.C., during the first 200-400 years of its existence it did not control the Ocotlán and Tlacolula subregions of the valley. To begin to examine the ways Monte Albán II administration affected Zapotec society, we should look for evidence suggesting both how elites operated as members of a social stratum and how they functioned as members of institutions. Data illustrating how different arms of the administration developed, and were peopled over time, allow us to consider better what kinds of material resources and knowledge the ruling and non-ruling elite had at their disposal. Fundamentally, how rulers decided to structure state administration may have had long-term consequences in terms of how well they were able to negotiate power with elite factions.

Chapter 2

Elite Behavior in the Early Zapotec State

Now I turn to an evaluation of data describing how elites functioned as social beings and operated as administrators in sixteenth-century Oaxaca. These data, in consideration of the broader themes addressed in the previous chapter, allow the proposal of several hypotheses, which will be tested in Chapters 3 and 4 with data from Monte Albán II.

Zapotec Polities in the Sixteenth Century

Descriptions of sixteenth-century Zapotec society are not as numerous or as detailed as those for central Mexico. It is noteworthy that over the course of the Postclassic period, the relatively small Zapotec and Mixtec states were in regular contact with one another. By the Late Postclassic, several researchers suggest that migration and sustained interregional contact contributed to the emergence of a pan-Mesoamerican elite (López Austin and López Luján 2001:269-91; Marcus and Flannery 1983). As royal families intermarried, elite culture developed shared aspects of its material culture and ideology. We have to consider how this "convergent evolution" might have affected the political organization of Oaxaca (Marcus and Flannery 1983:217-26).

Primary sources for Oaxaca include the *Relaciones Geográficas*, written between 1579 and 1582 (del Paso y Troncoso 1905), and evaluations of Zapotec behavior and beliefs by Burgoa (1670, 1674), Córdova (1578a, 1578b), and Balsalobre (1656). Many insightful analyses of Zapotec society at the time of contact and during the early Colonial period have been published (e.g., Carmagnani 1988; Chance 1978, 1989; Flannery 1983c:290-95; Flannery 1983d:318-22; Flannery and Marcus 1983c:295-301; Marcus 1983c:301-8; Marcus 1983d:345-51; Marcus 2006a; Marcus and Flannery 1996:12-22; Oudijk 2000; Paddock 1966; Spores 1965; Spores and Flannery 1983:339-45; Taylor 1972; Whitecotton 1977).

After the decline of Monte Albán, several towns in the valley probably emerged as the centers of independent polities and rulers created shifting political alliances (see Marcus 1983b; Oudijk 2000; Whitecotton 1977). During the Late Postclassic, the ruling family of Zaachila attempted to centralize power and may have replaced the conquered lords of two local Zapotec towns (Macuilxóchitl and Teitipac) with noble governors (Oudijk 2000; Whitecotton 1977:128). For a time, Zaachila probably controlled large, productive areas of the valley, but no single ruler succeeded in uniting the entire valley. After A.D. 1486, the Aztec, under the ruler Ahuitzotl, began their attempts to subjugate Mixtec and Zapotec polities (Marcus 1983b:302; 1983c:315). At the time of Spanish Conquest, the Aztec had imposed tribute demands on many Zapotec and Mixtec lords. Zapotec lords conquered by the Aztec were required to pay tribute, but were left in place as political leaders.

At the time of contact, there were approximately a dozen "autonomous" polities in the Oaxaca Valley. Each Zapotec polity consisted of a town and its subject villages. This basic political unit has been called a *señorío* or *cacicazgo*. Each polity had an estimated population of 2100 to 23,400 people, with a mean polity size of about 5000 people (Feinman 1998:115-21). The nature of these polities varied across the region. For example, the polities in the Etla branch had more dispersed populations than those in the Tlacolula branch. Flannery and Marcus (1983c:295-300) have used archaeological and historical data to reconstruct the Mitla polity, which "had a nucleated urban center with elegant ceremonial and civic buildings, a substantial suburban residential area, a rural hinterland or 'sustaining area' of 20 km², several hilltop forts, and a series of dependent hamlets up to eight leagues distant." Because these polities were small and the population was dispersed around one main town, there would have been little pressure on autonomous polities to develop additional administrative centers or a more complex bureaucracy when the ruler could directly administer the territory (Hodge 1996:59; Spencer 1990).

Zapotec Nobles

Ethnohistoric documents describing sixteenth-century society suggest that there was only one "legitimate" royal family in each Zapotec community and that it was composed of the ruler, his wives, and the ruler's offspring (Whitecotton 1977:144). The ruling family of each polity intermarried with other Zapotec and Mixtec (and occasionally Mexica) nobles, and ideally succession to rulership was based on primogeniture. The ruler and his family, the lesser nobility, their servants and slaves, and specialists such as priests, artisans, and merchants lived in the largest town.

The Spanish priest Juan de Córdova (1578a, 1578b, 1987) asked Zapotec informants about their nobles and recorded several phrases describing noble men and women. I want to look at these titles in terms of what they tell us about relationships *among* nobles. For the Zapotec, a simple "lord" was a *coqui* (female version is *coqui xonàxi*), while an "exalted lord" was the *coquitào* (female version is *coquitào xonàxi*). Even more important was an "exalted lord like an emperor" called a *coquitào huezàquiqueche*, a term that actually translates as "exalted lord triumphant in war." When Córdova asked the Zapotec to define the phrase "lord all powerful like god" he received a very literal translation, "lord who is a high being," *coquitào niquizàa latàca* (or *coquitào niquizàa lacòa*), but also was given the term *coqui huezàquiquèche* meaning "lord triumphant in war."

Below the highest-ranking nobles or ruling elite, Córdova recorded terms for lesser elite, similar to the Spanish "hidalgos" who were nobles by birth but not nobles of royal rank. For both men and women, these terms incorporate the concept of *joàna* meaning "first or principal occupant of a town." A male noble was a *joàna lahuiti* while a female noble was a *xonàxìxini joàna*.

Embedded in sixteenth-century Zapotec terminology is possibly a three-tiered nobility: the ruler (*coquitào*), other royal nobles (*coqui*), and non-royal nobles (*joàna lahuiti*). At the same time, in order for a ruler to become a truly powerful king, he had to be a successful war-leader and conqueror (*coquitào huezàquiqueche*).

Zapotec nobles and commoners had distinct origin myths and were treated very differently after death. Nobles were buried in elaborate tombs located beneath residences. These tombs could be reopened and added to, and often contained several generations of family members. Tombs also could have been reopened to provide additional offerings or to consult ancestors. After death, nobles became *ben zaa* or "cloud people," who were conceived of as existing in a divine or semi-divine state in close proximity

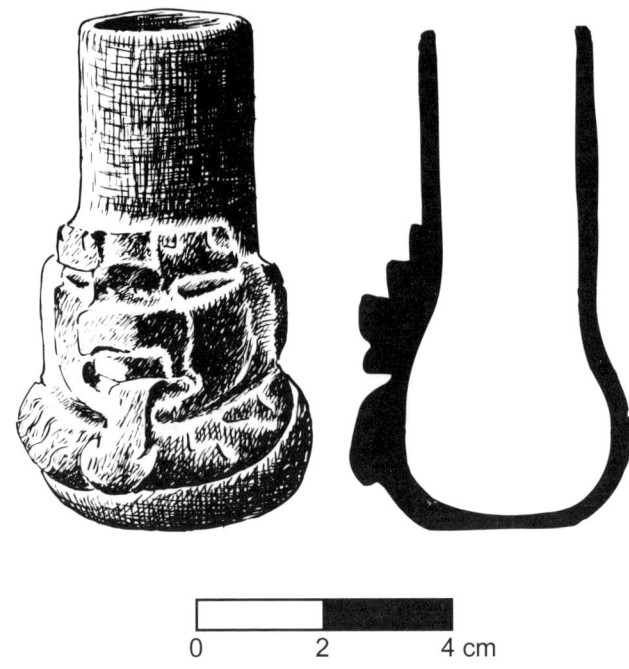

Figure 2.1. Formative Period gray-paste ceramic bottle depicting *Cociyo*; from Monte Albán Tomb 107 (see Fig. 3.7 for tomb's location) (adapted from Caso et al. 1967: Fig. 86c).

to supernatural beings. In particular, the sixteenth-century political ideology linked nobles with venerated ancestors who lived in close proximity to *Cociyo*, the preeminent Zapotec deity associated with lightning (Marcus and Flannery 1996; Oudijk 2000; Whitecotton 1977) (Fig. 2.1). Joyce Marcus (1992b:286-87) has evaluated pre-Hispanic and early Colonial period evidence that describes the concept of noble ancestor worship. In one example, records document the members of a town resorting to sacrifice and petition for the deceased nobles to intervene with supernatural forces and end a plague.

In the pre-Hispanic era, perhaps the most fundamental aspect of *Cociyo* was as a deity responsible for perpetuating the agricultural cycle (Marcus and Flannery 1996:18-19). The Oaxaca Valley is a semi-arid environment where even today over 80% of agricultural production relies solely on rainfall farming, and the valley experiences some level of drought and crop failure as frequently as one out of every four years (Feinman 2006). Modern ethnographic studies describe the continued existence of, and importance attached to, the performance of rituals petitioning *Cociyo* for rainfall (Beals 1975; Carmagnani 1988; Esparza 1994; González 2001; Leslie 1960; Parsons 1936). The existence of a sixteenth-century ideology linking nobles with divine ancestors and the fundamental importance of *Cociyo* suggest that Zapotec nobles did play a role in the performance of ritual—prayer and sacrifice—crucial for petitioning *Cociyo* to split the clouds and release rain (Flannery and Marcus 1976b; Marcus 2006b).

Zapotec Policy-Makers

In several *relaciones*, such as those recorded for the town of Mitla and a place called "Tlacolula" (possibly the archaeological site of Yagul), native informants state that the basis of government was "the will of the ruler." Beyond the ruler, the *relaciones* describe two kinds of officials. Elders drawn from the ruling family or from lesser noble families acted as the ruler's councilors and his intermediaries in dealing with the general populace (del Paso y Troncoso 1905:168). These councilors lived in the most important town and, possibly, in the same palace as the ruler, where they "held court" in a patio distinct from the one where the ruler received visitors. Here they heard the complaints and demands of subjects and received ambassadors from other polities. They declared the will of the ruler to the rest of the minor nobility and the townspeople.

The plan of the ruins of Yagul may reflect the activities described in the *relaciones* (Fig. 2.2). While Yagul was occupied continuously from Late Monte Albán I onward, the site in Monte Albán V was the center of a small polity organized much like Mitla (Bernal and Gamio 1974; Paddock 1955, 1957, 1960). In one area we find a large noble residence with six patios of varying sizes surrounded by rooms. The interior of each patio is delimited by a bench 1.6 m high and 30 cm wide; each patio is surrounded on all four sides by rooms and connected to other patios by passageways. Patio F is the largest and was open to the south, where a platform terrace and an I-shaped ballcourt can be seen. Both tombs and less elaborate burials were found under the palace's rooms (Bernal and Gamio 1974; Flannery 1983c:292-94).

Just south of the Palace of the Six Patios sat a large civic-ceremonial building, consisting of two long rooms facing onto a large patio. By "civic-ceremonial structure" I mean a discrete architectural unit whose floor plan is not known to have been that of a two-room temple but whose size, layout, and associated features (or lack thereof) suggest that it was not a residence either. One question we could ask is, to what extent is the plan of Yagul's ceremonial core consistent with elite architecture during earlier time periods? It would seem, for example, that hundreds of people could access the plaza of the civic-ceremonial building, but perhaps only a few dozen people could access the interior of the building. Still fewer could have entered Patio F of the palace, whose interior could have housed quite a large royal family and their retainers. One possibility is that the royal family used Patio F for private interactions and the civic-ceremonial building for more public interactions. As documented in the chronicles, the civic-ceremonial building also could have been used by councilors mediating between the ruler and the public.

A second office described in the *relaciones* is that of a "ward leader" or "village leader," possibly called a *golaba* ("lord's solicitor") in Zapotec (del Paso y Troncoso 1905:31-32; Flannery 1983b). The *relaciones* for Teocuicuilco, Nejapa, Ixtepec, and Huitzo provide us with a composite description of the duties of a *golaba*, which included collecting tribute in goods and labor, resolving land disputes, and deciding on some judicial matters. It is not clear whether this was a hereditary or appointed position. Whitecotton (1977:144) suggests that the sons of the ruler and other minor nobility would have administered over a ward or village, but trusted commoners might have been appointed to some lower-level offices.

Documents from sixteenth-century central and southern Mexico permit us to create an interesting and important point of comparison concerning the organization of sixteenth-century Zapotec, Nahua, and Maya communities, which may be relevant for understanding earlier time periods (see Lockhart 1992:41-44; Webster 2002:91-99; cf. Quezada 1993; Restall 1997; Thompson 1999). In both central and southern Mexico, people were born both into kin groups and (often) territorial units called *calpolli* (Nahuatl) or *cah* (Maya). While scholars still debate the particulars of these organizations, there could be one or several *calpolli* or *cah* in each town. The leaders of these units were called *teuctli* (Nahua) or *batabob* (Maya) and were always nobles, while the majority of the members of the *calpolli* or *cah* were commoners. There are interesting discussions in the literature regarding how the leader of a *calpolli* or *cah* obtained his position, but it is likely that within a *calpolli* or *cah*, factions of nobles came to agreements to support particular candidates (it is important to remember that for the most part all nobles in an area were related). In the Aztec heartland, the process of ongoing centralization meant that by the early 1500s several *calpolli* were under the political control of a *tlatoani* (king or ruler), and these in turn were ruled over by the Aztec emperor. Yucatán was less centralized, and some Maya *cah* functioned as independent political units, while others were ruled over by a *halach uinic* ("true man," a kind of glorified *batab*) who controlled several towns or provinces.

Underneath the *teuctli* or *batabob* were a series of ward officers who, as Lockhart (1992:43) aptly puts it, were "perhaps better imagined as citizens with some special duties than as functionaries." Some of these titles imply that one main duty of the position was organizing units of people. In this sense, the Zapotec *golaba* appears to be a condensation of the *teuctli/batab* and ward leader. The documents suggest that the *golaba* collected tribute in goods and labor, but also was charged with resolving land disputes and deciding on some judicial matters, powers typically reserved only for the nobility.

One question, then, is whether the positions of *coquitào, coqui, joàna lahuiti*, and *golaba* can be defined for earlier periods of Zapotec society. In the sixteenth century, the terms *coquitào* and *coqui* were most appropriate for describing royalty. The *joàna lahuiti* were lower-ranking nobles, and *golaba* could be used to describe any urban elite administrator. As will be discussed in the next chapter, Late Classic Monte Albán's urban landscape indicates the presence of wards or neighborhoods, each with its own elite residences and temples (Blanton 1978; Blanton et al. 1999). We should consider if there was a neighborhood level to religious and political organization, and what this might say about the organization of the urban elite during Monte Albán II.

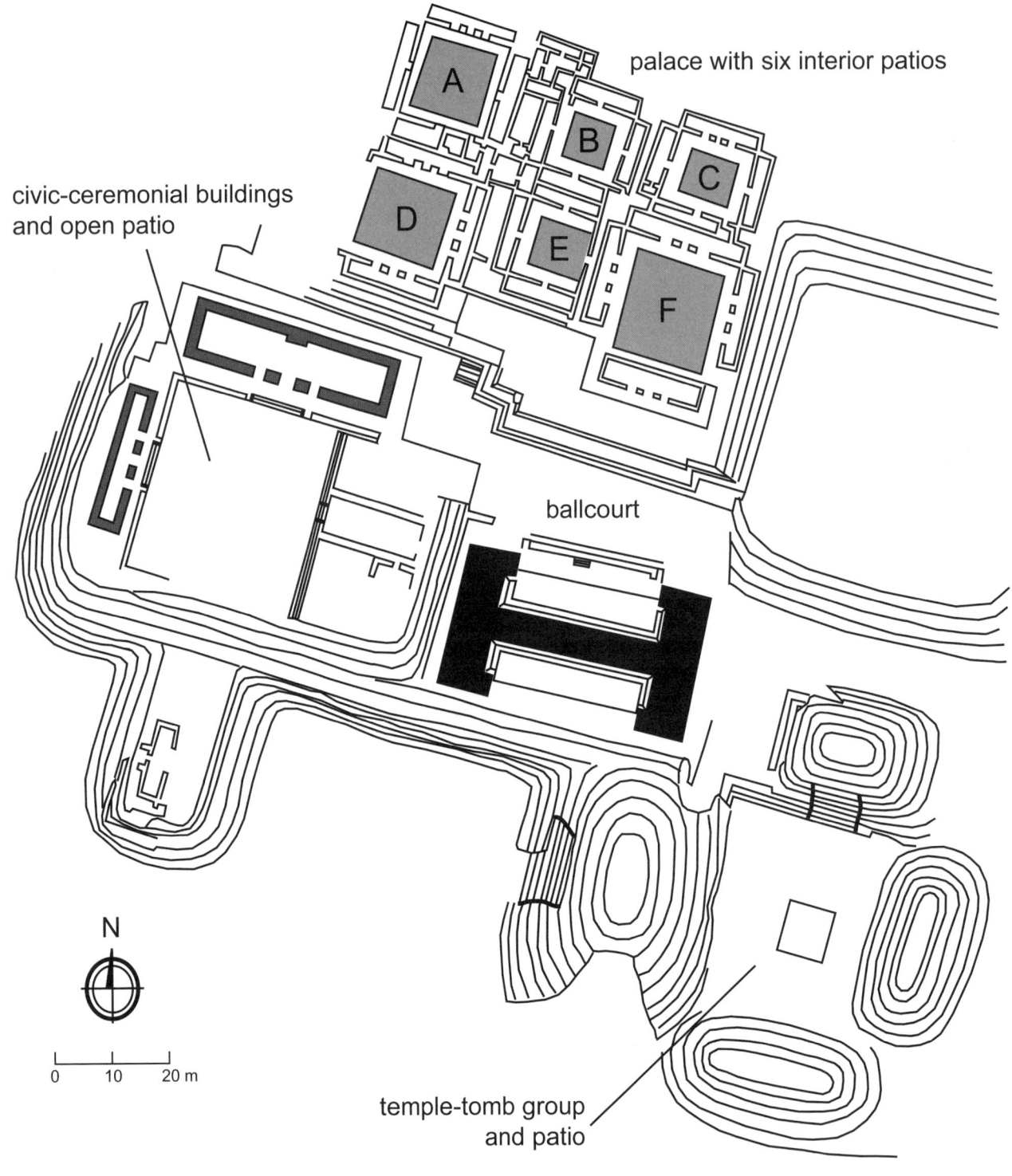

Figure 2.2. Plan of Yagul's ceremonial core showing the locations of palaces, civic-ceremonial buildings, I-shaped ballcourt, and temple mounds (redrawn from Bernal and Gamio 1974: Planos 1, 2).

Zapotec Priests

Ethnohistoric documents describe several levels or grades in the religious hierarchy and suggest that commoners filled lower-level positions in the priesthood (Marcus 1983d; Whitecotton 1977:146-48). I have already described Mitla as a small polity throughout the Postclassic. At some point in its history, Mitla evolved into a religious center somewhat like the Vatican in the sense that it was ruled by a priest called the "great seer," who was revered by all Zapotecs. The great seer, a noble by birth, consulted with the supernatural and advised the noble rulers of other polities. This office may have been inherited by sons or near relatives. In principle, high priests were chaste, but on certain festivals the high priest had intercourse with virgins and if one produced a male heir, that child would be trained to succeed his father (Marcus 1983d:350). This policy helped resolve the inheritance of political authority within the Postclassic Mitla polity and allowed religious bureaucrats to institutionalize descent-based organization. (We do not know if "custom" dictated chastity for the priestly class in earlier periods.)

Lower-ranking grades of priests had names such as "ordinary priest," "young" or "student" priest, and "sacrificer." The ordinary priests burned incense, performed minor sacrifices (including autosacrifice), and had contact with commoners. "Sacrificers" were specialized performers of human sacrifice. "Students" or "young" priests assisted older priests (Marcus 1983d:350).

By 100 B.C., Zapotec religious structures displayed an established architectural canon that lasted until the Conquest (Marcus and Flannery 1996). Temples had two rooms, "a more sacred inner room in which the priests performed their rites, and a less sacred outer room to which worshipers could come" (Flannery 1998:40). An example of this kind of temple, dating to Period II, was found on Mound X at Monte Albán and is shown in Figure 3.6. Many temples were set atop pyramidal mounds. Stone models of Zapotec temples show that feather draperies or curtains were used to shield the interior from view (Marcus and Flannery 1996:267). In general, floor space in temples was limited (under 100 m^2). Ethnohistoric documents state that some temples were supported by specific tracts of land, but it is not clear whether these lands were the property of the head priest of the temple or of the temple institution itself (Taylor 1972:41-44).

Descriptions of Zapotec priests state that some resided in the interior of the two-room temple where they officiated (Marcus 1983d:349-50). At the same time, historical accounts that describe Mitla's large and elaborate structures show that the "great seer" actually lived in a palatial residence attached to a temple. This temple-and-residence is called the "Hall of the Columns" and is located on the north side of a four-building patio. The outer room of the structure—the temple—was a long hall with interior columns. Behind this was an enclosed building that served as the residence of the priest and his assistants and as visiting quarters for Zapotec rulers and their retinues. Below the temple was an elaborate multi-chambered tomb (Flannery and Marcus 1983c:297-98).

At Yagul, a partially excavated four-mound group just south and east of the I-shaped ballcourt looks similar enough to have supported temples and also to have functioned as a priestly residence. In the eastern mound of the group, excavations uncovered three elaborate multi-chambered tombs (Flannery 1983c).

At Monte Albán, as I have pointed out, the city plan for Monte Albán IIIb-IV indicates a series of neighborhoods, each with its own platform mounds supporting both temples and residences. In the chapters that follow, specific details of the relationship between "temples" and "residences" on Monte Albán's Main Plaza and within the neighborhoods will be evaluated so that these data can be compared to the patterns at secondary centers.

Zapotec Warriors

The history of Postclassic period political intrigue provides ample evidence that nobles engaged in violent conflict, but not all of this combative interaction appears to be "warfare" in the explicit sense of conflict oriented to territorial conquest or expansion. As mentioned earlier, Zapotec rulers certainly were expected to be *coqui huezàquiquèche*. Many texts and carved stone monuments created after A.D. 700 express concern with maintaining noble genealogies; however, a notable exception comes from the site of Huitzo, where excavations uncovered a tomb with carved door-jambs showing warriors. The tomb held a young adult buried with a set of retouched obsidian blades that had likely been set in a wooden broadsword, now decomposed. Ten nearby burials contained other young men interred with obsidian blades and projectile points (Flannery 1983d).

Córdova (1987; see also Marcus 1992b; Whitecotton and Whitecotton 1993) provides us with several definitions for "war" and "the art of war." One is *china* (labor) *quelayè* (war/enemy); a second *xiquela* (human action in the present or future) *china* (labor) *peni* (having a personal, human quality) *quelayè* (war/enemy); and a third *xiquela* (human action in the present or future) *china* (labor) *pèni* (having a personal, human quality) *pèe* (vital force). All three definitions suggest that in one sense, the Zapotec saw the art of war as a kind of human labor; yet, the last of the three definitions suggests that one aspect of this ongoing labor was service to a "vital force."

Ethnohistoric documents suggest that Postclassic Zapotec rulers actively defended themselves from hostilities by local rivals, as well as from Mixtec and Aztec incursions. Commoners were regularly drafted to fight as footsoldiers. Sites such as Yagul and Mitla have defensible citadels on nearby hills, to which populations could retreat (Flannery 1983d).

Documents that describe Postclassic period violence state that nobles often fought each other for reasons other than territorial conquest. Some Zapotec rulers were expected to take captives to be sacrificed at their inauguration. Warfare might also be used to procure captives for sacrifice to deified ancestors, ensuring that the ancestors would be well-disposed toward dispensing courage and victory for future military endeavors. Sacrifices might also be made to *Cociyo* (Lightning) to petition him for rain. Such events were linked in Zapotec cosmology, where venerated ancestors lived in close proximity to *Cociyo*.

Let us consider these statements concerning warfare and agricultural abundance in light of recent theoretical approaches to understanding the institution of Classic Maya rulership in southern Mesoamerica. Maya kings, like their Zapotec counterparts, enacted rituals to maintain ongoing relationships with gods and royal ancestors (Marcus 1978; Webster 2002:119-136; Houston and Stuart 1996).

While the Zapotec and Maya were different cultures, both were Mesoamerican people and it is likely that they shared some aspects of a mental template that saw noble power stemming from the ability to access supernatural realms and to ensure cyclical abundance through ritual, including sacrifices that followed warfare. The underlying functions of elite competition and territorial expansion that lay at the heart of Zapotec warfare should not be downplayed.

We need also to consider how the Zapotec ballcourt may have functioned as a venue for conflict resolution and ritual behavior. While the game itself may be very old, I-shaped ballcourts first appear in Monte Albán II, which is consistent with the idea that the game was formalized by the state (Marcus and Flannery 1996:189-90). While the precise role of the ballgame in Zapotec culture is not known, Kowalewski et al. (1991) have proposed that it was used to maintain the readiness of armies, reinforce state ideology, and provide a setting for state-administered punishment and execution, while Redmond (1983) has proposed that it may have played a role in conflict resolution between feuding communities.

At Monte Albán V sites such as Yagul, I-shaped ballcourts are embedded within the civic-ceremonial core of the site. For Monte Albán II, I will examine the use of warrior imagery and the location of ballcourts in light of potential relationships between Zapotec warriors, nobles, and the natural world.

Zapotec Merchants

While there is evidence for trade and specialized production, ethnohistoric documents do not mention professional Zapotec traders. Commoners engaged in part-time craft specialization such as weaving, pottery-making, or lapidary work, and may have developed some special skills such as merchants, dancers, or musicians (Whitecotton 1977:148-50). Archaeological evidence shows that as early as the Formative period, certain villages specialized in crafts such as the reduced-firing of gray ceramics (Whalen 1981). However, there is no evidence for long-distance Zapotec merchants comparable to the Aztec *pochteca*.

Summary

Colonial-era documents provide some indication of how members of noble and commoner social strata functioned as specialized political/legal, religious, military, and economic administrators. Commoners could serve in some of the lower grades of the priesthood and were drafted to serve in organized warfare. The data suggest the presence of craftsmen, but not specialized traders.

Compared to the Aztec, Zapotec polities of the sixteenth century were just as socially stratified but had fewer levels of hierarchy or political bureaucracy. Within the boundary of a polity, the *coquitào* inherited his position and exerted ultimate authority over his subjects. Nobles presumably used genealogical distance from the ruler to distinguish among one another, with some claiming membership in royal lineages (*coqui*) and some belonging to families of lesser nobility (*joàna lahuiti*).

The *coquitào* lived in a large palace with attached civic-ceremonial structures and had a staff of noble relatives who advised him. He relied on the *golaba* to carry out royal mandates and collect labor and tribute from the neighborhoods. The *golaba* may have been the leader of a lineage, the leader of a ward, or both. Documents suggest that the *golaba* collected tribute in goods and labor, and was also charged with resolving land disputes and some judicial matters.

There are indications that Zapotec nobles successfully promoted an ideology in which they were uniquely suited to influence important supernatural forces; maintain cosmic order through the completion of certain rituals; perform autosacrifice, human sacrifice, and animal sacrifice; and act as military leaders. The performance of these cyclical activities created an overlap between nobles as social beings and as practitioners of state-sponsored ritual.

How might the role of the Classic Zapotec elite have differed from that of the Postclassic? These data bring us to an important point concerning the nature of Zapotec rulers in the sixteenth century. A recent study by Webster (2002) finds evidence that Postclassic Maya rulers were strong war leaders and responsible for the civic order of their communities. However, he argues (2002:102) that one major ideological change at the end of the Classic period was the collapse of "a tradition of divine or semi-divine kings who were responsible for the cosmos in general and for the well-being of their polities and subjects in particular." While Postclassic Zapotec rulers were also strong war leaders and responsible for civic order, we also see evidence that they claimed some authority over the performance of events related to the maintenance of cosmological order. At the same time, any cosmological order they might have had pales by comparison with the high priest of Mitla, who is described as important enough to advise the rulers of multiple polities. This high priest lived in a residence as elegant as that of a ruler, though it was attached to a temple. For the remainder of this volume I will look back at Monte Albán II, and use archaeological data to suggest the relationship between ruling and priestly elites at that earlier period.

Chapter 3

The Oaxaca Valley in Monte Albán II (100 B.C.–A.D. 200)

Archaeological Indicators of Elite Behavior

Let us consider, based on the evidence presented in Chapters 1 and 2, what kinds of archaeological remains might shed light on how ruling elites interacted with subordinates and what that might tell us about the shape of state administration for the 100 B.C.–A.D. 200 time period.

One line of evidence I will examine is the creation of infrastructure and monumental architecture. Monumental architecture is an important tool for conveying the perception of authority in the minds of subjects. Monumental architecture has also been viewed as a kind of conspicuous consumption that both signals the competitive advantage of the rulers over other members of their own social stratum and sends signals to commoners who might wish for a less hierarchical organization (Blanton 1989; Luttwak 1976; Ogburn 2004; Rapoport 1993; Trigger 1990). As Ogburn (2004) points out, a cycle of monument building can quickly get established as incoming rulers personalize architecture and refresh its message.

The way a capital or ceremonial center is laid out—its visual landscape—can say something about how different social groups interacted and what kinds of access these groups had to economic, religious, military, or political power. I examine these factors first for Monte Albán and then see how they were replicated in the visual landscape of regional centers. Data from regional survey provide information on the size and location of mounds and the presence of features such as ballcourts, walls, and carved stones. Without excavation, however, it is difficult to determine what kind of structure certain mounds supported, when those mounds or structures were first built, or for how many time periods they were used. In Oaxaca, I was able to draw not only on site plans, but also on excavated architecture and artifact assemblages from Cerro Tilcajete, San José Mogote, and Dainzú.

I have discussed buildings with functions related to specific administrative tasks: the residential palace, the two-room temple, the ballcourt, and the governmental palace. Postclassic period descriptions of palaces and data from excavated sites such as Yagul show that at the time of European contact, Zapotec rulers lived in grand, multifunctional facilities. Residential palaces like the Palace of the Six Patios held large families and contained both tombs and simpler burials. Patio areas might have been accessible to select outsiders, but most interactions between rulers and others probably took place in larger civic-ceremonial buildings with halls that faced onto open patios. Yagul's ceremonial core had a ballcourt as well as a mound group (probably supporting temples) that also contained tombs. Specific details of building plans can illuminate the relationship between elites and the performance of state functions.

In the case of recently subjugated areas, interaction between the capital and secondary centers depends, in part, on the nature of political incorporation and the strength of the local lord. Ruling elites may decide to replace the previous leadership with nobles appointed from the capital, local elites friendly to a state's expansionist design, or even prominent commoner bureaucrats. It is likely that the more resistance local elites show to political incorporation, or the more important that area is to the ruler's monopoly of resources, the less likely it is that local rulers will be left in place (Barker and Rasmussen 1998:226-67; Scullard 1980:61; Spencer 1982). In the early Zapotec state we may find that some areas of the valley and surrounding regions show little change in the local pattern. In areas that resisted political incorporation there may be more evidence for reorganization, including a shift in the settlement pattern of the region, evidence of violence, or a reduction in the size of the conquered polity's capital (Eisenstadt 1969:15-16).

The distribution of exotic goods should say something about the control of particular resources. The Zapotec may have controlled exotic resources by developing them through the conquest of polities or territories, or by dominating trade networks. For the Oaxaca Valley, non-local goods include obsidian, jade, and shell, as well as tropical fruits, feathers, and some agricultural products that can be cultivated only in warmer climates. To this we can add certain types of pottery with restricted functions that were made in the vicinity of Monte Albán and distributed to other areas. If Monte Albán's rulers controlled exotic/elite goods, they might differentially distribute them to their subordinates to reinforce the hierarchy of authority and to manipulate local elites and urban bureaucrats. In principle, there may be greater differentiation between ruling elites and intermediate elites and less material differentiation among intermediate elites. For example, local Zapotec elites might have access to obsidian, but not produce obsidian implements locally, instead acquiring such implements from the capital as finished products for use in particular contexts.

Occasionally, rulers may promote commoners to positions of authority to mediate the power of subordinate elites (Flannery 1999; Herskovits 1938; Offner 1983; Pollard 1993). While architecture, burials, and artifacts are good indicators of household "wealth" in Mesoamerica (Smith 1987), it is often difficult to demonstrate unambiguously when indicators of economic privilege were directly related to social strata. I have discussed how ethnohistoric documents indicate that commoners could serve the ruling elite (1) as administrators sent out from the capital to check on the local elite; (2) as military or economic advisors and agents; and (3) as trusted spies or close servants of the ruler. Many pre-modern states did have sumptuary laws, meaning that non-nobles could not use certain kinds of material goods. In the Aztec state, the *pochteca* may have lived in fine houses and acted as functionaries of the king, but they went about dressed poorly and hid their wealth (Smith 1996). I doubt that any group comparable to the *pochteca* existed in the early Zapotec state; however, it is useful to consider what kind of archaeological evidence might identify a privileged commoner versus a true noble.

In all likelihood, the Zapotec ruler had an important role in the state religion and military. I described the general outlines of the relationship between nobles and *Cociyo*, and we also want to evaluate archaeological data linking nobles with rituals of abundance and the practice of warfare. Ruling elites who establish themselves as "divinely selected" often exercise life or death control over their subjects (D'Altroy 2002; Lombard 1967; Marcus and Flannery 1996; Pollard 1993; Smith 1996). Iconography encapsulated in carved stone monuments and ceramic sculpture is one of our primary means for evaluating the presence of sacrifice, warfare, and conflict.

Over the long term, however, most intermediate elites—commoner and noble—develop into groups defined by kinship and social solidarity (perhaps even more than social strata), and these groups strive to accumulate wealth and institutionalize their positions as administrators by creating multigenerational bonds. We should look for information indicating (1) the possible expansion of elite groups at the capital and secondary centers, and (2) the affiliation of position and kin unit. In many past cases, both noble and commoner bureaucrats could pass their offices on to their heirs with the ruler's approval (Bossler 1998; Herskovits 1938; Hsu 1995; Paludan 1998; Pollard 1993).

The diversity of burial practices in large palace complexes such as Yagul suggests that people of different social strata lived together within the palace (Bernal and Gamio 1974; Flannery 1983c:292-94). Valley-wide comparisons of "eliteness" (palace size, burial patterns, material goods) may allow us to detect some distinctions in wealth between the local elite who administered different kinds of territories.

On the one hand, factionalism within the nobility may be likely to affect negatively the administrators at the capital; dynastic coups, for example, may result in the replacement of one group of urban functionaries by another more dependent on the new ruler. On the other hand, we might find evidence that factionalism allows subordinate nobles to develop the kinds of resources they needed to intimidate and control the ruler. These distinctions may be difficult to detect without written records, but archaeologically we can look for several factors. First, the proliferation of elite groups at the capital may demonstrate the development of a top-heavy bureaucracy. Second, elite consumption or display, as seen in the plan and location of elite residences and burials at the capital, may show that subordinate elites are effectively developing resources that are not under the direct control of the ruler, resources that they can use to force the ruling elite to negotiate or concede some aspects of decision-making power. Finally, urban bureaucrats or local elites may attempt to challenge the dominant ideology through increased elite-to-elite propaganda. Rulers may use the same tactic to demonstrate the strength of their sociopolitical position.

The Regional Picture

Regional data are an important source of information for evaluating the valley's settlement hierarchy, the distribution of I-shaped ballcourts, and the broad outlines of the pottery production and distribution network.

The Settlement Hierarchy

Cerro Tilcajete's predecessor, El Palenque, was a 71.5 ha center with a 1.6 ha plaza surrounded by thirteen mounds. Cerro Tilcajete (located about 200 m upslope) covers 24.5 ha (Fig. 3.1), while Dainzú (Tlacolula) covers 45.6 ha and San José Mogote (Etla) 60-70 ha (Kowalewski et al. 1989: Appendix VI; Marcus and Flannery 1996:178-80). Based on the number of terraces mapped at Cerro Tilcajete and a rough population estimate of

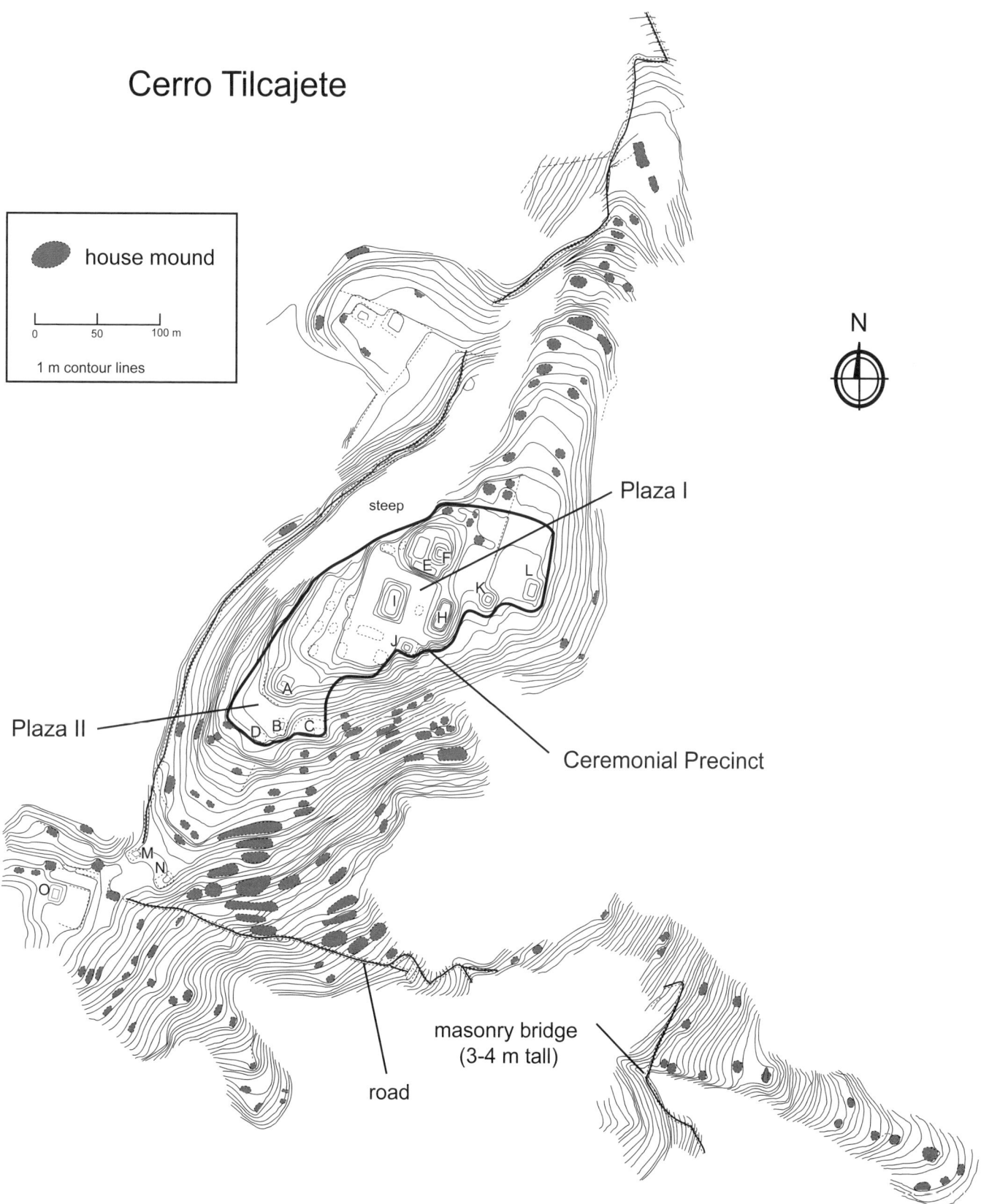

Figure 3.1. The plan of Cerro Tilcajete showing residential terraces and mound groups. The black line delimits an area of high-status residences and civic-ceremonial architecture that make up the site's ceremonial precinct (map by Charles Spencer and Elsa Redmond).

5-10 persons per terrace, the site's population could have been 800-1600 persons.

The loss of 47 ha of population at Ocotlán's largest center from Late Monte Albán I to Monte Albán II is also evident in the general loss of population and a change in the settlement hierarchy of the Valle Grande-Ocotlán subregion (Fig. 3.2). Table 3.1 presents data on the number of sites and the population of Tier III-V sites in Late Monte Albán I and Monte Albán II in the Valle Grande-Ocotlán subregion (Kowalewski et al. 1989: Tables 6.3 and 7.5). These figures suggest that the subregion lost half of its population, notwithstanding the loss of nearly 50 ha of population when El Palenque was conquered and the secondary center shifted to Cerro Tilcajete.

A closer look at the settlement pattern data in light of recent excavations at El Palenque and Yaasuchi, a small site with Late Monte Albán I and Monte Albán II occupation (Fig. 3.2), indicates the settlement hierarchy of the Valle Grande-Ocotlán also changed from Late Monte Albán I to Monte Albán II (Sherman 2005; Spencer and Redmond 2001a). Spencer and Redmond (2001a:205-7; see also Feinman 1998:128-29) argue that in Late Monte Albán I, the El Palenque polity would not have controlled sites west of the Atoyac River nor would it have controlled sites in the northern Valle Grande. They suggest that one site that fell outside El Palenque's control during Late Monte Albán I was San Bartolo Coyotepec. San Bartolo's main mound group has Early Monte Albán I (500-100 B.C.) through Monte Albán IIIa (A.D. 200-500) diagnostics (Blanton et al. 1982:442, Fig. A.XI-11). Site size estimates suggest that San Bartolo covered 0.1 ha in Early Monte Albán I, but jumped dramatically to 34.1 ha in Late Monte Albán I (Blanton et al. 1982: Appendix I). It is only slightly smaller in Monte Albán II and Monte Albán IIIa periods (about 32 ha). It is likely that San Bartolo Coyotepec was controlled by Monte Albán in Late Monte Albán I and marked the boundary between the El Palenque-Ocotlán polity and the Monte Albán-Central Valley polity.

For the northern Valle Grande, Spencer and Redmond's (2001a) analysis and Sherman's (2005) excavations at Yaasuchi can be examined in light of the settlement pattern analyses that looked at how sites grouped at different scales during different time periods. In Late Monte Albán I, when sites were grouped using 1500 m divisions, Yaasuchi grouped with Monte Albán and this site may have been outside El Palenque's control (Kowalewski et al. 1989: Fig. 6.2; Sherman 2005). In Monte Albán II, several sites in the northern Valle Grande cluster with the Tier III site of Cuilapan. Cuilapan is much closer to Monte Albán than to Cerro Tilcajete and it may be that Monte Albán administered Cuilapan in Monte Albán II and that sites in the northern Valle Grande were directly administered by Cuilapan, not Cerro Tilcajete.

Several ideas may explain the changes in the subregional population and settlement pattern. It is possible that the populations did not drop dramatically, but were distributed differently. For example, Monte Albán could have dispersed some people to small, scattered agricultural hamlets that can be difficult to detect or are covered by later sites. Regional survey located four hamlets (each less than 1 ha in size) southeast of Cerro Tilcajete, in an area that later became part of the massive site of Jalieza (Finsten 1995; Kowalewski et al. 1989: Table 8.5). Breaking up the population amassed around large sites such as El Palenque would have aided Monte Albán's rulers in establishing control over the subregion. Of course, some of the population could have fled Monte Albán's domination. Several factors including localized over-farming (particularly in the Central Valley) and Zapotec colonization of areas outside the valley could have contributed to the removal of the local population (Blanton et al. 1999:110). I have noted that the rulers of many ethnohistorically known states often relocated some or all of the members of conquered elite families (often including their servants and retainers) to the capital, where they could keep a watchful eye on their activities.

I suggest that these data favor a model in which Monte Albán not only dictated the forced abandonment of El Palenque, but also either moved populations out of Ocotlán or shifted people into small villages. In stark contrast to Etla and Tlacolula, there are no Tier III centers in Ocotlán south of Cerro Tilcajete (we have noted that the site of Cuilapan in the northern Valle Grande was probably administered directly by Monte Albán). The secondary representatives situated at Cerro Tilcajete would have interacted with the leaders of villages with fewer than 350 persons, such as Santa Ana Zegache, Santa Inés Yatzeche, and Ocotlán.

Table 3.1. Settlement hierarchy and population ranges for Late Monte Albán I and Monte Albán II sites in the Valle Grande-Ocotlán.

Level in Hierarchy	Number of Sites	Site Size (ha)	Population Range	Total
Late Monte Albán I (300-100 B.C.)				
Tier 2	El Palenque	71.5		
Tier 3	3		555-879	1665-2637
Tier 4	7		233-496	1631-3472
Tier 5	11		102-221	1122-2431
Total Population*				4417-8540
Monte Albán II (100 B.C.-A.D. 200)				
Tier 2	Cerro Tilcajete	24.5		
Tier 3	1		387-727	387-727
Tier 4	9		180-343	1620-3087
Tier 5	7		101-161	707-1127
Total Population**				2714-4941

*Excludes El Palenque.
**Excludes Cerro Tilcajete.
(From Kowalewski et al. 1989: Tables 6.3 and 7.5; Spencer and Redmond 2001a)

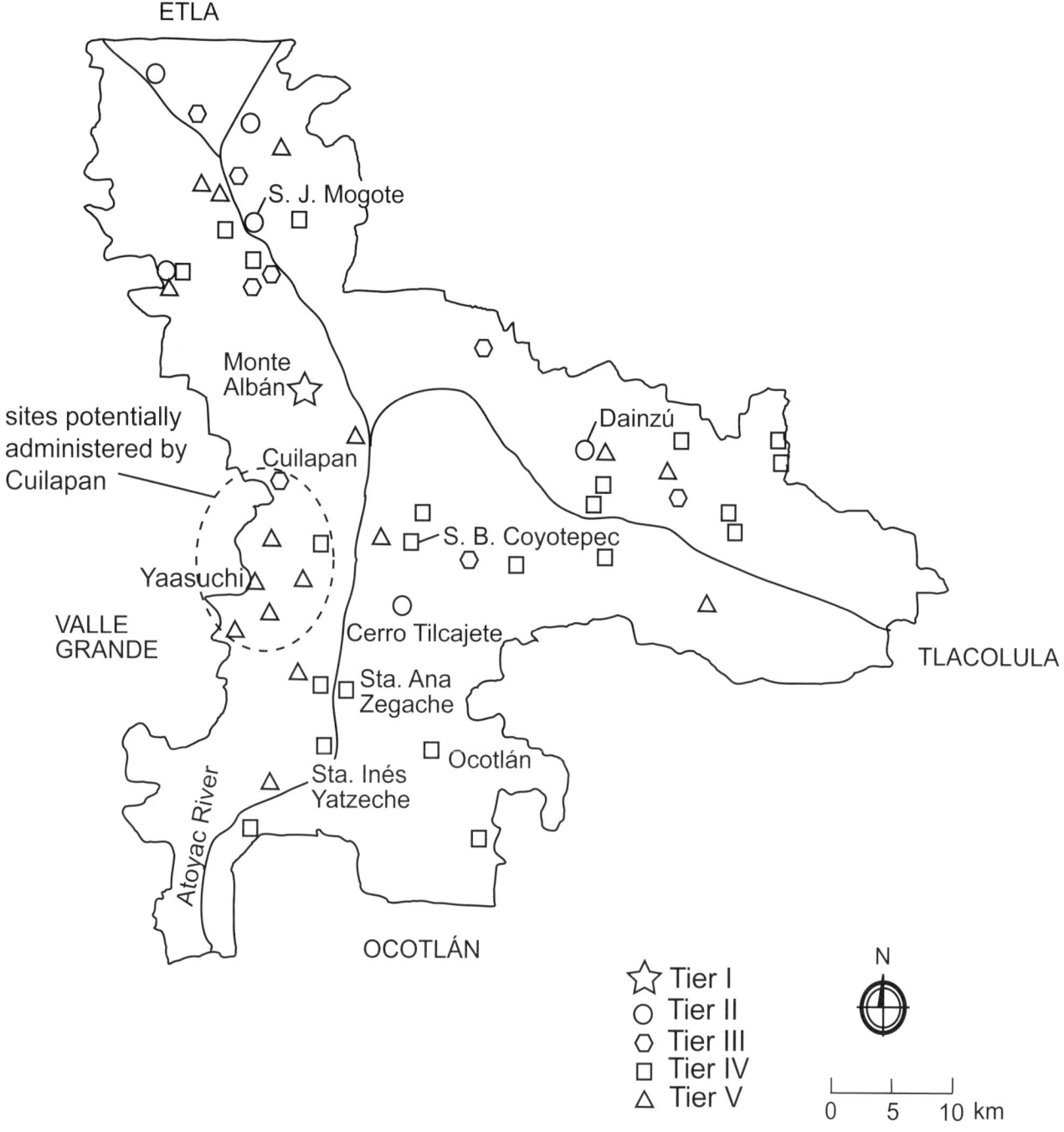

Figure 3.2. The Monte Albán II settlement hierarchy in the Oaxaca Valley (adapted from Kowalewski et al. 1989: Fig. 7.20). Monte Albán, a Tier 1 site, is the largest site in the valley (see Table 3.1 for population estimates).

Figure 3.3. The I-shaped ballcourt at the northeast corner of Monte Albán's main plaza (photo courtesy of Anthropology Division, American Museum of Natural History).

I-Shaped Ballcourts

I have already looked at several hypotheses for the function of the I-shaped ballcourt in Zapotec society. The ideology of the game can be associated with ritualized conflict, and the appearance of the courts in Monte Albán II is consistent with the idea that the game was formalized by the state. Regional survey has provided information on the distribution of ballcourts in the valley, allowing us to suggest where these structures were built and, just as importantly, where they were *not* built (Fig. 3.3). It should be stressed, however, that ballcourts cannot be reliably dated with surface sherds; without excavation, we do not know when a ballcourt was built.

The earliest excavated I-shaped ballcourts in Oaxaca have been found at Monte Albán and San José Mogote, and these excavated courts can be dated to Monte Albán II. The I-shaped ballcourts at both sites are nearly identical: both have high sloping walls to either side of a 41 m long by 21 m wide playing area, and both have a central court 26-27 m long. Despite the fact that earlier figurines and carved stones depict ballplayers, no I-shaped courts earlier than 100 B.C. have been excavated.

In contrast, neither Cerro Tilcajete nor Jalieza (the Monte Albán IIIa site that became Ocotlán's secondary administrative center after A.D. 200) have I-shaped ballcourts. If we look more closely at the Valle Grande/Ocotlán subregion, we find that San Bartolo Coyotepec—suggested in the previous section as a boundary-marking site during Late Monte Albán I—does have an I-shaped ballcourt. As it is still unexcavated, we do not know when this court was constructed; it might have been built in Monte Albán II or Monte Albán IIIa, since San Bartolo Coyotepec covered about 32 ha in both periods. If the court was built in Monte Albán II, it may be that formal ballplaying rituals were one of the means used to integrate Ocotlán with the Valle Grande. If, on the other hand, the court was built in Monte Albán IIIa, it means that the Ocotlán subregion had no I-shaped ballcourt during the first three hundred years of its incorporation into the Monte Albán state.

In Tlacolula, Dainzú has an I-shaped court, but excavations determined that it was not built until circa A.D. 900 (Bernal and Oliveros 1988). To be sure, stone carvings at Dainzú dating to Late Monte Albán I or Monte Albán II depict ballplayers. Thus, an early form of the ballgame was evidently played in Tlacolula, but during Monte Albán II, the game was not yet played on a formal I-shaped ballcourt. Regional survey has located an I-shaped ballcourt at what seems to be a small, single occupation site (with a population estimated at under 200) some 4 km northeast of Dainzú (Kowalewski et al. 1989: Fig. 7.23), but until this site has been excavated, the court cannot be dated.

In both Ocotlán and Tlacolula, we must consider the possibility that I-shaped ballcourts were not located at Monte Albán II

 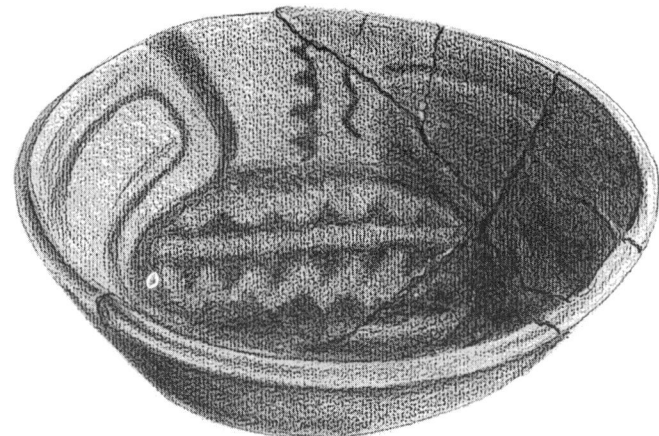

(*Left*) Figure 3.4. Cream-paste bowl with bulbous supports, found in Tomb 77 at Monte Albán (see Fig. 3.10 for tomb's location). The bowl has both incised zigzag and rectangular designs (adapted from Caso et al. 1967: Fig. 205).

(*Right*) Figure 3.5. Orange-paste bowl with red-painted designs (type A.9); found in Burial 2 at Cerro Tilcajete (drawing by Miriam Vallesteros).

secondary centers, but rather at smaller specialized sites nearby. It will take excavation to confirm this, however. We need to know exactly what state function I-shaped ballcourts were designed for, and whether it was a function that Monte Albán preferred not to delegate to elites at Dainzú and Cerro Tilcajete.

Pottery Production Network

Several kinds of Monte Albán II ceramics are distinctive in terms of paste, form, and decoration. One kind of pottery made of a cream paste (called *crema* in the Oaxaca ceramic vocabulary) appears to have been produced only in the vicinity of San Lorenzo Cacaotepec and Sta. María Atzompa, two towns situated just north of Monte Albán (Feinman 1986:356; Shepard 1967:447-48; Sherman et al. 2004; Thieme 2001). Recent trace element analysis of a selection of cream ceramics from the Ocotlán region indicates that they are indeed compositionally similar to those found at Monte Albán and are likely to have been made in the Cacaotepec/Atzompa region (Sherman et al. 2004).

Cream-paste ceramics are very scarce at the El Palenque sector of Tilcajete between 300 and 100 B.C. As described in greater detail below, the most elaborate Monte Albán II cream-paste vessels are bowls with fancy rims, large hollow cylindrical feet, red or black paint, and exterior incised designs that often take the form of step-frets or zigzags. Elsewhere, Jason Sherman and I have argued that these designs symbolize Lightning or the deity *Cociyo* (Elson and Sherman, in press). These bowls were time-consuming to produce and costly to transport (Fig. 3.4) yet they are fairly standardized, suggesting that they were produced with some degree of central organization (Kowalewski et al. 1989:167). Cream-paste ceramics appear to have been an elite ware; thus, information on these ceramics from Cerro Tilcajete can tell us something about how they were used and what role they played in relationships between local and Monte Albán elites.

One additional ceramic type largely destined for the elite was fired to an orange color in an oxidizing environment and decorated with red-painted designs that sometimes included step-frets and zigzags (Fig. 3.5). In contrast to the localized cream paste, the paste used to make the red-painted orange ware (called *amarillo* in the Oaxaca ceramic vocabulary) is generally available throughout the valley. On regional survey, red-painted orange ware is concentrated on the surface of sites in the Valle Grande/Ocotlán and Tlacolula subregions, and is largely absent from sites in the Etla subregion. Red-painted orange ware is, however, found at Monte Albán, primarily around the Main Plaza and on an eastern spur of the site called Monte Albán Chico (Kowalewski et al. 1989:168-79). Data from Cerro Tilcajete now allow me to evaluate the distribution of red-painted orange ware at that site and to compare and contrast its distribution with that of cream-paste ceramics.

Next, to better understand the administrative structure of the early Zapotec state and to determine how Monte Albán's rulers interacted with local elites in all three branches of the valley, I consider site-specific data from the Zapotec capital and three of its secondary centers: San José Mogote in Etla, Dainzú in Tlacolula, and Cerro Tilcajete in Ocotlán.

Monte Albán

Data from decades of research at Monte Albán provide clues about the changing sociopolitical landscape of the Zapotec capital (for the location of buildings, tombs, offerings, and excavated areas described in the text, see Figs. 3.6, 3.7, and 3.10). During Monte Albán II, Monte Albán is estimated to have covered about 416 ha (Blanton 1978:44). While the site had been occupied for at least four hundred years, major new construction projects (described below) were undertaken in the ceremonial-administrative core.

Outside this core there were other discrete mound groups (Blanton 1978), and excavations confirm that at least four of these were in use during Monte Albán II. In general, these groups outside the ceremonial core consisted of one or two mounds on a "closed" patio, accompanied by one or two mounds on an "open" patio. One interpretation of this pattern is that each mound group functioned as the center of a neighborhood with its own elite administrator, who lived in the "closed" patio group and oversaw public ceremonies taking place on mounds in the "open" patio group (Blanton 1983:129). I will not address the question of whether or not these "neighborhoods" were present from the onset of the site's occupation; I will simply review evidence concerning their nature during Monte Albán II and discuss what that tells us about Monte Albán's organization. Let us begin, however, by examining the ceremonial core of the site.

The North Platform Governmental Palace

In Monte Albán II, the North Platform was the focus of extensive renovations involving the site's most important civic-ceremonial structures and temples. As stated above, a civic-ceremonial structure is a discrete architectural unit whose floor plan does not seem to have been that of a two-room temple, but whose size, layout, and lack of burial features suggest that it was not a residential palace either. A civic-ceremonial building can function (among other things) as a reception area where nobles meet with staff or other groups outside their private residence. It is easy to imagine a whole range of formal or ritualized activities that might take place in a civic-ceremonial structure, including the exchange of goods, consumption of food or drink, and presentation of information (see Flannery 1998).

In essence, the architecture of the North Platform (Fig. 3.6) suggests to researchers that this area functioned as a massive governmental palace (Blanton 1978:46, 63; Caso et al. 1967:90-106, Plan 1; Flannery 1998). Figure 3.7 presents a detailed view of the North Platform and the main arteries of traffic flow through the building. In order to reference the mounds, I have numbered them. It is not clear how many of the mounds supported two-room temples; the point is that the complex contained areas for large groups to assemble, smaller private areas where the ruler could receive select groups of people, and temples where rituals were conducted.

The complex was approached from the Main Plaza by a steep set of stairs leading to a colonnaded portico. Both sides of the portico may have been open areas, and as such would have been ideal vantage points for observing the Main Plaza. Another set of stairs descended from the portico into a large sunken patio. A low platform sat in the center of the patio. To the west, a stairway led to Mound 1. To the east, a stairway led to a platform (the east side of the portico) and Mound 2. To the north, a set of stairs led to a series of rooms through which one passed to reach Mound 3.

These constructions were dedicated with elaborate offerings. Excavations in Mound 3 confirm that it was first built in Monte Albán II and was dedicated with a rich offering including shell, a pair of jade earspools, and two masks made of jade, greenstone, shell, and pyrite (Caso et al. 1967:137-40). One offering in the patio east of the portico (and south of Mound 2) contained zoomorphic vessels, cream-paste ceramics, and two burned whale ribs with notches (Caso et al. 1967:90-106). More elaborate Monte Albán II offerings were placed under the Sunken Patio and the stairway leading up to Mound 1, including a sculpture of a bird (perhaps a macaw) in a temple, crafted in red-slipped cream paste (Caso 1935:6, 1938:179; Marcus and Flannery 1996:184-85).

The north section of the platform was accessed by a narrow hall passing east of Mound 3. This route led first to a very private patio, enclosed on three sides by platform mounds (Mounds 4, 5, and 6). This was the most inaccessible point at the site as determined by ekistic analysis. An offering associated with Mound 5 contained what has been interpreted as two female sacrificial victims buried with ceramic vessels, two greenstone and shell necklaces, and a mother-of-pearl mosaic (Acosta n.d.; see also Marcus and Flannery 1996:183). Passing along the corridor brought one to the north end of the platform, where recent excavations have uncovered a Monte Albán II temple atop Mound 7 (Winter 1994).

To date, excavations on the North Platform have not located tombs within any of the mounds. The nearest residence/tomb units are just north and west of the North Platform on a terrace set at a lower level. I will return to this area of the site when I discuss elite residences.

The Main Plaza

Monte Albán II saw a renovation of the Main Plaza, which provided its final 6 ha extent (300 m north-south by 200 m east-west); its surface was completely leveled and plastered (Acosta 1965:818; Flannery 1983a:103). In some cases it is not clear whether certain of the mounds surrounding the Main Plaza held two-room temples, civic-ceremonial buildings, or residences. I will describe what is known about Monte Albán II structures on the Main Plaza, starting with Platform IV North and working counterclockwise (see Fig. 3.6).

Recent excavations on Platform IV North confirm the earlier indications that it held a residence entered from the plaza. Tomb 162 was located below the eastern side of the residence (Caso et al. 1967: Table 7). Seven other burials (not located in tombs) were located just outside (west of) the residence. Many of the burials had associated offerings, and two of the individuals had dental mutilations or inlays signifying a relatively high social status (Martínez López et al. 1995:237).

Just north of Platform IV north, the so-called PNLP platform supported a number of rooms around an interior courtyard. One of these rooms has been interpreted as a temple or ritual area (Martínez López and Markens 2004; Martínez López et al. 1995; Winter 1995). The debris associated with the PNLP platform shows that ceramic production (involving kilns), shell working, and chipped stone production (involving obsidian, silex, and quartz) all took place here (Martínez López and Markens 2004:80-88). Mound K, to the south of Platform IV North, contained a tomb dating to Monte Albán I, as did a terrace located just west of Mound K.

Building L is best known for its Monte Albán I construction stage, when it was covered with hundreds of carved slabs depicting slain and sacrificed captives (Marcus 1992b). In Monte Albán II, Building L was remodeled and these slabs were either covered up or reused in other construction projects. It is likely that the Building L platform once supported either a two-room temple or a building with a civic-ceremonial function. In Monte Albán II, the east side of the Main Plaza and the terraces directly west of the Plaza were occupied by associated residences, civic-ceremonial buildings, and two-room temples.

There is little or no information concerning the kinds of buildings that occupied Areas Q, S, P, and U on the eastern side of the plaza. One offering from this side of the plaza contained an 85 cm tall ceramic statue of a jaguar or puma. Indeed, jaguar or puma imagery—on ceramic urns, statues, and figurines—is found with greater frequency throughout Monte Albán during Monte Albán II (Caso and Bernal 1952:55).

Platforms G, H, I, and J lie in the center of the Main Plaza. During later time periods at least, it is likely that G and H supported two-room temples. Between Buildings H and P sat a low platform with an offering containing five skeletons of young adults (possibly sacrificial victims) entombed with jade and shell, including an extraordinary bat mask of jade and shell. Two of the skeletons were associated with Monte Albán II pottery, including cream-paste bowls with tripod feet (Acosta 1974:76-77, 82; Marcus and Flannery 1996:183-84, Plate 1).

Platform I faced south toward Building J, an odd, arrowhead-shaped structure whose function is not clear, but whose outer walls were covered in hieroglyphic inscriptions thought to depict territories claimed by the Zapotec state. This building may have served as a kind of war memorial intended to honor past military victories (Blanton 1978:47; Marcus 1976b; Marcus 1983e:106-8; Marcus and Flannery 1996:195-98). Archaeological data, however, suggest that not all the areas depicted needed to be incorporated into the Zapotec state by force.

The northeast corner of the Main Plaza was occupied by an I-shaped ballcourt, with high sloping walls to either side of a 41 m long by 21 m wide playing area and a central court 26-27 m long. We have already stated that the appearance of I shaped ballcourts in Monte Albán II is consistent with the formalization of the game by the Zapotec state (Marcus and Flannery 1996:189-90). Some suspect that these courts may have served as venues for performing acts of ritual conflict that served to further state ideology (Kowalewski et al. 1991). Others suspect that the games may have served to resolve factional or community affairs conflict in a ritual context (Redmond 1983).

The Mound of the Carved Stone

Let us now turn to an examination of mounds and temples with Monte Albán II occupation outside the Main Plaza. The first is a zone of residences and tombs located just off the northwest corner of the North Platform, and associated with a tall mound the excavators called "The Mound of the Carved Stone" (see Figs. 3.6 and 3.7). This mound supported a palace measuring about 18 × 20 m (Caso 1938:68-83). Three tombs were found in the mound, while three more were found on the adjacent architectural terrace. The presence of one tomb dating to Monte Albán I (Tomb 107), three tombs dating to Monte Albán II (Tombs 102, 113, and 118), and two tombs dating to Monte Albán III (Tombs 103 and 104) attest to a long history of elite occupation; it is likely that many Zapotec royal families resided here.

Caso's pit into the east side of the mound passed through five plaster floors and reached a depth of almost 3 m before it struck Tomb 107 (Caso 1938:74-75). This tomb was a simple, stone-lined rectangle with no door but with a corbelled roof. Its floor was the original bedrock upon which the mound had been built. The single adult skeleton was accompanied by two Monte Albán I style *Cociyo* urns (see Fig. 2.1) (Caso et al. 1967: Fig. 86*c*).

Another important Monte Albán I tomb (Tomb 33) was located on one of the terraces slightly north and east of the Mound of the Carved Stone. I mention this tomb because it contained at least thirty-four ceramic vessels, including many elaborate zoomorphic and anthropomorphic vessels and figurines, and the skeleton of a young girl. Many vessels occurred in pairs lip to lip, with one vessel right-side up and its companion placed upside down (Caso 1933:646; Martínez López et al. 1995:236). Of the five Monte Albán I tombs with substantial offerings excavated thus far at Monte Albán, three were located in this area.

Tomb 118, dating to Monte Albán II, contained at least twenty-five vessels including cream-paste bowls with incised designs and bulbous feet. The contemporaneous Tomb 113 contained pottery (including red-painted cream-paste bowls with incised designs and bulbous feet) and three standing polychrome figures (Caso 1942:183; Caso and Bernal 1952:336-39; Caso et al. 1967:167; Redmond 1983:171-76). Two of these figures are warriors dressed in apparent military costumes (Fig. 3.8). They wear headdresses that have feline imagery ("Glyph C," which is interpreted as the nose and mouth of a feline) (see Caso 1928:29). The third polychrome figure, originally interpreted as female and perhaps depicting a priestess, wears a headdress incorporating *Cociyo* (Caso and Bernal 1952).

Tombs 103 and 104 date to Monte Albán III (A.D. 200-700) and were tombs of Zapotec royalty. Tomb 104 may have been reused over several generations. The tomb's antechamber contained an urn representing a young lord wearing a headdress with a central figure of *Cociyo* and a jaguar or puma head at either side (Fig. 3.9). The lord is richly attired and carries a copal bag.

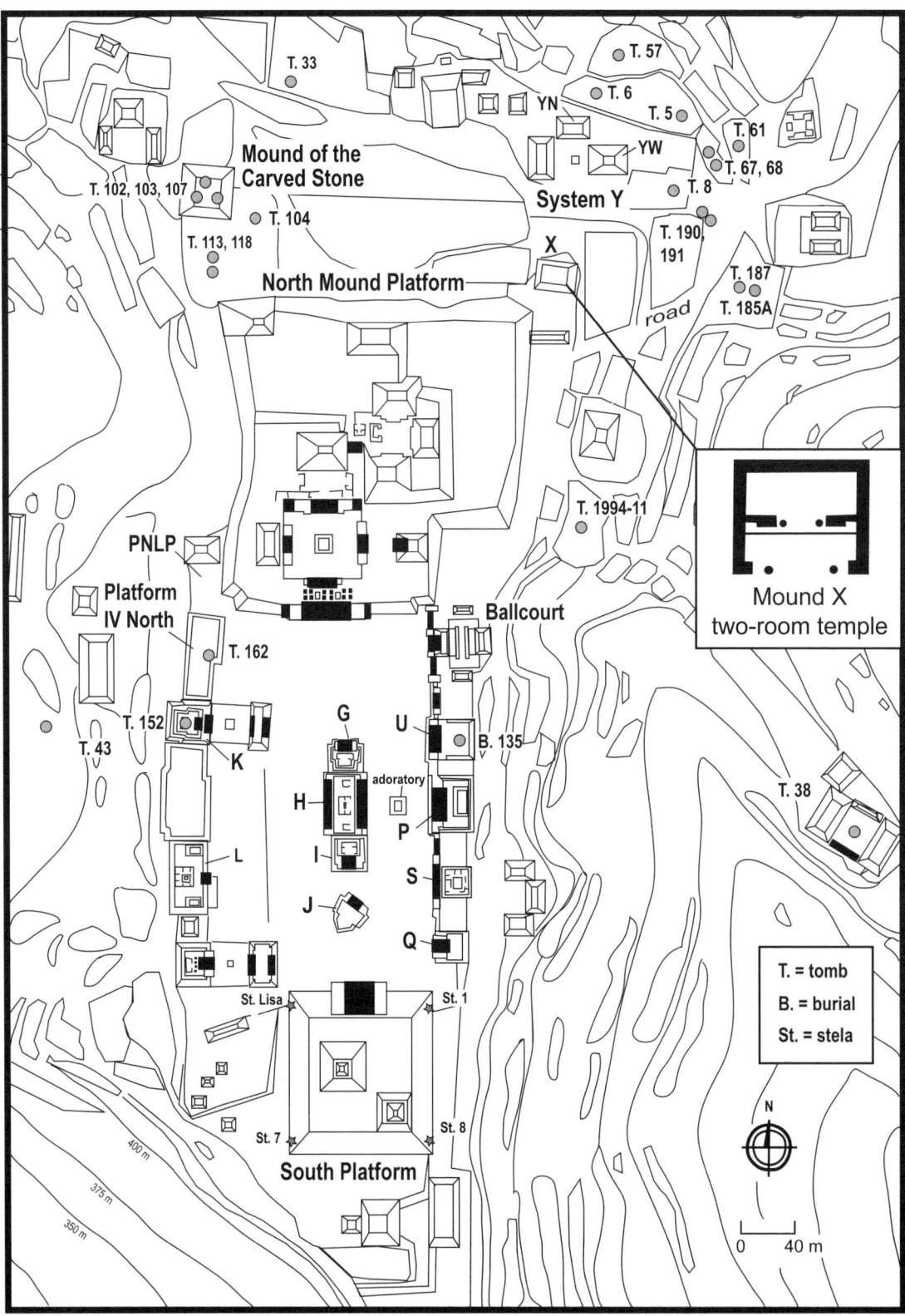

Figure 3.6. Plan of Monte Albán's ceremonial core showing the location of buildings, carved stones, burials, and tombs discussed in the text (redrawn from Blanton 1978: Appendix VI).

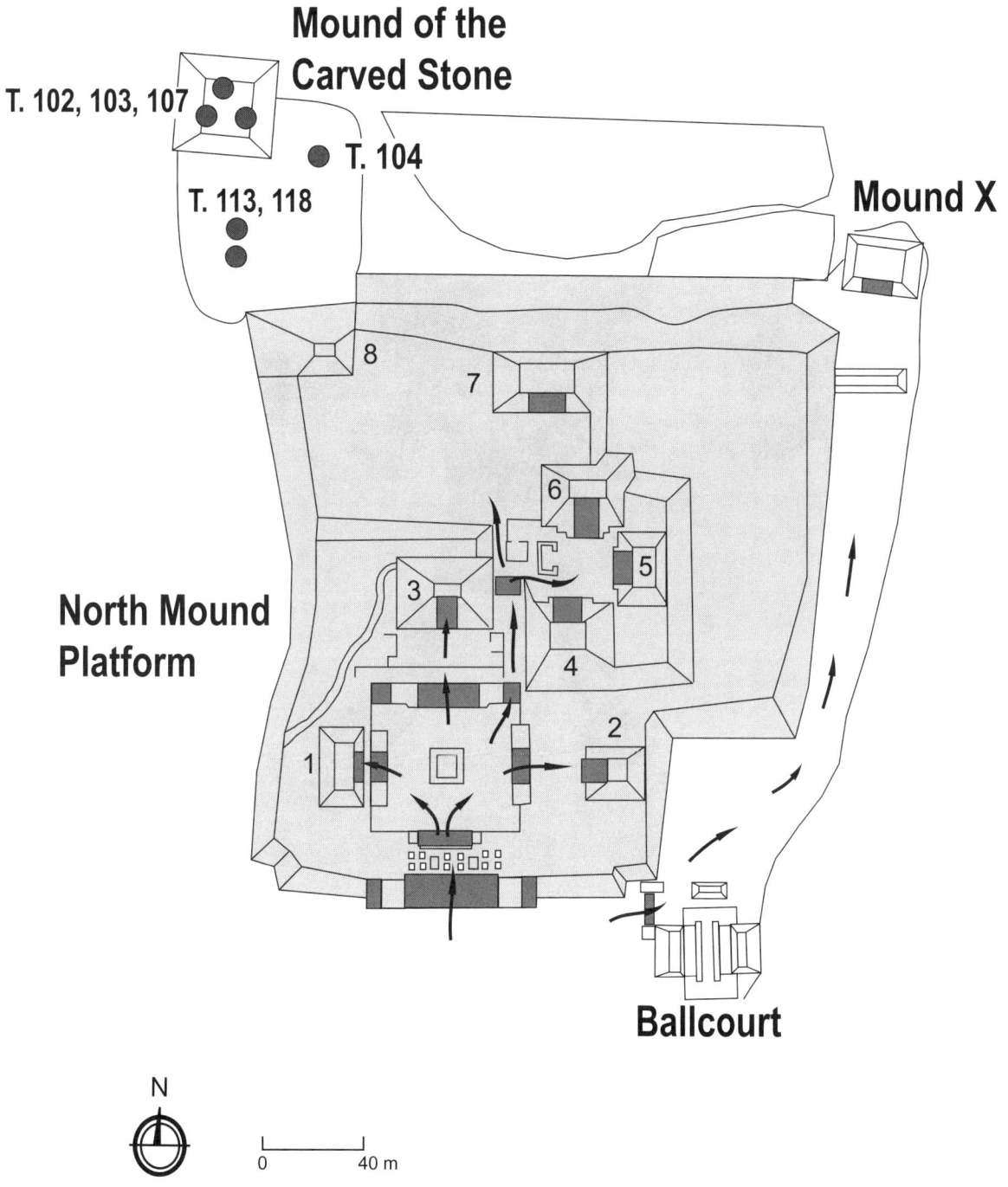

Figure 3.7. A detailed view of buildings on the North Platform (shaded) and the areas just north and east. To the north of Building 8 is a large terrace and mound where elaborate tombs dating to Monte Albán I, II, and III have been excavated. The arrows show likely routes of traffic onto the North Platform and its buildings from the Main Plaza.

Figure 3.8. Three ceramic statues from Tomb 113, a Monte Albán II tomb at Monte Albán (see Fig. 3.7 for tomb's location) (redrawn by Miriam Vallesteros from Caso and Bernal 1952: Figs. 498 and 499; Caso and Bernal 1965: Fig. 8; no scales given).

Figure 3.9. An urn, showing a noble lord, from the antechamber of Tomb 104 at Monte Albán. Tomb 104 dates to Monte Albán III (see Fig. 3.7 for tomb's location) (photo courtesy of Anthropology Division, American Museum of Natural History).

He sits cross-legged on a pedestal with additional jaguar or puma imagery (Caso and Bernal 1952:51; Marcus 1983f:140). Inside the tomb are wall murals depicting the relatives or royal ancestors of the tomb's occupant (Marcus 1983f:140). There are two important glyphs in the tomb: a stylized depiction of the nose and mouth of a feline (Glyph C), and a motif called "the jaws of the sky," which has been interpreted as indicating noble descent (Caso 1932:29; Marcus 1983f:137).

Tomb 103 was a very rich, very elaborate Monte Albán III tomb constructed of large stone blocks. It was painted inside with glyphs; it contained ceramics, several polychrome urns, and a jade bird head (Caso 1938:69-74; see also Miller 1995:72-73). In the patio of the Tomb 103 palace was a complicated offering depicting a deceased individual surrounded by large, elaborately dressed figures and accompanied by other smaller "assistants" (Caso 1942:181-82).

Over time, the mortuary treatment, residences, offerings, and iconography associated with the Mound of the Carved Stone became very elaborate. During Monte Albán I, there was imagery linking elites with *Cociyo*. By Monte Albán II, some elites used avian and feline imagery. Several scholars have suggested that the proliferation of jaguar or puma imagery (statues, urns, and figurines) at Monte Albán during Monte Albán II indicates that the use of feline imagery had become the particular right of the ruling elite, who also fulfilled important roles as military leaders (Marcus 1989; Spencer and Redmond 2000). If this is the case, it would not be surprising to find such imagery explicitly displayed in an area housing ruling elite families.

The Northeast Zone

The Mound of the Carved Stone can be contrasted with the area northeast of the North Platform (see Fig. 3.6), where excavations uncovered an area of elite residences stretching for 100 m east of the System Y Mound Group and at least 75 m in a north-south direction (Caso 1932, 1935:16-31; Caso et al. 1967:106-41). It is unclear what most of these residences would have looked like during Monte Albán I or Monte Albán II since they were covered by later periods of occupation. Early tombs, however, were found when exploratory pits were used to examine the earlier stratigraphy. The System Y mound group itself—one focus for ritual expression by residents living in this area—was built in Monte Albán II.

Based on the grouping of tombs, there were at least four concentrations of Monte Albán II residences within this area. We can begin with Tomb 5, a simple slab-lined rectangular crypt containing the remains of two people buried with at least eight vessels. Tomb 6, found on the same terrace, had been built in sections and contained at least seven people, demonstrating the reuse of the tomb over generations.

Tomb 57 was found in a separate residence. This elaborate tomb had a vaulted roof and five vessels including a bowl with painted stucco ("al fresco" decoration). Yet another residence contained Tomb 68, a simple tomb with the remains of one individual accompanied by various offerings, including several cream-paste vases.

This same residence contained Tomb 67, a tomb with a vaulted roof holding two individuals accompanied by a cream-paste bowl with large hollow supports, a cream-paste vase, and a bowl with a painted stucco decoration in green, yellow, and red.

A more recent investigation of tombs, burials, and residences to the southeast (and downslope) of this area has found that most probably date to A.D. 100 and later, and that the residences contained several types of interments (Martínez López 1998). For example, excavations on one terrace uncovered the remains of several attached residences and two Monte Albán II tombs (Tombs 187 and 185A), each containing one or more adults accompanied by urns and other objects. Other burials were placed in trash pits and under the floors of rooms; some of these individuals were accompanied by relatively abundant offerings. Burial 1991-83 (an adult in a simple pit) was interred with seven vessels, seven obsidian blades, a bone point, two water-smoothed stones, and a ceramic tray with red paint and cinnabar (Martínez López 1998:55-66, 101-3).

The area northeast of the Main Plaza shows a great deal of variation in terms of burial features and residences, and it does appear that over time, elite residences proliferated and are thus more densely packed within this area.

Zone East of Building P

Excavations have located another Monte Albán II tomb, Tomb 38, in a four-mound group 300 m east of Building P (Caso et al. 1967) (see Fig. 3.6). This mound group is set on a terrace covering 3969 m^2; work there has produced pottery from all time periods. The four-mound group may have been a discrete residential area complex as early as Monte Albán I. Surface collections from this mound group and the Main Plaza had the highest concentrations of Monte Albán II red-painted orange ware at the site (Blanton 1978:37-38, 83; Kowalewski et al. 1989:168-80). Tomb 38 contained at least seven vessels, including two cream-paste vases, one with a lid (Caso et al. 1967). Surface collections in this area also produced evidence for shell working and large-scale food production, but it is difficult to date these activities from surface remains (Blanton 1978:83).

The El Pitahayo Mounds

Far from the Main Plaza, near a defensive wall on Monte Albán's north slope, is a mound cluster called the El Pitahayo Group (Fig. 3.10). This mound group was originally constructed in Late Monte Albán I or II and sits on a 15,200 m^2 terrace (Blanton 1978:156; Caso 1935:23-27; Caso 1938:32-36). Seven tombs dating to Monte Albán I or II were excavated in this area: Tombs 77 and 78 in Mound F (Fig. 3.11); Tomb 94 in (or very near to) Mound A; Tombs 95 and 96 in Mound B (Fig. 3.12); and Tomb 85 in (or very near to) Mound C or Mound D. Tomb 98 was located about 100 m northwest of Mound B. Other, simpler burials were located in pits at the bases of these mounds or on the roofs of the tombs (Tombs 77 and 95). Initially, the excavators dated Tombs 94, 95, 96, 85, and 98 to Monte Albán II; however,

The Oaxaca Valley in Monte Albán II   29

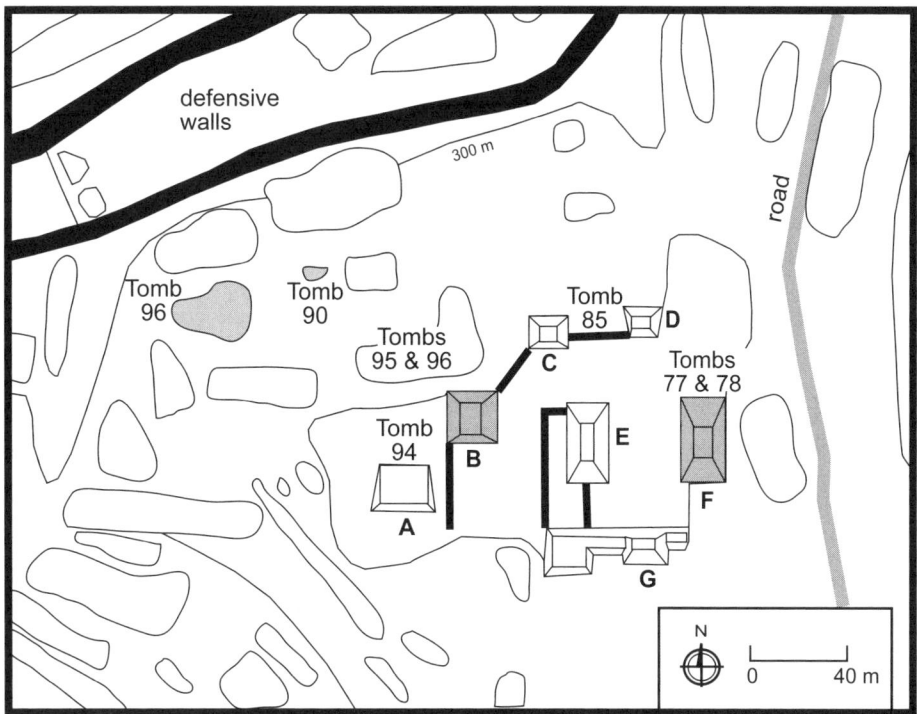

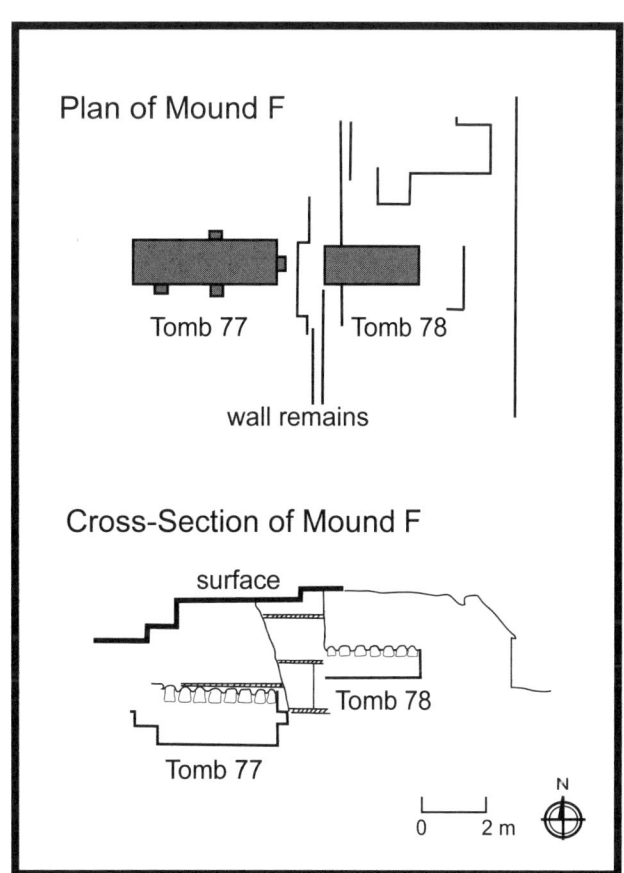

(*Above*) Figure 3.10. Plan of the El Pitahayo mound group at Monte Albán showing the location of excavated tombs. Tomb 98 is not shown; it was located about 100 m northwest of Mound B (redrawn from Blanton 1978: Appendix VI).

(*Right*) Figure 3.11. Plan of Tombs 77 and 78 in the El Pitahayo mound group at Monte Albán (redrawn from Caso et al. 1967: Plan 8).

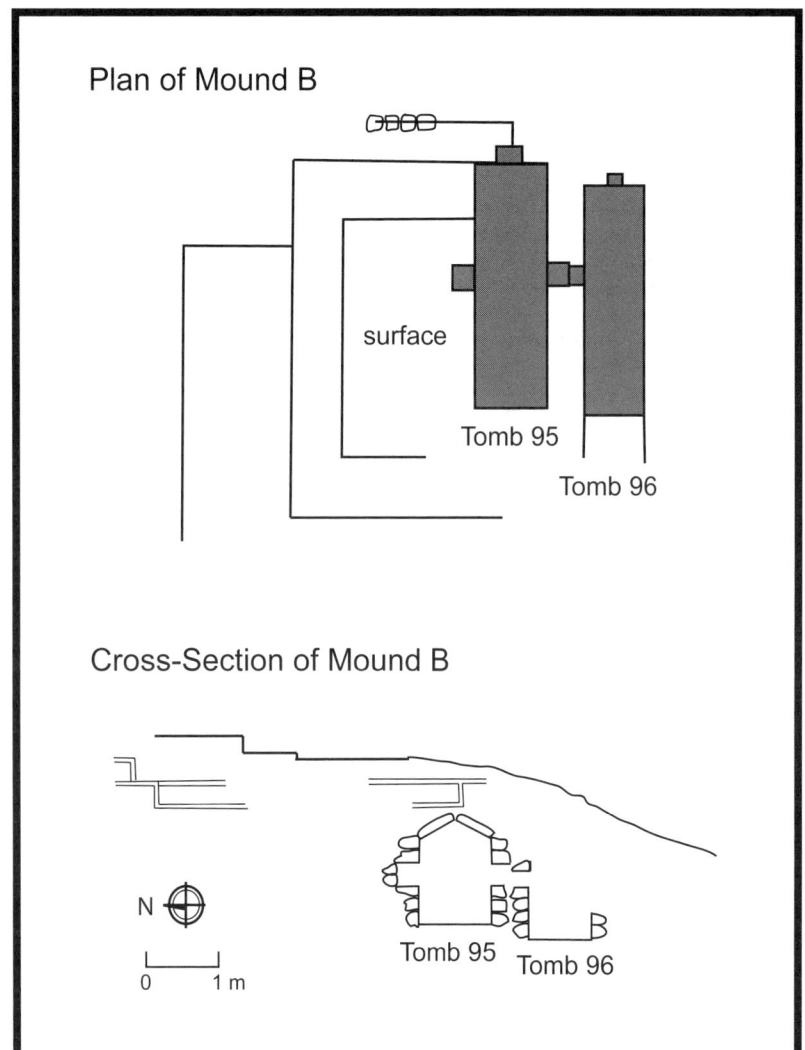

Figure 3.12. Plan of Tombs 95 and 96 in the El Pitahayo mound group at Monte Albán (redrawn from Caso et al. 1967: Plan 9).

later analysis identified Tomb 94 as a Monte Albán I tomb (Caso et al. 1967: Table 4; Caso 1938:33-36).

Tomb 85 (Mound C or D) contained at least fourteen objects, including a cream-paste bowl with bulbous supports, a vase, and an incense burner. Tomb 95 (Mound B) had three niches and an antechamber, an architectural layout suggesting that it was built during Monte Albán II or later. The plan of Tomb 96 shows fifty-five objects, including twenty-five ceramic vessels placed in and among scattered bones (Caso et al. 1967: Plan 9). The Tomb 96 offering included at least two incised bowls that are most common during the Monte Albán I time period, suggesting that this tomb may date either to Late Monte Albán I or to early Monte Albán II.

Tomb 94 in Mound A contained at least eighteen objects, including a *Cociyo* bottle, a cream-paste vase possibly depicting a monkey, and elegant bowls and plates. Tomb 78 was found next to Tomb 77, but several facts suggest that the former pre-dates the latter. Tomb 78 was relatively simple, stone-lined, and rectangular, while Tomb 77 had elaborate niches and a vaulted roof (Caso et al. 1967: Plan 8). Tomb 78 had been partially looted but its architecture was structurally intact, suggesting to Caso (1938:82) that objects might have been removed from Tomb 78 at the time Tomb 77 was built. Tomb 78 still contained at least twelve ceramic objects, jade earspools, the remains of a shell and obsidian mosaic, and at least one bowl type more frequent in Monte Albán I than in Monte Albán II (Caso et al. 1967:32).

The most spectacular tomb in the El Pitahayo area was Tomb 77, an elaborate construction with niches and a vaulted roof, which probably served as the final resting place of an important person. Besides its many ceramic vessels, Tomb 77 contained a beautiful urn portraying a warrior whose head was enclosed in a helmet depicting a raptorial bird, and faux eagle claws carved in shell (Caso 1935:26; Marcus and Flannery 1996:199).

The distribution of tombs suggests that the El Pitahayo terrace and at least Mounds A and F were built in Late Monte Albán I and were the scene of elite residences. During Monte Albán II, the complex probably was expanded, and additional mounds and residences were constructed on surrounding terraces. We do not know if any of the mounds supported two-room temples, but the relatively small area atop most of the mounds (less than about 100 m^2) suggests that they likely were temples rather than larger civic-ceremonial structures. The imagery in the tombs—individuals wearing avian "warrior" headdresses and vessels depicting *Cociyo*—mirrors that of Monte Albán II tombs at the Mound of the Carved Stone.

Mounds and Terraces on the North Slope

About 500 m northwest of the Mound of the Carved Stone are a series of terraces and low mounds. During the Monte Albán urban survey, ceramics from all time periods were noted on the surface in this area (Blanton 1978:274). Excavations on parts of three of the terraces associated with these mounds uncovered the remains of residences and features. These excavations show that the first occupation of the area took place in Early Monte Albán I (Winter 1974; Winter et al. 1995:14-78). Architectural remains suggest that there were up to five distinct domestic units of that period on the terraces. One Early Monte Albán I tomb was cut into bedrock and had sections of adobe walls. It contained the remains of four individuals accompanied by fifty-nine objects: fifteen ceramic vessels, four pieces of worked bone, and forty pieces of shell and worked shell pendants (Winter et al. 1995:60-72).

The distribution of Monte Albán II tombs and burials suggests the presence of at least four domestic units on the terraces. The only Monte Albán II tomb, Tomb 173, was located in the patio area of one of the units (Winter et al. 1995:53-56). This tomb had been cut into bedrock, and the walls were finished with large, roughly cut blocks of stone. Tomb 173 contained the remains of one individual buried with eight vessels, including a gray-paste effigy bowl, a cream-paste incense burner, and a cream-paste bowl with incised decoration and large hollow supports. Two simpler burials (one infant and one adult) were found in the same general area, but neither contained any offerings. Other burials nearby, however, either had multiple interments or included many offerings. Burial 1972-16 was a simple hole dug into bedrock; it contained the remains of three individuals, six vessels, four pieces of shell (some worked), and five greenstone beads. Burial 1972-17, also a simple hole in the earth, had one individual accompanied by five vessels and shell fragments. Burial 1973-23 was placed in a modified oven dug into bedrock; this simple feature contained a man with tabular cranial deformation and accompanied by more than twenty-four pieces of shell, bone needles, and four pieces of rabbit mandible. In general, the excavators suggest that people living in this area suffered from declining fortunes (in terms of access to elite goods) after 100 B.C. (Winter et al. 1995:73-75).

Summary

The combined evidence for the Monte Albán II occupation of Monte Albán points to three important trends. First, most of the site's ceremonial center was rebuilt to suit a particular aesthetic: an elevated civic-ceremonial palace was placed at the north end of a large open plaza, surrounded primarily by mounds supporting buildings with ritual functions. (The one exception to the ritual emphasis is the PNLP area, a residence that had occupation going back to Monte Albán I.) Public buildings and temples were dedicated with elaborate offerings, including multiple sacrificial victims and exotic goods (jade, whale bone, obsidian). An I-shaped ballcourt was placed near the plaza's northeast corner.

A second trend was evidence for increasing hierarchy within the noble social stratum. The North Platform civic-ceremonial complex contained both reception areas and temples and was closely associated with the residential palaces of the Mound of the Carved Stone. The individuals in the tombs under these palaces, buried with *Cociyo* urns, jaguar or puma imagery, and fancy cream-paste vessels with Lightning iconography, probably belonged to the city's ruling families.

Other Monte Albán II nobles lived in areas associated with mound groups: (1) the System Y mound group was affiliated with a dense cluster of residences north and east of the North Platform; (2) the area east of Building P incorporated a smaller number of terraces; and (3) the El Pitahayo zone was located along a major road connecting Monte Albán with the valley floor, and positioned directly behind a double defensive wall on one of the gentlest slopes of the site. Tombs in these areas show that individuals received both urns with *Cociyo* iconography and cream-paste vessels with Lightning iconography. Finally, an area of mounds and terraces on the north slope of the site also contained tombs and burials. This area may have declined in fortune during Monte Albán II; however, a few individuals did merit burial with cream-paste ceramics and exotic goods. The north slope residential area lay relatively far from the Main Plaza and can be contrasted with the El Pitahayo zone, where multiple tombs and large mounds were constructed.

Finally, a third trend involves evidence that some lower-ranking elites may have had specific involvement with military and economic activities. The dense concentrations of shell and chipped stone debris in Area PNLP (and possibly shell in Area P) suggest that Monte Albán had considerable control over access to obsidian and dominated the production of worked shell (Martínez López and Markens 2004:90; see also Winter 1989:352). For their part, the residents of the El Pitahayo Mound Group were buried in elaborate tombs with warrior effigies, offering the possibility that they were deeply involved with defensive or military functions.

Indirect evidence for ritual specialization can be derived from the placement of temples in mound groups associated with distinct "neighborhoods" at Monte Albán. These data are more difficult to interpret, but could indicate: (1) the presence of a hierarchical organization of priests (in essence, high-ranking priests served in temples on the Main Plaza while lower-ranking priests were assigned to serve "neighborhoods"); (2) a system in which the highest-ranking elite family in each neighborhood was involved with the conduct of local ritual; or (3) some combination of these situations. For example, the temples on the Main Plaza may have employed priests from the highest levels of the hierarchy to direct state ritual, while the temples situated in urban neighborhoods were under the joint supervision of noble families and lesser priests.

San José Mogote

Excavations at San José Mogote were directed by Kent Flannery and Joyce Marcus (Flannery and Marcus 1983a, 1994, 2005; Marcus and Flannery 1996). Virtually abandoned when the bulk of its population moved to Monte Albán around 500 B.C., San José Mogote was reborn around 100 B.C. and was repopulated as the main secondary administrative center for the Etla region (Fig. 3.13). Excavation data suggest that the site's Early Monte Albán II renaissance was directed by elites from Monte Albán (Marcus and Flannery 1996:178-80).

During Monte Albán II, the site came to cover 60-70 ha and was given a Main Plaza with roughly the same dimensions as Monte Albán's. An I-shaped ballcourt with dimensions identical to Monte Albán's was built on the west side of the Main Plaza. A governmental palace built on a natural rise on the north side of the plaza had, in microcosm, a layout reminiscent of the one on Monte Albán's North Platform: both structures have colonnaded porticos, a sunken patio, and reception rooms, and both may have been used for elite assembly.

Like Monte Albán, San José Mogote had many temples. There are at least ten mounds at the site that probably held two-room temples; some of these were paired temples that faced each other along the east-west path of the sun. The offerings associated with one stratigraphic sequence of Monte Albán II temples demonstrate the elaborateness of the dedication ceremonies that took place after the site was renovated. Temple 35 had an interior floor space of approximately 88 m². Forty-two prismatic obsidian blades and two sacrificial knives were found *in situ* on the floor of the temple; several offering boxes were found below the floor. One of these boxes held two jade figures, the larger of which (49 cm tall) may represent a sacrificed noble. A second box under the same room held seven ceramic figures arranged in a scene. The centerpiece of this offering was a figure in a miniature tomb; his necklace and large ear ornaments identify him as a member of the nobility. On the roof of the tomb was a flying figure wearing a Lightning mask. The four remaining ceramic figures may represent Clouds, Rain, Hail, and Wind, the four companions of Lightning. The excavators suggest that "this scene may depict the metamorphosis of a deceased Zapotec lord into a 'Cloud Person' (*ben zaa*) or 'Flying Figure' who was now in contact with Lightning. He could represent a royal ancestor of the kneeling man in the miniature tomb, or even the partial

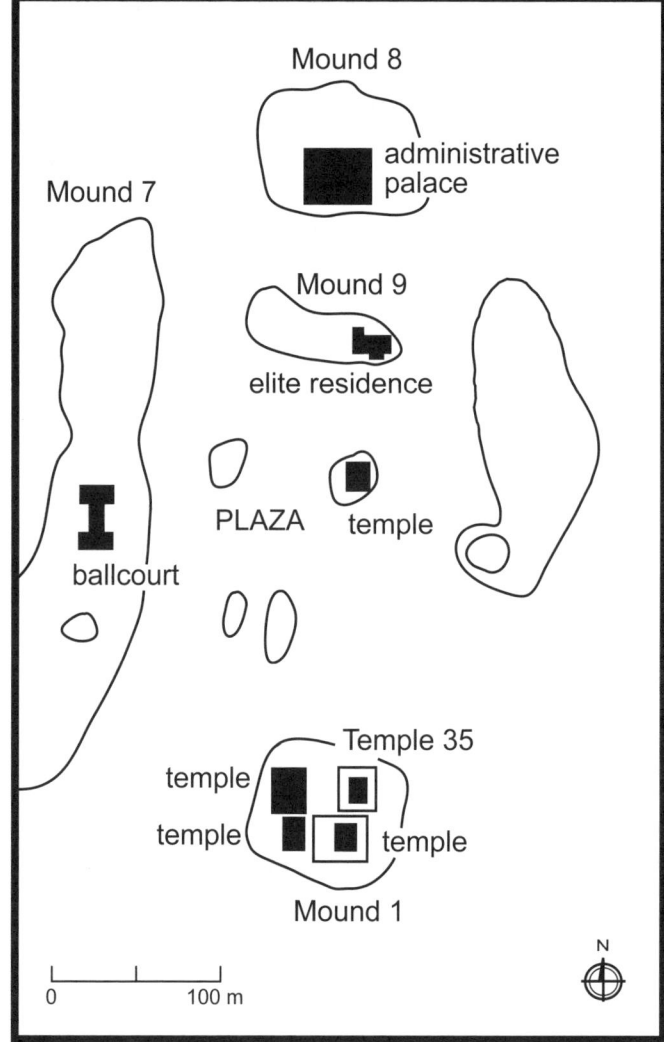

Figure 3.13. Map of San José Mogote (redrawn from Flannery and Marcus 1983a: Fig. 4.19).

metamorphosis of that same individual, caught at a stage where his body is still that of a human but his face is *Cociyo's*" (Marcus and Flannery 1996:188).

Apart from these structures, an elite residence was located on Mound 9 (just south of the governmental palace), and a fragmentary residence south and west of the Main Plaza may have belonged to a family of less elevated status (Flannery and Marcus 2005). The layout and architecture of San José Mogote, as well as the dedicatory offerings associated with the Monte Albán II buildings, indicate close ties between the local elite and the elite at Monte Albán. Both San José Mogote and Monte Albán had governmental palaces and I-shaped ballcourts (see Fig. 3.13). The local elite of San José Mogote seem to have had access to a great deal of wealth and disposed of it in elaborate dedicatory offerings, suggesting that they were interested in (1) establishing their status as persons with ties to venerated noble ancestors, and (2) promoting an ideology that closely linked themselves to elites at the capital.

Dainzú

Dainzú in the Tlacolula region was excavated under the direction of Ignacio Bernal (Bernal 1967, 1968, 1973, 1981; Bernal and Oliveros 1988). Dainzú was first occupied in Monte Albán I, a period when the regional center of Yegüih (a little over 8 km to the east of Dainzú) was the largest site in the Tlacolula area. During Monte Albán II, some population shifted from Yegüih to Dainzú, but the former site was not abandoned; it still covered at least 24.5 ha. For its part, Dainzú grew from a site occupying less than 2 ha to one covering 45.6 ha; simultaneously, the number and density of sites in the central Tlacolula subvalley increased (Kowalewski et al. 1989:162).

Bernal's excavations allowed him to determine when different kinds of administrative buildings appear at the site (Fig. 3.14). In Area A, ceramics from the fill date the earliest buildings to Late Monte Albán I. These were platforms supported by walls 1.25 to 5.25 m tall. Along the southern portion of the lowermost wall, excavations uncovered a number of carved stone monuments depicting ballplayers. Bernal suggests that these monuments were placed in the wall at the end of Late Monte Albán I (Bernal and Oliveros 1988:20, 40; see Bernal 1967).

Excavations in Area A also uncovered two "hidden" stairways that lead from a large open area to an upper patio. This kind of stairway was found also at San José Mogote, and Monte Albán had hidden tunnels; both features would have allowed priests to suddenly appear or disappear (see Marcus and Flannery 1996:184). One stairway at Dainzú was sealed during Monte Albán II and re-used as a tomb; it contained the scattered bones of an individual with five ceramic objects, including a cream-paste bowl with large hollow supports (Bernal and Oliveros 1988:28). The other stairway at Dainzú led to a room that opened onto a patio. This room (originally a one-room structure) had been modified to resemble the plan of a two-room temple: the outer room faced the patio, while the inner room was flanked by two adobe columns.

Area B, a series of terraces downslope from Area A, contained other civic-ceremonial buildings and elite residences. The original constructions here date to the Late Monte Albán I-II transition (Bernal and Oliveros 1988:10). All of these constructions were eventually covered or destroyed by later renovations; however, using trenches and pits, the excavators uncovered enough data to reconstruct the earliest stages of the platforms.

On one small terrace, Bernal and Oliveros uncovered the remains of a yellow-painted temple-like structure (3.25 × 1.25 m), reconstructed to have two columns in the entranceway and a small niche in the north wall. The northernmost platform was accessed by means of a "hidden" stair. Its west-facing retaining wall was at least 4 m tall and took the form of a sloping, stuccoed *talud*. Two carvings, Reliefs 85 and 86, were set into the base of this stucco-covered wall. One is a ballplayer standing on a series of footprints indicating "travel." The other sculpture is the only one of its kind at the site, and represents an individual with an elaborate headdress and closed eyes standing on a hill glyph (Bernal and Oliveros 1988:49). The placement of these two carvings together suggests competition and defeat, perhaps formally symbolized through ballplaying. Just who these individuals were, or where they were from, is unknown.

During Monte Albán II or early Monte Albán III, these same platforms were converted from open spaces to complexes of several rooms reached by a broad stairway. At the top of this stairway was a portico with five adobe columns supporting a roof. Behind the portico was a room, and underneath the floor of this room the excavators found a very elaborate tomb that had been disturbed in antiquity. The façade of the tomb was carved to depict the head and forelegs of a puma or jaguar. Sherds in the tomb date its initial use to the Monte Albán II-IIIa transition (Bernal and Oliveros 1988:27-28).

South and east of these platforms, excavations uncovered roughly half of a sunken plaza that would have been flanked on the north, east, and (probably) west by long platforms. The plaza's dimensions would have been about 20 m (along the north-south axis) by about 30 m (along the east-west axis). It is possible that by the end of Monte Albán II, this plaza had become the central court of an elaborate elite residence. Rooms were built on the north and east platforms of the plaza. Two burials (one an infant and one an adult) accompanied by Monte Albán II vessels were found outside the southwest corner of the north room, and an elaborate (but unfortunately disturbed) tomb dating to the Monte Albán II-III transition was located under the platform on the east side of the plaza.

The data from Dainzú suggest that during Monte Albán II, the site grew rapidly and was outfitted with two-room temples and residential palaces. Dainzú did not have an I-shaped ballcourt at this time, but it did have ballgame imagery, including suggestions of conflict and defeat symbolized by ballplaying.

Regions Outside the Valley

Before summarizing Monte Albán II in the valley proper, I will look at two regions, one north and one south of the valley. Both were incorporated into the Monte Albán state by the end of Monte Albán II. Archaeological research in these outlying areas provides evidence that the Zapotec used different methods to incorporate each, and treated their populations differently.

The Cuicatlán Cañada

Research in the hot, low-lying (*tierra caliente*) Cuicatlán Cañada was directed by Elsa Redmond and Charles Spencer, who surveyed the broad canyon and excavated two sites (Redmond

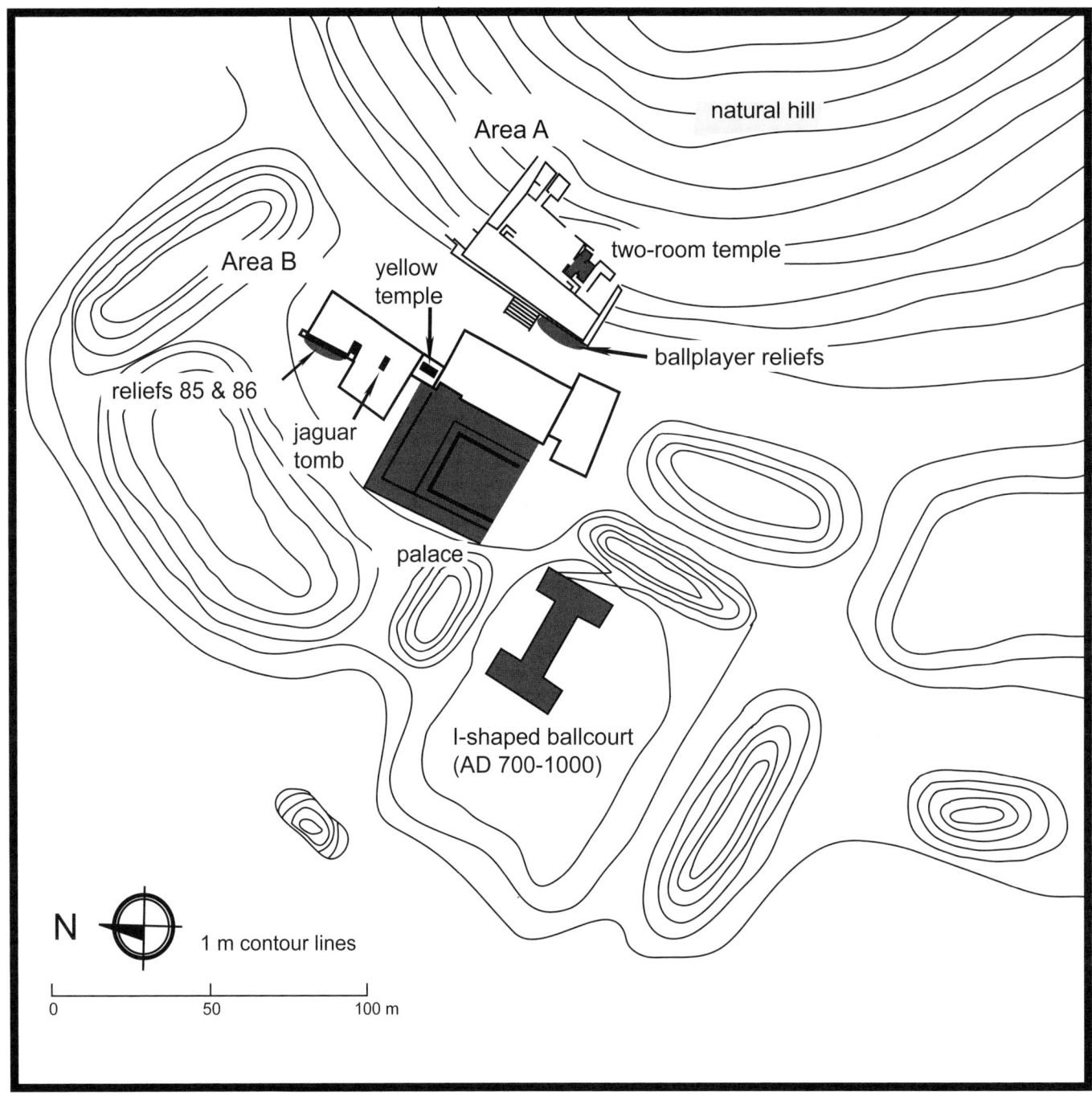

Figure 3.14. Map of Dainzú's ceremonial core. The area shaded in gray and labeled a palace is a complex of rooms and walls constructed during Monte Albán Late I-II and used during subsequent periods. Excavation dated the I-shaped ballcourt to after A.D. 700 (redrawn from Bernal and Oliveros 1988: Láminas 2-5).

1983; Spencer 1982; Spencer and Redmond 1997, 2001b). By A.D. 1521, the indigenous populations of the Cuicatlán Cañada were speakers of the Cuicatec language, but their linguistic affiliation during the Late Formative is unknown. Excavations at the sites of Llano Perdido and La Coyotera show that about 300 B.C., the beginning of the Lomas phase (300 B.C.-A.D. 200), Monte Albán took control of the Cuicatlán Cañada. Llano Perdido was burned and abandoned, and the population was moved to the hilltop site of La Coyotera. Comparative data from excavations at La Coyotera and Llano Perdido show "major changes in local economic, social, political and religious behavior" (Spencer and Redmond 2001b:186-87). Differences in the layout of the two sites suggest that administrators may have "pursued a deliberate policy of breaking up residential compounds in order to allow for easier control of the conquered population" (Spencer and Redmond 2001b:187). In addition, a skull rack with at least sixty-one human skulls was placed prominently in the middle of La Coyotera's main plaza (Spencer and Redmond 1997:520-24).

Carbonized plants suggest that there was a shift from subsistence agriculture to specialized cropping, especially the production of tropical fruits and nuts that could not be grown in the cooler Oaxaca Valley (Spencer and Redmond 2001b:186-87). There is a decline in evidence of craft-related activities and a reduction in the relative amounts of imported ceramics, obsidian, and shell. Far fewer ceremonial artifacts such as figurines and obsidian blades were found at La Coyotera than at Llano Perdido and the elite administrators of the Cañada were using ceramics like those used by elites in the Oaxaca Valley, particularly cream-paste wares (Spencer and Redmond 1997:505-29).

During the same period (or perhaps toward the latter part of the period), the Fortress of Quiotepec was built at the northern terminus of the Cañada, along two sides of a natural pass leading to the Tehuacán Valley (Spencer and Redmond 2001b:184). Quiotepec was a fortified 44 ha complex, and at the base of the site was an enormous (75 m long) I-shaped ballcourt, thought to have been in use during the Monte Albán II occupation (Redmond 1983). Quiotepec served as the northern frontier of the Zapotec state and monitored an important route to the Central Mexican highlands.

Ejutla

Research in the Valley of Ejutla was conducted by Gary Feinman and Linda Nicholas (1990), who surveyed the region and excavated at the Ejutla site. Ejutla is separated from the Valle Grande subregion of the Oaxaca Valley by a low range of hills, and the indigenous population there spoke Zapotec. The route leading from Monte Albán to Ejutla and from there to the Pacific coast was important for traffic in feathers, cloth, cacao, animal pelts, tropical fruit, resins, and shell.

Feinman and Nicholas have presented a picture of how this region developed over the course of the Late and Terminal Formative. Monte Albán I settlements had populations of less than 350 people each, and smaller ceremonial constructions (in terms of mound volume) than similar sites in the Oaxaca Valley. No one site was significantly larger than any other, so it appears that no single center in Ejutla dominated the others (Feinman and Nicholas 1990:230).

After 100 B.C., there was a marked discontinuity in settlement location, accompanied by the growth of three strategically positioned centers: Amatenango, located on the Atoyac River; Yogana, located on the Miahuatlán River near the pass where it begins its descent to the Pacific; and Ejutla itself. The remaining settlements in the Ejutla Valley shifted to defensible hilltop locations that overlooked the most direct route between Monte Albán and Ejutla; the latter site grew twice as large as any other and became a center for the conversion of Pacific shell to ornaments (Feinman and Nicholas 1990:231). Ejutla, Amatenango, and Yogana all show greater frequencies of cream-paste pottery than do the smaller hilltop sites in their hinterland.

Feinman and Nicholas (1990:234) recognize that the relationship between Monte Albán and Ejutla underwent a "significant transition" in Monte Albán II. At the same time, they suggest that Ejutla may not have been conquered outright, as was the Cuicatlán Cañada. One interpretation is that until circa 100 B.C., Ejutla may have been shielded from Monte Albán's aggression by the presence of the Ocotlán polity centered at El Palenque (Tilcajete). Once Ocotlán had been brought under Monte Albán's control, Ejutla's residents may have begun to feel the pressure of Monte Albán's expansion. During Monte Albán II, some of Ejutla's population (at the very least, the Ejutla site) appears to have come under the direct control of Monte Albán; however, other segments of the Ejutla population might initially have retreated to the defensible hilltop centers. Instead of succumbing to military conquest, Ejutla's elite may have been drawn into the Zapotec state through intermarriage; or, as Feinman and Nicholas (1990:234) have suggested, the area may have undergone various episodes of co-option and rebellion. After A.D. 200, however, Ejutla appears to have been well integrated into the hierarchy of the Monte Albán state.

Summary

In this chapter I have presented data describing the Valley of Oaxaca and two nearby areas during Monte Albán II. There is convincing evidence that a class of hereditary nobles, based at Monte Albán, ruled the Oaxaca Valley and put together a small empire that included the Cuicatlán Cañada and Ejutla.

At Monte Albán itself, a monumental building program was carried out to convey the ruler's roles as a political decision-maker, warrior, and ritual leader. The distribution of different types of architecture across the site argues for the presence of an urban elite and for some degree of specialization or hierarchical organization of these elites as administrators, warriors, and ritual leaders. The urban elites associated with the System Y Mound group could have functioned as political administrators. The urban elites in the El Pitahayo neighborhood may have functioned (in some sense) as military leaders. The urban elites situated in the PNLP probably functioned to manage the production of shell and obsidian.

When we look at data from the three major subregions of the valley, it is clear on the one hand that until 100 B.C., each branch of the valley had a different kind of relationship with Monte Albán. On the other hand, after 100 B.C., major building campaigns were enacted at San José Mogote (Etla) and Dainzú (Tlacolula), and both sites were outfitted with two-room temples and palaces. The Etla subregion probably contributed much of Monte Albán's initial population, leading to San José Mogote's virtual abandonment for four hundred years. When San José Mogote was resettled, it was rebuilt to closely reflect the splendor of Monte Albán. San José Mogote is the only one of the valley's three major subregional centers to have an I-shaped ballcourt. Dedicatory offerings in the Monte Albán II temples there indicate that the local elites were interested in demonstrating (1) their ability to acquire and dispose of exotic goods, and (2) their knowledge of and participation in an ideology promoted by elites at the capital, linking nobles with *Cociyo*.

In Tlacolula, the incorporation of the subregion resulted initially in the establishment of a secondary center closer to the Central Valley (although the previous center for the region, Yegüih, was not abandoned). Dainzú was chosen for this purpose, remodeled, and outfitted with two-room temples and palaces with tombs. Dainzú's elite acquired cream-paste pottery from the Cacaotepec/Atzompa region through Monte Albán. Although Dainzú lacked an I-shaped ballcourt during Monte Albán II, carved stones at the site show ballplaying, possibly involving ritualized conflict and sacrifice. By Monte Albán IIIa, one tomb at Dainzú had been carved with jaguar or puma iconography.

Monte Albán conquered the capital of the rival Ocotlán polity, El Palenque (Tilcajete), circa 100 B.C. The El Palenque site was burned and abandoned, and a new secondary center was set up at Cerro Tilcajete nearby. The population of the Ocotlán subregion may have decreased by as much as one-third, as Monte Albán dispersed the people formerly concentrated at El Palenque to smaller agricultural hamlets, or moved them to other colonized regions. Some populations could even have fled Monte Albán's control.

Neither Cerro Tilcajete nor Dainzú have I-shaped ballcourts. I propose such buildings may deliberately have been denied to those secondary centers, and placed instead at "special purpose" sites nearby. This arrangement might have made made it harder for local elites to organize or participate in ballplaying rituals, or exercise direct authority over military personnel.

The longstanding "hostile" relationship between the Ocotlán subregion and Monte Albán probably influenced how Monte Albán's rulers decided to administer the subregion after 100 B.C. Outside the valley proper, one of Monte Albán's initial conquests was the Cuicatlán Cañada, probably because it was a source of exotic foods and lay along an important trade route with Central Mexico. Radiocarbon dates suggest that the Cañada was conquered circa 300 B.C., before Monte Albán had been able to overcome all resistance within the valley proper (for example, from Tlacolula or Ocotlán). Monte Albán's harsh administration of the Cañada included (1) abrupt relocation of settlements, accompanied by violence; (2) the breakup of former residential compounds; (3) the reduction of craft activities and local ritual; and (4) the use of terror tactics (sacrifice and the public display of crania on skull-racks).

The next chapter describes Cerro Tilcajete in detail. I look at how the site's layout and buildings shed light on the kinds of policies the elites at Monte Albán enacted to administer Ocotlán, and how those initial decisions may have affected the historical trajectory of that subregion over the next centuries.

Chapter 4

Cerro Tilcajete during Monte Albán II (100 B.C.–A.D. 200)

The Surface Data

Site Layout and Occupational History

My fieldwork at Cerro Tilcajete was designed to acquire data on elite and commoner residences and civic-ceremonial structures, which could then be compared to similar buildings at other secondary centers. In 1994, Spencer and Redmond mapped the site and made intensive surface collections. My analysis of those collections provided an outline of the site's occupational history and informed my selection of areas for excavation.

Figure 4.1 shows the relationship of El Palenque, Cerro Tilcajete and Jalieza. Figures 3.1 and 4.2 show Cerro Tilcajete's layout and the location of surface collections, mounds, and plazas. The highest point on the site, the summit of Mound F, lies 1850 m above sea level. Intensive surface collections were made at 47 locations on the site (Fig. 4.2) and took the form of 10 × 10 m squares or 5 × 20 m rectangles, depending on the terrain. Surface collections were placed in areas likely to yield good samples of material, particularly in areas associated with mounds, terraces, and other features. Table 4.1 presents data on the dimensions of some of the mounds, plazas, and terraces mapped at the site. Tables 4.2-4.4 present data from the surface collections. Appendix A provides descriptions and illustrations of the pottery types mentioned throughout the text.

Surface evidence suggests that the initial occupation of Cerro Tilcajete took place about 100 B.C.; by A.D. 200, the site covered an irregular 24.5 ha. Cerro Tilcajete was abandoned for the next three hundred years and was reoccupied around A.D. 500. The later (Monte Albán IIIb-IV) occupation was much smaller and was directly associated with Plaza I—around which several large mounds (Mounds E-K) were constructed or refurbished—as well as with the terraces located north and east of Plaza I. After A.D. 1000, Cerro Tilcajete was all but abandoned, although I did find some Monte Albán V ceramics associated with Mound L, which probably supported a temple.

Mounds and other structures exhibited two distinct orientations: those dating to Monte Albán II were oriented 22° east of magnetic north, while those dating to Monte Albán IIIb-IV were oriented 17° east of magnetic north. Monte Albán I buildings at Cerro Tilcajete's predecessor, the site of El Palenque, were oriented 17° east of magnetic north (Spencer 1999); it seems that the orientation of the post-A.D. 500 buildings reverted to an earlier pattern found in the Ocotlán subregion. At Monte Albán and San José Mogote, buildings dating to the Late Formative period were generally oriented north-south (Marcus and Flannery 1996).

A central element of Cerro Tilcajete was a pre-Hispanic road that climbed the hill from the northwest and along whose path the domestic occupation was arranged. The road is (at most) 1.5 m wide and in many places had a hard-packed earth surface. At two points, the road passed niches. The north niche lies along a steep slope, and both the niche and the road were carved into bedrock on the side of the hill. Collection squares associated with the niches (Collection Squares 163 and 165) yielded Monte Albán II pottery, figurine fragments, urn fragments, and shell. It appears that these niches marked points of entry into the site. Travelers leaving or entering the site may have stopped here to conduct rituals.

The road continued along the western side of the site to a natural saddle with three small platforms (Mounds M-O). This was a natural point of access to the ceremonial precinct, which I defined as Plazas I and II and the terraces between the two

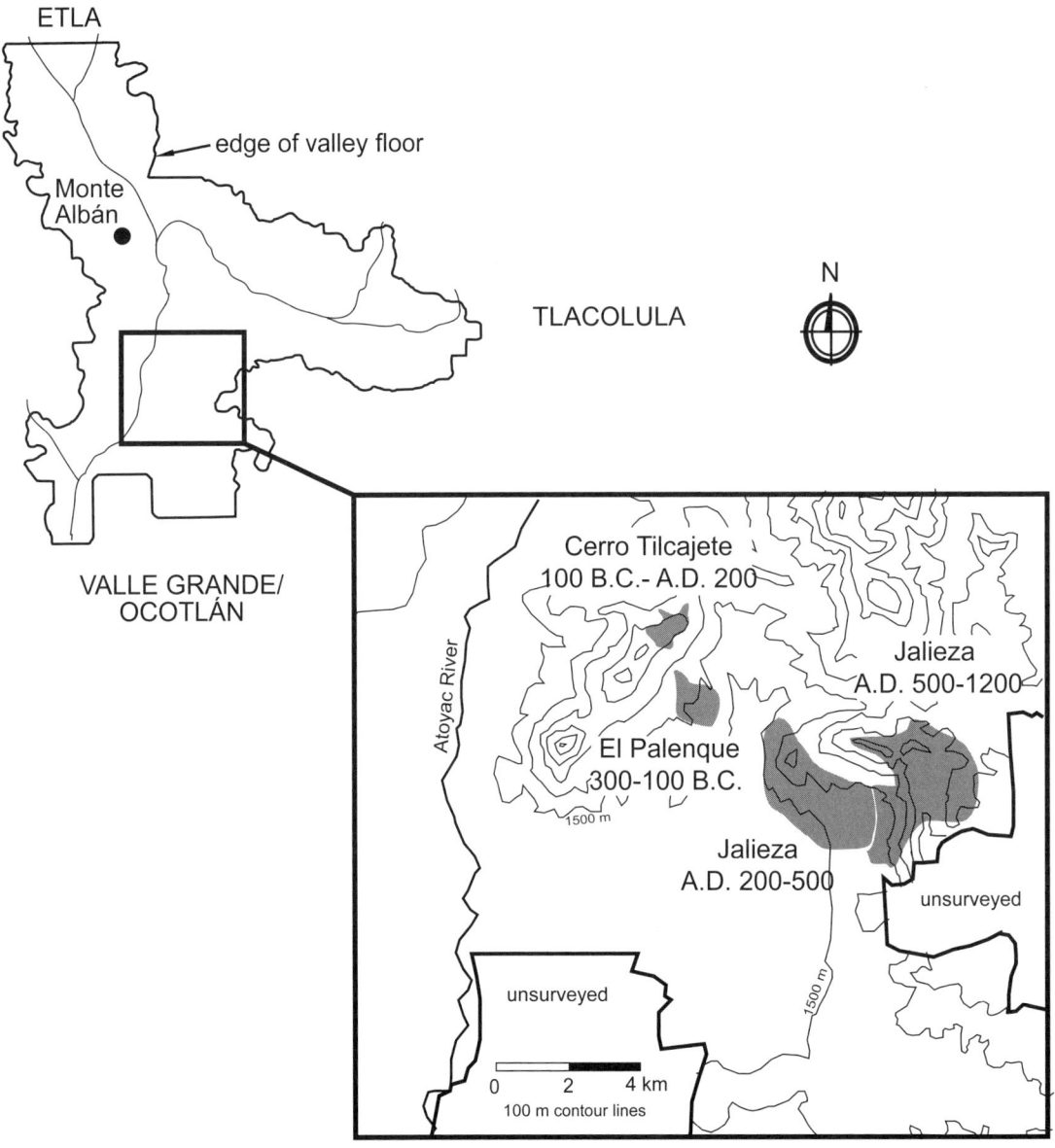

Figure 4.1. Topographic map of a section of the Ocotlán subregion showing the relationship between the subregional capitals: El Palenque (300-100 B.C.), Cerro Tilcajete (100 B.C.-A.D. 200), Early Classic Jalieza (A.D. 200-500) and Late Classic-Early Postclassic Jalieza (A.D. 500-1200).

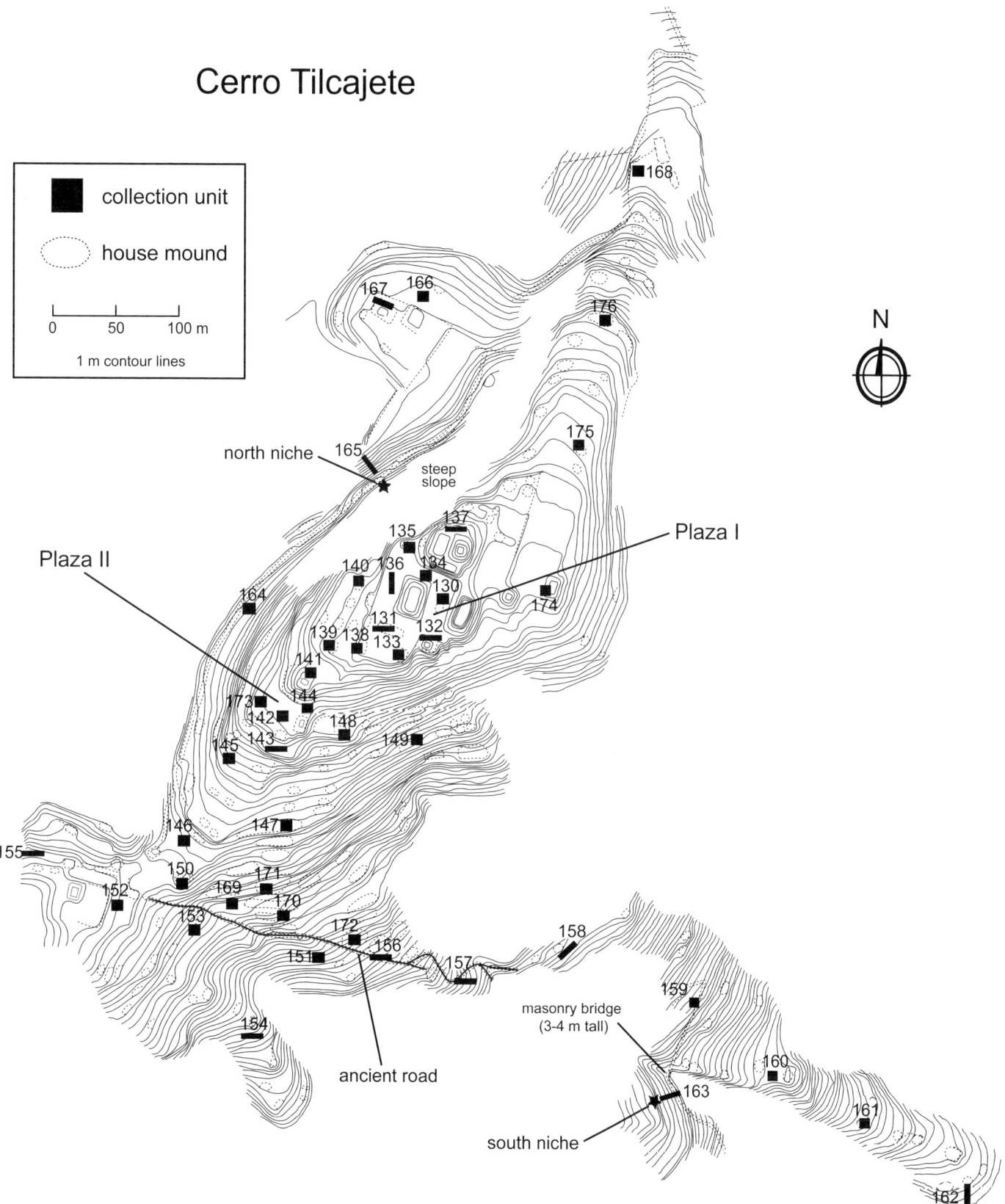

Figure 4.2. Plan of Cerro Tilcajete showing the location of surface collections. The site's mound groups are labeled in Figure 3.1 (map and surface collections by Charles Spencer and Elsa Redmond).

Table 4.1. Mound and plaza dimensions at Cerro Tilcajete.

Location	Base (m)	Top (m)	Height (m)	Total Area (m²)	Room Area (m²)
Plaza II	30 × 40			1200	
Mound A*	25 × 30	12 × 14	5	750	144
Mound B*	6.4 × 14.4	7 × 10.4	2.75	92	36
Mound D	10 × 7	6 × 3	1	70	18
Plaza I	53 × 22			1166	
Mound E*	40 × 15	20 × 5	5	600	100
Mound F	20 × 25	5 × 5	5	500	25
Area G	20 × 10			200	
Mound H	25 × 40	23 × 7	4	1000	161
Mound I	25 × 35	20 × 9	3	875	180
Mound J	17 × 12	3.5 × 4	2	204	14
Mound K	12 × 13	5 × 4	2	156	20
Mound M	10 × 7	3 × 5	1	70	15
Mound N	8 × 16	5 × 5	1	126	25
Mound O	10 × 15	5 × 10	1	150	50

*Data from excavation.

plazas. Surface data, confirmed by later excavation, suggested that Plaza II had only Monte Albán II occupation. Excavation of the largest mound in Plaza II, Mound A, produced a residence, and excavation of Mound B produced a two-room temple. The small surface area of the South Mound, Mound D, suggests that it also supported a temple. The west side of Plaza II was open, and the frontispiece of this Memoir shows what a clear view of Monte Albán one has from this vantage point.

Collection squares inside the ceremonial precinct yielded a high frequency of the cream-paste ceramic types that I consider elite wares (see below). One collection square also yielded a remarkable find. Collection Unit 173 was placed on the southwest corner of Plaza II, where site reconnaissance had noted a feature (which subsequently had been looted) eroding from the slope. The collection contained red and black colored cream-paste pottery, shell, mica, and bone. Later analysis showed that one of the bone fragments was a partial human maxilla from an adult (forty years old or less) that had been defleshed so as to not leave cut marks, and was then smoothed by grinding (Appendix B). Duncan et al. (2006) interpret this object as a trophy—in essence, a keepsake from a sacrificial victim. Four similar objects have been recovered at Teotihuacán, for example, from the Feathered Serpent Pyramid (Spence et al. 2004). These mandibles and maxillae are interpreted as trophies taken by warriors during combat; these warriors themselves were later sacrificed for the dedication of the pyramid.

Poor architectural preservation makes it difficult to determine the context of this unique object. On the one hand, I did not notice plaster floors or stone architecture, so the bone might be part of an offering placed at the southwest corner of the plaza. On the other hand, the presence of other bone fragments may indicate that the maxilla was part of a mortuary offering or human sacrifice buried at this location. In any case, this trophy clearly suggests elites were interested in showing their success at violent confrontation.

The terraces north of Mound A and south of Mound I yielded a very high frequency of cream-paste sherds, as well as gray-paste sherds of a pottery type typical of Monte Albán IIIb-IV (A.D. 500-1000). It is clear there were a number of elite households here during Monte Albán II, but some of the constructions may have been substantially modified or reoccupied in Monte Albán IIIb-IV.

In Plaza I, excavations focused on Area G, Mound E, and the adoratory (a low, ritual platform) associated with Mound H. (An adoratory is usually set in front of a temple; any worshipper approaching the temple would pass the adoratory before climbing the temple's staircase. Temple-adoratory complexes were common at Monte Albán during the Classic period.) Recent looting into Mounds H and F provided an opportunity to examine the interior of the mounds and to recover data on the construction sequence. Work in Plaza I determined that the adoratory and Mound F were single component buildings constructed in Monte Albán IIIb-IV. Mound E did have Monte Albán II constructions, and it is likely that Mounds H, I, and J also were first built in Monte Albán II. I do not have sufficient data to evaluate the initial construction of Mounds K and L. In general, it is likely that during Monte Albán II, Plaza I was surrounded by a four-mound group.

The majority of the site's residential terraces were located on its northern and eastern slopes. Terraces northeast of Plaza I, along the crest of the ridge, showed definite Monte Albán II occupation and possibly some scattered Monte Albán IIIb-IV occupation. The eastern side of the site had a dense scattering of occupational terraces, most placed along the road and on small natural spurs. Surface collections here yielded fewer red-painted orange ware and cream-paste sherds than did the collections inside the ceremonial precinct. I suggest that residences on the eastern slope belonged to families lower in status than those occupying residences on the crest of the ridge. I chose one terrace in this section for excavation. This terrace, the location of Collection Square 147, is located 29 m downslope and 240 m south of Plaza II.

Based on the number of house mounds or probable residential areas mapped on the surface, I estimate that there were 15-20 households in the ceremonial precinct. At 5-10 persons per household, the population estimate for this zone would be 75 to 200 persons.

Outside the ceremonial precinct, Spencer and Redmond mapped 143 house mounds on terraces. It is evident that some house mounds were much larger than others. However, architectural surface debris ranged only from about 1 to 3 m² in area.

Table 4.2a. Surface data from Cerro Tilcajete by collection unit: units 130-148.

Collection Unit:	130	131	132	133	134	135	136	137	138	139	140	141	142	143	144	145	146	147	148
gray undec. body	51	274	200	103	99	425	25	270	226	378	114	425	60	268	259	592	705	432	624
café undec. body	17	111	108	41	27	96	3	57	116	200	61	240	28	65	117	230	659	366	293
gray rims	17	40	17	5	9	42	10	19	35	63	8	81	12	42	34	84	88	58	83
gray base	8	18	6	2	8	29	1	8	14	24	8	36	3	14	16	37	32	16	29
gray body	11	3	4	1	0	1	0	0	1	6	0	6	0	5	5	5	4	4	5
gray other	2	1	0	0	0	0	1	1	1	1	0	6	1	0	0	3	6	0	2
total gray diagnostics	38	62	27	8	17	73	12	28	51	94	16	129	16	61	55	129	130	78	119
G.12	1	9	8	3	0	12	0	2	6	20	6	29	8	23	12	33	28	24	28
G.12 rims	1	6	4	1	0	4	0	2	4	14	0	20	6	16	8	23	18	19	14
G.12 base	0	3	4	2	0	8	0	0	2	6	6	9	1	7	4	10	10	5	14
G.12 "sloppy" base	0	2	0	0	0	2	0	0	1	3	2	1	0	0	0	2	5	0	4
G.12 "fine" base	0	0	1	0	0	0	0	0	0	0	0	5	1	4	1	3	1	1	4
G.12 indeter. dec.	0	1	3	2	0	6	0	0	0	3	2	3	0	3	3	5	4	5	6
G.21	0	0	0	0	0	0	0	0	0	0	0	1	0	0	0	2	3	4	3
G.25	0	0	1	0	0	1	0	0	5	4	0	0	2	4	2	0	5	0	1
G.29	0	3	2	0	0	1	0	0	0	0	0	3	0	4	0	3	0	1	4
G.15	0	0	0	0	0	0	0	0	0	0	0	0	0	0	0	2	0	0	0
G.34	0	0	0	0	0	0	0	0	0	0	0	0	0	0	0	0	0	0	1
G.35	16	7	2	0	12	12	2	12	4	5	5	0	0	0	0	4	2	2	4
G.35 rim	9	5	2	0	4	5	2	7	3	4	1	3	0	0	0	1	2	2	0
G.35 base	7	2	0	0	8	7	0	5	3	1	1	0	0	0	0	3	0	0	1
G.35 foot	20	0	0	0	4	3	0	2	3	1	2	0	0	0	0	2	0	0	0
gray apaxtle	1	3	1	0	0	0	1	1	0	3	0	7	0	0	0	4	7	1	6
G.9	0	1	0	0	0	0	0	0	0	0	0	1	0	0	0	1	0	0	0
G.23	0	0	0	0	0	0	0	0	0	0	0	0	0	0	0	0	0	0	0
G.16	0	0	0	0	0	0	0	0	0	0	0	0	0	0	0	0	0	0	0
gray jar	0	0	0	0	0	0	0	0	0	3	0	0	0	1	0	6	1	1	8
gray incurved bowl	0	0	1	0	0	0	0	0	0	0	0	8	1	3	1	1	1	2	0
gray exterior inc.	0	0	0	0	0	0	0	0	0	0	0	0	0	1	3	2	0	0	4
gray plates	0	0	0	0	0	0	0	0	0	1	0	0	0	0	0	1	2	0	3
gray molded	0	0	0	0	0	1	0	0	0	0	0	2	0	0	0	0	0	0	0
orange rim	2	0	0	2	0	0	0	0	1	3	0	0	1	0	0	10	2	0	4
orange base	1	0	0	1	0	0	1	0	0	4	0	0	0	0	0	7	3	3	1
orange body	0	0	0	3	0	0	0	1	2	1	5	5	2	0	1	4	1	0	6
orange other	0	0	0	0	0	5	0	2	7	1	0	0	0	0	0	1	5	2	0
total orange diagnostics	3	0	0	6	0	7	1	3	19	9	20	46	3	7	0	22	11	5	11
orange incising	0	0	0	1	0	2	0	2	6	2	9	13	1	3	1	14	8	5	0
A.9	0	6	0	4	1	5	1	1	10	21	9	25	3	3	0	10	52	8	17
G.35 (oxicized)	0	0	0	1	0	0	0	0	0	3	1	5	2	3	0	3	11	2	30
cream rim	0	11	5	2	1	0	0	2	0	23	5	12	1	4	0	12	33	6	14
cream base	0	2	1	1	1	1	0	0	2	10	3	8	6	3	0	10	14	2	10
cream body	0	4	13	3	0	5	1	1	7	27	15	26	2	0	3	11	35	2	33
cream other	0	0	0	0	0	1	0	0	0	0	0	0	0	0	0	0	0	0	0
total cream diagnostics	0	17	19	6	1	7	1	3	19	60	20	46	8	7	3	33	82	10	57
C.6	0	6	4	4	1	2	0	2	6	21	9	13	2	5	2	14	19	8	17
C.7	0	11	11	1	0	5	1	1	10	31	9	25	0	3	1	10	52	2	30
C.11	0	0	1	4	0	0	0	0	0	3	3	5	2	3	0	3	11	0	7
C.12	0	0	2	1	1	0	0	1	0	4	1	1	0	0	0	5	0	0	3
C.20	0	0	3	0	0	0	0	0	3	4	0	2	0	1	0	0	0	0	1
café rims	0	7	1	0	2	7	0	4	5	15	5	23	6	9	9	34	51	16	39
café base	0	0	1	0	0	1	0	0	0	1	3	0	0	1	2	0	0	0	0
café dec. body/other	0	0	0	0	0	0	0	0	0	0	0	3	2	5	0	4	0	3	0
total café diagnostics	0	7	2	0	2	9	0	4	5	16	8	26	8	15	11	38	51	19	39
café K.2	0	0	0	1	0	0	0	0	1	0	0	0	0	5	0	0	0	3	0
café comal	0	0	0	0	0	0	0	0	0	2	2	3	1	2	1	8	16	5	13
café jar	0	0	0	0	0	0	0	0	0	4	0	3	0	4	0	4	6	2	2
K.3	0	0	0	0	0	0	0	0	0	0	2	1	1	1	1	8	7	0	0
K.7	0	0	0	0	0	0	0	0	0	0	0	0	0	0	0	0	0	0	0
K.17 like C.11	0	0	0	0	0	0	0	0	0	0	0	0	0	0	0	0	5	0	3
K.17	0	0	0	0	0	0	0	0	0	0	0	1	1	0	0	0	0	0	0
K.22	0	0	0	0	0	0	0	0	0	0	0	0	0	0	0	0	0	0	0
café braziers	0	0	0	0	0	0	0	0	0	0	0	0	0	0	0	0	0	0	0
white rim blackware	0	0	0	0	0	0	0	0	0	0	0	0	0	0	0	0	0	0	0

Table 4.2b. Surface data from Cerro Tilcajete by collection unit: units 149-166.

Collection Unit:	149	150	151	152	153	154	155	156	157	158	159	160	161	162	163	164	165	166
gray undec. body	180	213	207	278	509	322	104	250	129	147	136	226	131	90	36	257	10	260
café undec. body	172	230	129	161	352	360	74	163	120	145	178	139	75	25	19	151	8	110
gray rims	22	39	32	47	17	34	22	29	7	12	21	19	13	21	7	61	6	31
gray base	6	13	5	13	54	15	4	10	2	7	6	8	5	10	3	18	3	11
gray body	7	0	2	0	2	0	0	2	1	0	1	0	0	3	0	1	1	1
gray other	1	3	0	0	3	7	0	1	0	0	1	0	0	0	1	0	2	1
total gray diagnostics	36	55	39	60	76	56	26	42	10	19	29	27	18	34	11	80	12	44
G.12	5	18	21	19	71	8	6	11	3	6	6	6	4	13	1	17	3	5
G.12 rims	3	10	11	14	45	6	4	8	2	3	6	5	1	9	0	14	1	4
G.12 base	2	8	10	5	26	2	2	3	1	3	0	0	3	4	1	3	2	4
G.12 "sloppy" base	0	2	1	0	7	0	1	2	0	0	0	0	0	1	0	2	1	0
G.12 "fine" base	0	0	0	0	1	0	0	0	0	0	0	1	1	1	0	0	0	0
G.12 indeter. dec.	2	6	9	5	18	2	0	1	0	3	0	0	2	2	0	0	0	1
G.21	0	1	0	1	1	0	0	0	0	0	0	0	0	0	0	0	0	0
G.25	0	2	1	1	5	1	0	0	1	0	0	0	0	3	0	2	0	0
G.29	0	0	1	1	5	0	0	6	0	0	0	0	0	0	0	1	0	0
G.15	0	0	0	0	1	0	0	0	0	0	0	0	0	0	0	0	0	0
G.34	0	0	0	0	0	0	0	0	1	0	0	0	0	3	0	0	0	0
G.35	0	0	0	0	3	0	0	2	0	3	0	0	0	0	0	3	1	0
G.35 rim	0	0	0	0	0	0	0	1	0	0	0	0	0	0	0	3	0	1
G.35 base	0	0	0	0	3	0	0	0	0	3	0	0	0	0	0	3	1	1
G.35 foot	0	0	1	0	1	0	0	0	0	0	0	0	0	0	0	3	1	1
gray apaxtle	4	0	0	3	0	0	0	0	0	0	0	0	0	0	0	0	2	0
G.9	0	0	0	0	0	0	0	0	0	0	0	0	0	0	0	0	0	0
G.23	0	0	0	0	2	1	0	1	0	1	0	0	0	0	0	0	0	0
G.16	0	0	0	0	0	0	0	0	0	0	0	0	0	0	0	0	0	0
gray jar	1	0	0	1	5	1	2	2	1	0	6	0	1	0	0	5	2	2
gray incurved bowl	0	0	0	0	1	0	0	2	0	1	0	0	0	0	0	3	0	0
gray exterior inc.	0	0	0	2	2	0	0	0	0	0	0	0	0	3	0	4	1	0
gray plates	0	0	0	0	2	0	0	0	0	0	0	0	0	0	0	2	0	0
gray molded	0	0	0	0	0	0	0	0	0	0	0	1	0	1	0	0	0	0
orange rim	3	1	0	3	4	0	0	1	0	0	0	1	0	0	1	6	0	0
orange base	2	0	0	1	0	0	2	0	1	3	0	1	0	0	0	2	0	0
orange body	0	0	3	0	5	3	0	1	0	3	4	0	0	0	0	7	0	0
orange other	0	1	0	0	4	0	0	0	0	0	0	1	0	0	0	1	0	0
total orange diagnostics	5	2	3	4	13	0	4	2	0	6	8	2	1	0	3	16	0	1
orange incising	3	0	0	0	0	0	0	2	3	1	4	2	0	0	3	0	0	0
A.9	0	0	1	1	2	0	0	0	0	0	3	0	0	0	1	7	0	0
G.35 (oxidized)	0	0	0	0	0	0	0	0	0	0	0	2	0	0	0	0	0	0
cream rim	3	12	2	13	10	4	2	3	1	0	4	2	5	0	1	2	0	5
cream base	1	2	2	4	7	3	0	0	0	3	0	0	1	1	0	4	0	0
cream body	5	25	8	10	10	7	2	5	2	3	4	1	0	2	0	1	0	0
cream other	0	0	1	0	0	0	0	0	0	0	0	0	0	0	0	0	0	0
total cream diagnostics	9	39	12	27	27	14	4	8	3	6	8	3	6	3	2	7	0	5
C.6	3	10	8	6	13	6	4	2	3	4	4	3	0	0	2	0	0	0
C.7	6	23	4	26	11	7	0	6	2	5	3	0	0	1	0	4	0	0
C.11	0	3	2	4	1	3	0	0	1	3	1	0	0	0	1	2	0	0
C.12	0	0	0	0	2	1	0	0	0	0	0	0	0	0	0	0	0	0
C.20	0	2	0	0	0	0	0	1	0	0	0	0	0	0	0	1	0	0
café rims	4	15	11	27	35	16	8	10	13	8	8	12	5	0	0	17	0	3
café base	0	2	0	1	1	0	1	0	0	0	0	0	1	1	0	1	0	0
café dec. body/other	0	0	0	3	0	1	1	1	0	3	2	1	0	2	0	2	0	1
total café diagnostics	4	17	11	31	36	17	9	11	13	8	10	13	6	2	0	20	0	4
café K.2	0	0	0	1	0	0	0	4	0	0	2	0	0	0	0	1	0	0
café comal	0	5	5	10	5	3	1	1	2	5	2	4	0	1	0	6	0	0
café jar	1	1	3	4	3	1	1	4	3	0	5	1	0	0	0	0	0	0
K.3	0	0	0	0	0	0	0	1	1	5	4	0	0	0	0	6	0	0
K.7	0	0	0	0	0	0	0	0	0	0	0	0	0	0	0	0	0	1
K.17 like C.11	0	0	1	0	0	0	0	0	0	0	0	2	0	0	0	0	0	0
K.17	0	0	0	0	0	0	0	0	0	0	0	0	0	0	0	0	0	0
K.22	0	0	0	0	0	0	0	0	0	0	0	0	0	0	0	8	0	0
café braziers	0	0	0	0	0	0	0	0	0	0	0	0	0	0	0	0	0	1
white rim blackware	1	0	0	0	0	0	0	0	0	0	0	0	0	0	0	0	0	0

Table 4.2c. Surface data from Cerro Tilcajete by collection unit: units 167-176.

Collection Unit:	167	168	169	170	171	172	173	174	175	176
gray undec. body	823	804	57	43	70	57	195	110	215	146
café undec. body	365	165	47	35	54	57	146	14	62	63
gray rims	83	164	12	11	6	16	48	10	23	26
gray base	28	58	4	1	4	4	17	5	11	14
gray body	1	3	1	1	0	0	5	3	1	0
gray other	3	1	0	0	0	0	1	1	2	2
total gray diagnostics	115	226	17	13	10	20	71	19	37	42
G.12	14	27	4	3	3	3	15	1	4	10
G.12 rims	9	20	2	3	0	2	11	0	3	8
G.12 base	5	7	2	0	3	1	4	1	1	3
G.12 "sloppy" base	0	2	2	0	2	0	2	0	1	2
G.12 "fine" base	3	1	0	0	1	1	2	0	0	1
G.12 indeter. dec.	2	4	0	0	0	0	0	1	0	0
G.21	1	0	1	0	0	1	0	0	0	1
G.25	1	2	1	2	0	0	0	0	0	0
G.29	0	0	0	0	0	0	3	0	2	7
G.15	0	0	0	0	0	0	0	0	0	0
G.34	0	0	0	0	0	0	4	0	0	0
G.35	9	37	0	0	0	0	0	0	1	0
G.35 rim	3	13	0	0	0	0	0	0	0	0
G.35 base	6	24	0	0	0	0	0	0	0	0
G.35 foot	3	19	0	0	0	0	0	0	1	0
gray *apaxtle*	2	4	0	0	0	1	3	0	1	0
G.9	0	0	0	0	0	0	4	0	0	0
G.23	0	0	0	0	0	0	0	0	0	0
G.16	0	0	0	0	0	0	0	0	0	0
gray jar	8	1	2	2	2	0	2	0	0	0
gray incurved bowl	1	12	0	0	0	1	1	3	0	0
gray exterior inc.	1	1	1	1	0	0	1	1	0	0
gray plates	0	1	0	0	0	0	1	0	0	0
gray molded	0	0	0	0	0	0	1	0	0	0
orange rim	0	4	1	1	1	0	1	0	4	1
orange base	0	1	0	0	0	2	1	0	0	1
orange body	0	2	0	1	2	0	1	0	1	1
orange other	0	0	2	0	0	0	0	0	0	1
total orange diagnostics	0	7	3	2	3	2	3	0	5	4
orange incising	0	0	0	0	1	0	0	0	0	0
A.9	0	2	0	0	1	1	1	0	2	1
G.35 (oxidized)	0	0	0	0	0	0	0	0	0	0
cream rim	13	11	0	2	2	3	27	0	6	4
cream base	5	2	10	0	5	1	9	0	2	3
cream body	0	16	0	1	0	3	7	0	2	10
cream other	1	0	0	0	0	0	0	0	0	0
total cream diagnostics	18	29	10	3	7	7	43	0	10	17
C.6	10	12	8	1	4	1	11	0	2	2
C.7	5	8	1	2	3	4	22	0	2	9
C.11	3	4	1	0	0	2	0	0	0	2
C.12	0	4	0	0	0	0	1	0	1	1
C.20	0	0	0	0	0	0	10	0	0	0
café rims	18	37	0	2	3	13	24	2	7	10
café base	1	0	0	0	2	1	1	1	1	0
café dec. body/other	1	0	1	0	0	0	9	0	1	0
total café diagnostics	20	37	1	2	5	14	34	3	9	10
café K.2	0	0	0	0	0	0	0	0	0	0
café *comal*	0	0	0	0	0	0	0	0	1	1
café jar	0	3	0	0	1	0	5	0	0	2
K.3	0	0	0	0	0	0	14	0	0	0
K.7	0	0	0	0	0	0	7	0	0	0
K.17 like C.11	0	0	0	0	0	0	0	0	0	0
K.17	0	0	0	0	0	0	9	0	0	0
K.22	0	0	0	0	0	0	0	0	1	0
café braziers	0	0	0	0	0	0	0	0	0	0
white rim blackware	0	0	0	0	0	0	0	0	0	0

Table 4.3. Surface data by collection unit (non-vessels).

Collection Unit	mano	metate	figurine	urn	kiln waster	sherd disk	shell	mica	bone	daub	adobe	burned daub	plaster	lime
130	0	0	0	0	2	0	0							
131	0	0	0	0	0	0	0							
132	0	0	0	1	0	0	0		present					
133	0	0	0	0	0	0	1				present			
134	0	0	1	0	0	0	0							
135	0	0	0	0	0	0	0							
136	0	0	0	0	0	0	0							
137	0	0	1	0	0	0	0							
138	1	0	0	0	2	0	0							
139	0	0	2	0	0	0	1		present				present	
140	0	0	1	0	0	0	0	present						
141	1	0	5	0	1	0	1						present	present
142	0	0	0	0	0	0	0							
143	1	0	0	0	0	0	0	present	present					
144	0	0	3	0	0	0	0	present	present					
145	1	0	3	0	0	1	4	present						
146	0	0	7	0	0	1	1							
147	0	0	0	2	0	0	2							
148	0	0	1	0	0	0	0	present	present					
149	0	0	1	1	0	0	0							
150	0	0	3	1	0	0	0		present					
151	0	0	1	0	0	0	0							
152	0	0	8	0	0	0	8	present						
153	1	0	8	2	0	0	2							
154	0	0	3	1	0	0	1							
155	0	0	1	0	0	0	1							
156	0	0	1	0	0	0	0							
157	0	0	1	2	0	0	1							
158	0	0	1	0	0	0	0							
159	0	0	0	0	0	0	1							
160	0	0	0	0	0	0	0							
161	0	0	1	0	0	0	1							
162	0	0	1	0	0	0	0							
163	1	0	0	3	0	0	0							present
164	0	0	3	0	0	0	0		present					
165	0	0	1	1	0	0	2							
166	0	0	1	0	0	0	0							
167	0	0	13	4	0	0	3						present	
168	0	0	4	0	0	0	0	present						
169	0	0	1	1	0	0	0							
170	0	0	0	0	0	0	0							
171	0	0	0	0	1	0	1							
172	0	0	0	0	0	0	0							
173	0	0	1	0	0	1	1	present	present					

Table 4.4. Surface ceramic categories by zone at Cerro Tilcajete.

Ceramic Category	Outside Precinct (%)	Inside Precinct (%)	Mounds M-O (%)
cream-paste	1.28	1.98	2.80
gray *apaxtle*	0.44	0.40	0.88
gray jar	0.70	0.25	0.48
all gray	64.04	70.18	52.48
café *comal*	1.15	0.51	2.47
café jar	1.21	0.09	1.04
all café	32.60	25.56	41.33
Total Ceramics	14,180	4625	3039

At 5-10 persons per house structure, an estimated 715 to 1430 people may have lived outside the ceremonial precinct. The site's total population can thus be estimated as between 790 and 1630 persons.

Surface Ceramics as Possible Clues to Status

Archaeologists often assume that people living closer to the ceremonial core of a site have a higher social, political, or economic status than those living further away. Data from intensive surface collections made inside and outside the ceremonial precinct allowed me to evaluate this assumption. As seen in Figure 4.2, forty-seven surface collections were made across the site, employing standard units of 100 m². Thirty-one units lay in areas outside the ceremonial precinct; sixteen units were from areas inside the precinct. All sherds from these collection units were counted and tabulated in the field, and all diagnostic sherds were brought to the lab for further analysis. The comparisons described here are based on the total number of sherds (both diagnostic and non-diagnostic) recovered.

Clearly, preservation, topography and many other factors affecting the distribution of ceramics on the surface make it prudent to use caution when translating surface data into behavioral patterns. That said, the surface data do point to some differences in how ceramics were used across the site. My analysis concentrated on determining (1) the amount of cream-paste pottery, and (2) the frequency of gray-paste wares (which tended to be used for serving vessels) versus café-paste wares (which tended to be used for cooking and other food preparation).

In order to evaluate the way cream-paste consumption compared with the site areas posited as potential "elite" or "non-elite" habitation zones, I tabulated and plotted on the site map, for each collection square, the proportion that cream-paste vessels made up of the overall ceramic assemblage. As seen in Figure 4.3, cream-paste ceramics made up 0.0-4.78% of the total ceramics collected in each unit.

Not all units collected in the ceremonial core had a high frequency of cream-paste pottery. Units near Plaza I had fewer cream-paste ceramics, but I suspect that these figures were diluted by a significant concentration of Monte Albán IIIb-IV pottery, which tends to be undecorated and made largely of gray paste. The average frequency for cream-paste pottery in the ceremonial zone was 1.98%. Cream-paste pottery was more abundant than this in five units associated with Mounds M-O and the terraces just east and downslope of these mounds; the average frequency for this part of the site was 2.80%. The rest of the site (excluding Unit 176, which had an above-average frequency of cream-paste pottery) had an average frequency of only 1.23%. The frequency of cream-paste sherds trailed off particularly in those units placed on the southeastern spur of the site.

My evaluation of gray-paste and café-paste pottery also indicated that Mounds M-O may have been in an area for special activities of some kind. I say this because previous studies of regional ceramic production and exchange indicate that during Monte Albán II, some gray-paste wares probably were exchanged, while most café wares were made and used locally (Feinman 1982). At Cerro Tilcajete, gray pottery tended to occur more frequently inside the ceremonial zone than outside. Café pottery, on the other hand, made up a relatively high frequency of the ceramics collected in the five units associated with Mounds M-O. It is possible that café ceramics were being produced in this area. I coded only one café kiln waster on Terrace 141, but pottery making in Oaxaca did not produce high numbers of wasters.

A more detailed look at the data shows that Mounds M-O may, in fact, have been a location where utilitarian pottery was made or used more frequently, possibly in activities including food preparation (Table 4.4). In this area, café-paste tortilla griddles (*comales*) and gray-paste basins (*apaxtles*) occur in relatively high frequencies within their respective paste types. *Comales* were used to cook tortillas, known to be part of the Oaxacan diet by Early Monte Albán I. *Apaxtles* can be used for many functions, but they probably were used mainly to soak the corn (for making tortillas) in lime water. *Comales* account for 2.47% of the café pottery near Mounds M-O, 1.15% of the café pottery found outside the ceremonial precinct, and only 0.51% of the café pottery inside the ceremonial precinct. *Apaxtles* account for 0.88% of the gray pottery near Mounds M-O, 0.44% of the gray pottery found outside the ceremonial precinct, and only 0.40% of the gray pottery inside the ceremonial precinct.

Thus, the distribution of cream-paste ceramics suggests that higher-status families likely occupied residences in the ceremonial precinct. A second elite zone was centered at Mounds M-O. Ceramics near Mounds M-O suggest that corn was soaked in lime water and tortillas were prepared on *comales* more frequently in that area than elsewhere. Ceramics also suggest that many lower-status families lived farther from the ceremonial core, on the lower terraces and on the southeastern spur of the site.

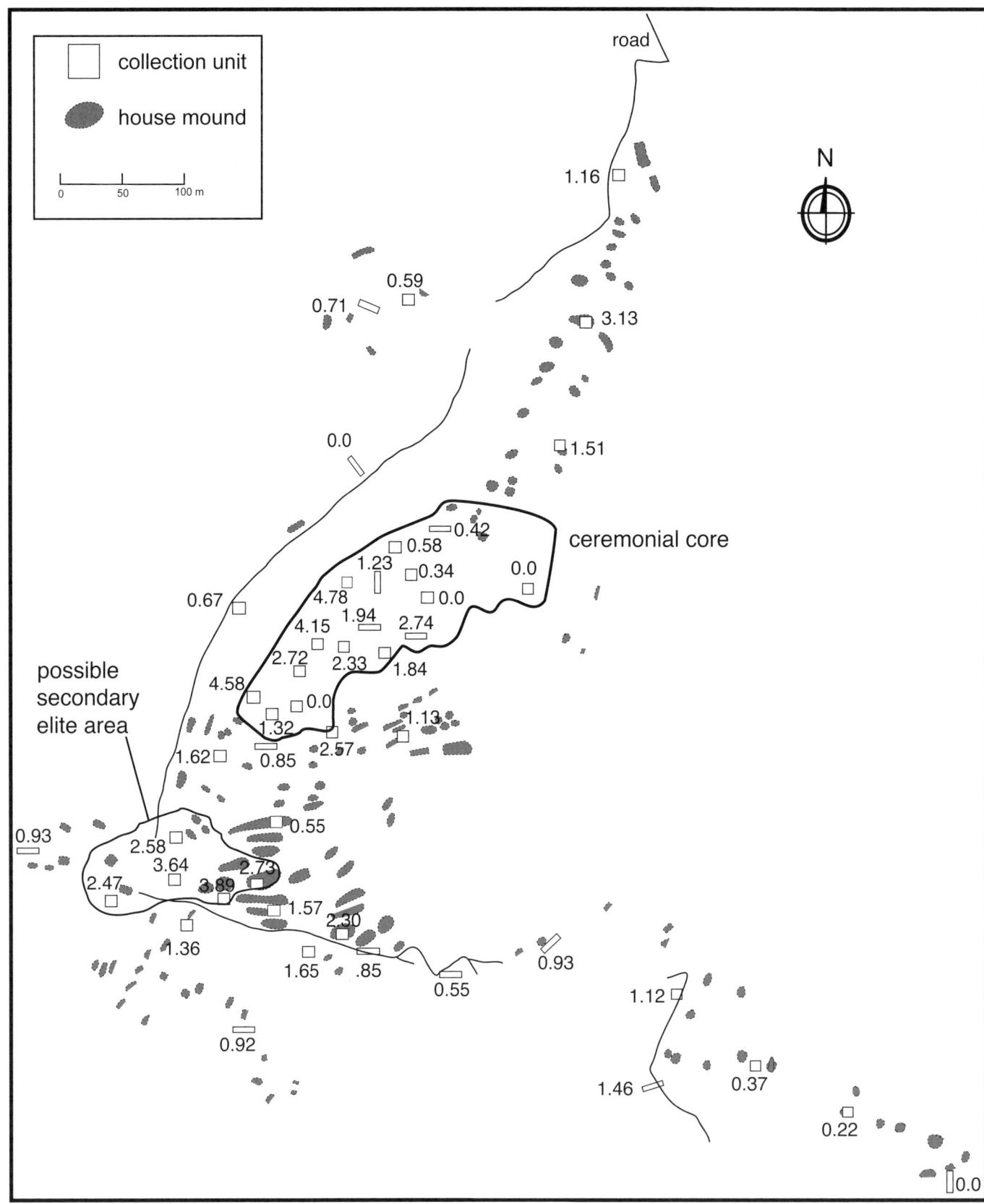

Figure 4.3. Map showing the frequency of cream-paste ceramics as a percentage of all ceramics coded in a surface collection across the surface of Cerro Tilcajete.

Other Materials from the Surface

Most non-ceramic material occurred in low frequency across the surface of the site, making it difficult to use the data for statistical analysis (Table 4.3). Figurine fragments tended to occur on the surface more frequently than urn fragments. Interestingly, shell was found more abundantly on the surface around Mounds M-O than in other areas of the site; for example, in the Mound M-O area, Collection Unit 152 contained eight pieces of shell. Shell was an imported commodity and, like the cream-paste wares, may have reached this area of the site before it was distributed to households (see Appendix C).

Summary

Cerro Tilcajete, the smallest of the valley's Monte Albán II secondary centers, was newly built—and placed in a position that allowed it to maintain visual contact with Monte Albán—around 100 B.C. A road linked the site with both the Ocotlán subregion and the Central Valley. Cerro Tilcajete had as many as a dozen temples, palaces, and administrative buildings placed on mounds around three distinct plazas. Two of these mound-plaza groups were placed inside an area I have defined as a ceremonial precinct; the third was placed in such a way as to monitor access to that precinct.

Surface Collection 173 produced a worked human maxilla, placed in an offering or burial at the southwest corner of Plaza II (see Appendix B). This artifact suggests human sacrifice, possibly of a captured warrior. While it is not clear whether this individual was sacrificed at Cerro Tilcajete or simply had his maxilla brought to the site, such evidence of human sacrifice can be interpreted as one of the powerful tools local elites used to demarcate their position as successful warriors, and to demonstrate life and death control over their subjects.

The distribution of surface data in relation to site layout and building placement indicates gradations in social status. Lower-status residents occupied households on terraces on the eastern slope of the site. Households in the M-O Mound Group area likely fulfilled administrative or regulatory functions related to intra-valley transport and possibly the production and distribution of food, shell, and ceramics. Households inside the ceremonial precinct belonged to high-status individuals and were closely associated with administrative and ceremonial architecture.

Excavation Data

Excavation was conducted with a *barreta* (a steel digging bar), trowel, ice pick, shovel, and scoop. In almost all contexts, dirt was passed through a 6 mm screen mesh. Excavation was carried out in 1 × 1 m squares or in cultural units (a room, a midden, and so on) and thick cultural levels were subdivided into 10 to 20 cm arbitrary levels. All artifacts recovered from the screens, including charcoal, bone, pottery, and chipped, polished, and ground stone, were saved. Flotation, pollen, and radiocarbon samples were taken from units that seemed appropriate for additional analyses.

Plaza II at Cerro Tilcajete was ideal for large-scale horizontal exposure because the remains are close to the surface and the structures date to a single period of occupation. The multiphase sequence of Plaza I meant that it was more difficult to obtain complete plans of earlier buildings there. In all, just over 700 m^2 were excavated in six different areas of the site. Each of these areas was gridded with chalkline into one-meter squares, and a set of datum points established around the excavations. Since Cerro Tilcajete is part of the same three-dimensional grid system established by Spencer and Redmond for El Palenque and El Mogote, the exact location of any excavated area can be determined by referring to (1) the number of meters north and east of an arbitrary reference point southwest of the site, and (2) the number of meters above an arbitrary elevation.

The most specific unit designated during excavation was the *provenience*. Each provenience was assigned a unique number. Often, a provenience was part of a larger unit such as a *structure*. Structures were numbered individually. Proveniences could also be part of *features*, such as middens or burials, which were also numbered individually. The information recorded for each provenience included the context and association of the unit and the kinds of artifacts recovered. Forms were also filled out for structures, middens, and burials—more general analytical units including many provenience numbers. In all, we excavated 494 proveniences; of these, 150 proveniences had particular associations with structures and features.

In the sections to follow, I use the proveniences associated with structures to date those structures and to assess differences in status among residences. I use data from proveniences associated with the burials, middens, and storage rooms in Structures 3 and 4 to generate hypotheses about household "wealth," mortuary practices, and subsistence activities.

Temples and Civic-Ceremonial Buildings

Structure 2

My excavations atop Mound B exposed 138.50 m^2, including the remains of a two-room temple designated Structure 2 (Fig. 4.4). The platform supporting Structure 2 measured 6.40 m (north-south) by 14.40 m (east-west); its southern and eastern sections were constructed with considerable fill and stone retaining walls to accommodate the natural slope of the terrain. The southern retaining walls were constructed in at least two tiers and were faced with cut stone blocks. The eastern retaining wall defined and separated Area B from Terrace Area C. This wall was 1 m thick and at least six courses (70 cm) high, and its lowest courses sat on sterile ground (Fig. 4.5).

The plaza-facing (west) wall of Mound B stood almost 1 m high and was constructed of 5-6 courses of neatly faced stone

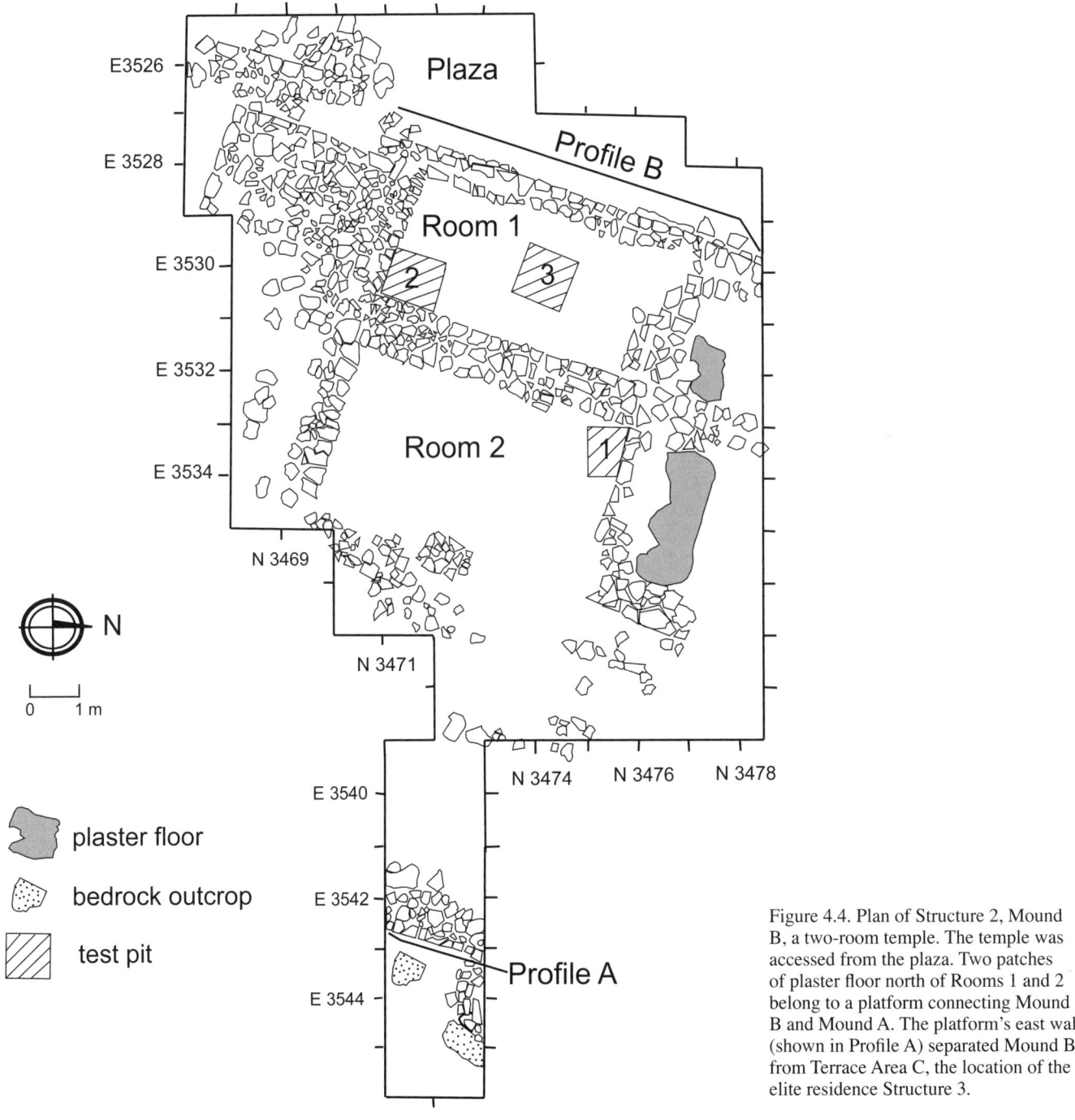

Figure 4.4. Plan of Structure 2, Mound B, a two-room temple. The temple was accessed from the plaza. Two patches of plaster floor north of Rooms 1 and 2 belong to a platform connecting Mound B and Mound A. The platform's east wall (shown in Profile A) separated Mound B from Terrace Area C, the location of the elite residence Structure 3.

blocks (Fig. 4.6). Sections of the wall sat on bedrock. Recent erosion and plowing had destroyed the floors of Structure 2, but it was possible to obtain a plan. The interior of Room 1 measured 3.2 m by 5.2 m, and the interior of Room 2 measured 3.8 m by 5.2 m, creating a total of 36.4 m^2 of interior space. The inner room (Room 2) of the temple was some 30 cm higher than the outer room (Room 1).

Several clues indicated a platform had been built as a base to link the north side of Structure 2 with Mound A. The east wall of Structure 2 continued in an unbroken line beyond the northwest corner of Structure 2 toward Mound A. Test Pit 1, placed along the north wall of Structure 1, determined that this wall was a nine-course retaining wall almost 2 m high. It is unclear whether or not there had been a building on top of the platform, but wall fall from Structure 2 had preserved the remains of a 6 cm thick plaster surface on the platform. Test pits placed into the mound fill did not recover the remains of any earlier constructions, so Mound B appears to have been built in a single construction phase.

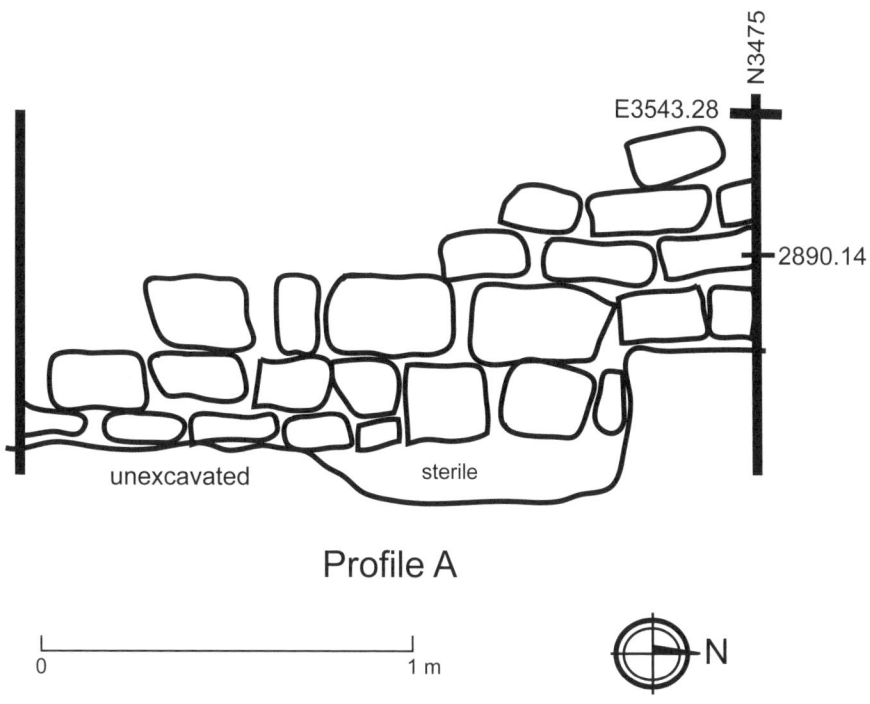

Figure 4.5. Profile of the east wall of Mound B, supporting Structure 2, a two-room temple (see Fig. 4.4 for the mound's plan and wall's location).

Mound E

The excavation of Mound E (Plaza I) determined that its last phase of construction dated to after A.D. 500. That phase, which included Structure 5, is described in the next chapter. Below this Monte Albán IIIb-IV building, I located the remains of earlier Monte Albán II buildings. These were examined with *sondages*, taking advantage of damaged areas of the overlying building (Fig. 4.7).

The overall plan of the Monte Albán II construction is not clear, but differences in elevation on the western and eastern sides of the mound suggest that it was either (1) one multilevel construction, or (2) several associated but separate structures. Neither the "eastern" nor the "western" structure probably exceeded 50 m². The western structure was placed atop a 1.57-1.70 m platform, while the eastern structure was close to plaza level. Both structures are made of cut stone and have plaster floors.

Test Pits 2 and 8 helped locate the remains of the "western" structure, 29 cm below the base of the overlying Monte Albán IIIb-IV building (Structure 5). In Test Pit 2, excavations uncovered a flagstone surface containing an oval stone-lined hearth filled only with fine ash and carbon chunks. Test Pit 8 located a section of wall and a plaster floor. Carbon found on the floor provided a radiocarbon sample (Beta-1654787) dated to A.D. 70-370 (2 sigma calibrated).

Test Pits 1 and 5 encountered the remains of the "eastern" structure, 77 cm below the base of Structure 5. Test Pit 1 located a section of wall associated with a plaster floor. This test pit produced the only significant sample of ceramics from the mound fill (that is, from above the Monte Albán II plaster floor to the base of the Monte Albán IIIb-IV structure). In Test Pit 5, excavations uncovered walls or platforms and a possible stone-lined canal. Test Pit 7 reached the same level as Test Pit 1, but failed to locate a plaster floor, so it probably did not extend into this area.

These contexts produced so little material that all ceramics, not just diagnostics, were saved for later study in the laboratory. Table 4.5 lists the ceramics from Test Pit 1, which include a few Monte Albán II diagnostics. The total weight of all ceramics was as follows: 780 g of gray ware, 980 g of café ware, 180 g of cream ware, and 20 g of orange ware. The paucity of domestic refuse and the general layout of the buildings suggest that they functioned as temples or civic-ceremonial structures.

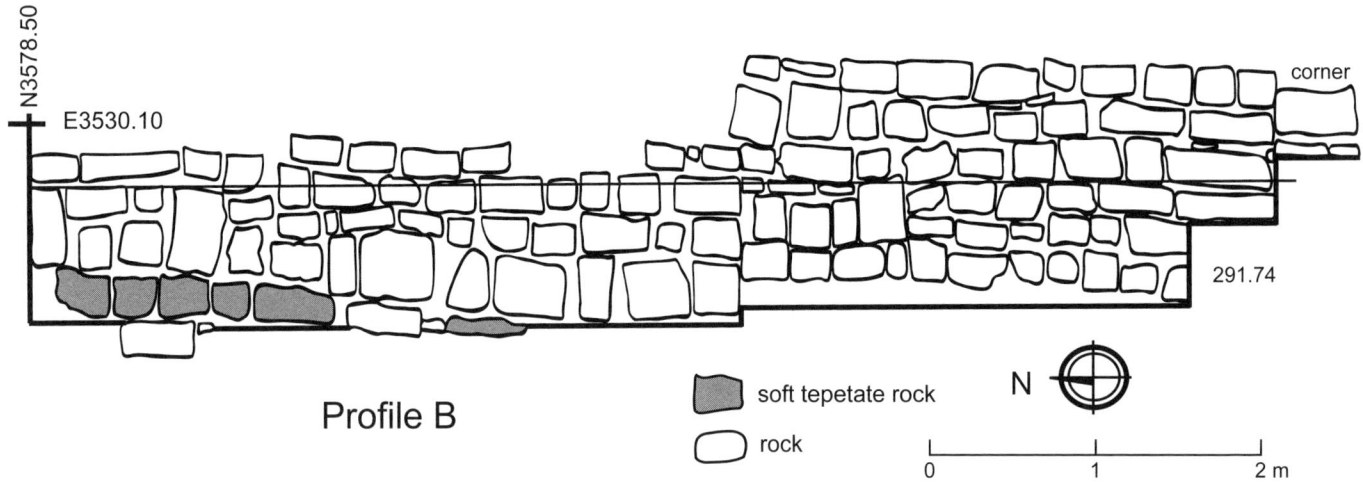

Figure 4.6. Profile of the west (plaza-facing) wall of Mound B, supporting Structure 2, a two-room temple (see Fig. 4.4 for the mound's plan and wall's location).

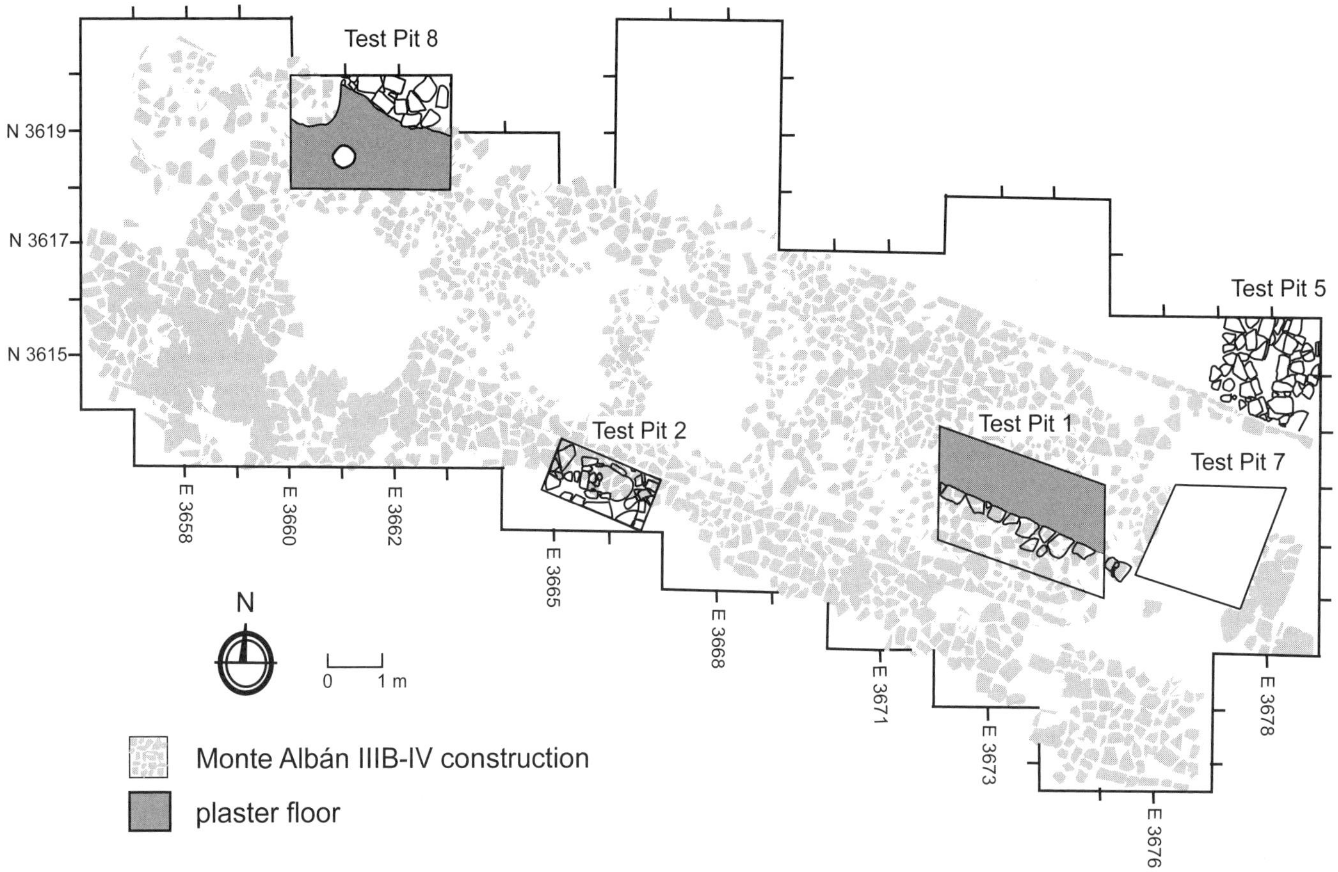

Figure 4.7. Plan of the Monte Albán II phase structures on Mound E. Test Pits 2 and 8 located a building 29 cm below the base of the Monte Albán IIIb-IV building's flagstone floor. Test Pits 1 and 5 located a building 77 cm below the base of the Monte Albán IIIb-IV building's flagstone floor.

Table 4.5. Ceramics coded in Test Pit 1, Mound E, Cerro Tilcajete.

Ceramics	Number of Sherds
G.12	9
other diagnostic grays	14
gray body sherds	253
K.4	1
other diagnostic cafés	8
café body sherds	209
C.12	3
C.20	2
C.6	21
C.7	14
A.9	1
undecorated orange	3
Total	538

Residential Excavations

Structure 1

Mound A is the largest mound on Plaza II and was built to take advantage of the natural north-south slope of the terrain. The base of Mound A measured at least 25 m (north-south) by 30 m (east-west); the plaza-side retaining wall had been built up 5 m above the level of the plaza. This operation created a roughly L-shaped 600 m² area.

Excavations on top of Mound A exposed an area of 150 m². We successfully obtained a plan of the structure in spite of the fact that the mound had suffered from subsequent erosion, plowing, and looting (Fig. 4.8). The overall dimensions of Structure 1 were 11 × 12 m (the western side of the structure was eroded, so the original dimensions may have been 12 × 12 m). No occupation floors were preserved, but the wall foundations show that Structure 1 consisted of four to six rooms enclosing a central patio.

The quality and layout of the architecture supports the interpretation that the residence housed an elite family. The walls of Structure 1 were built of cut stone blocks, and were well preserved in places. For example, the southern (plaza-facing) wall was 1.8 m thick and at least 1.6 m high (Fig. 4.9). Between this wall and the Mound A retaining wall was a 2 m wide corridor—a good vantage point from which to observe activities taking place in the plaza below. Here I found large fragments of adobes with 3 to 5 cm of smoothed plaster coating, apparently fallen from the structure's walls (Figs. 4.10-4.11).

A large, modern looters' pit intruded into the residence from the west side of Mound A. This looting had destroyed an irregular area of about 7 m², and in some places the looters' pit reached 2 m in depth. It was easy to distinguish the fill in the looters' pit from that of the mound because the fill was so loose that it could be shoveled out with plastic scoops, while the mound itself was hard-packed earth. I cleaned out the looters' pit and placed six test pits below the surface of Structure 1; these pits afforded a view of the interior of Mound A. It is clear that Mound A was built in one phase with adobe blocks, some of which measured 30 × 20 × 10 cm. A radiocarbon sample (Beta-143356) taken from below the interior of Mound A produced a date of 5 B.C. to A.D. 330 (2 sigma calibrated).

Excavations did not produce any evidence that a tomb had been incorporated into Structure 1. The looters' pit did contain a hodgepodge of ceramics, chipped stone, shell, and fragments of both human and animal bone (see Appendix B), but did not contain evidence of nicely faced stone construction or restorable pieces of smashed vessels. No tombs or burials were found in any of the test pits. It may be that some kind of offering or burial had attracted the looting, but whatever the case, similar residential palaces at Monte Albán commonly contain stone masonry tombs and multiple burials, and it would not have been surprising to find such features in Structure 1.

One truly fascinating object, a modeled sherd with a human head, was associated with the rubble of the northwest corner of Room 2 (Fig. 4.12). The sherd shows the head of a person with multiple ear piercings, a closed eye, and an open mouth. The sides of the sherd are unbroken edges, suggesting that it was an appliqué on some kind of vessel or other object. Similar kinds of objects are known from a few locations in the Oaxaca Valley and have also been found in Monte Albán I offerings at Monte Albán. They depict deceased individuals, possibly either ancestors or sacrificed individuals (Caso et al. 1967:150-51). This object suggests that such depictions could have lasted into earliest Monte Albán II. This modeled sherd may be an heirloom.

Structure 3

Terrace Area C was easily accessible only from the east side of the plaza, specifically by passing between Mounds A and B. Creating Terrace Area C required the construction of retaining walls, especially at the southeast corner, which had been raised at least 1.23 m using several layers of stone and adobes (Fig. 4.13). Excavations exposed 147 m² of the terrace and determined that Structure 3, which sat atop it, would have had at least 88.56 m² of living and patio space. The floors of Structure 3 were not well preserved, and it is difficult to describe the original layout of the building except to say that it appears to be a Monte Albán II residence. The rubble of the house contained fragments of plaster and plastered adobes, and there are suggestions that it may have been added onto or refurbished (Fig. 4.14). The house platform measured at least 11 m by 8.5 m, and part of its initial construction was a massive central wall 1 m thick and 10 m long. This wall was constructed with both cut stone and large adobes, some measuring 50 cm by 30 cm. One room, at the northwest corner of the structure, measured 3.2 × 3.2 m. The exterior walls

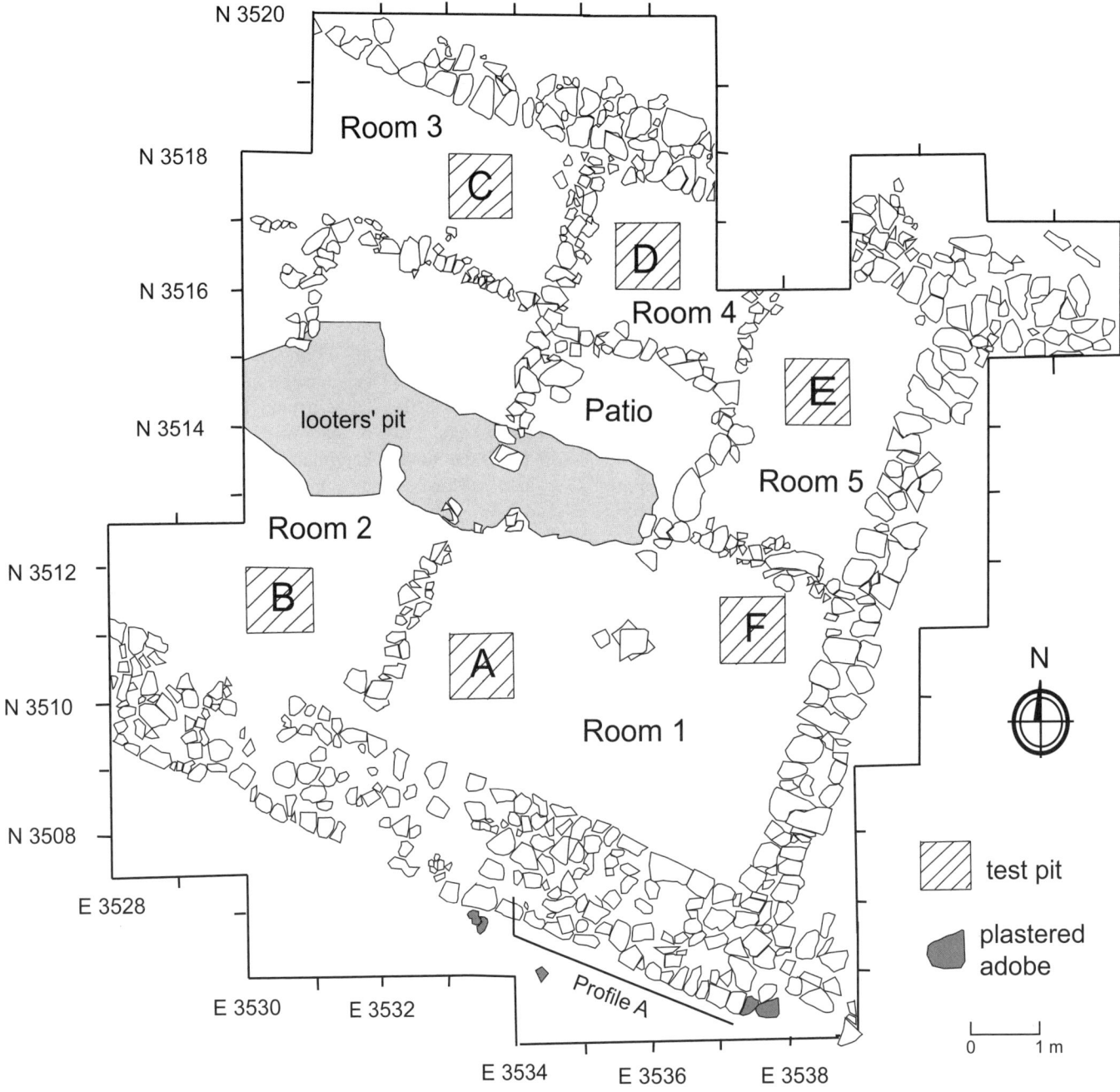

Figure 4.8. Plan of Structure 1, Mound A, a residential palace. The southern wall is 1.8 m thick and built of nicely faced stone. Floors were not preserved and the looters' pit destroyed the walls of some interior rooms, making it difficult to conclusively assess the western room arrangement.

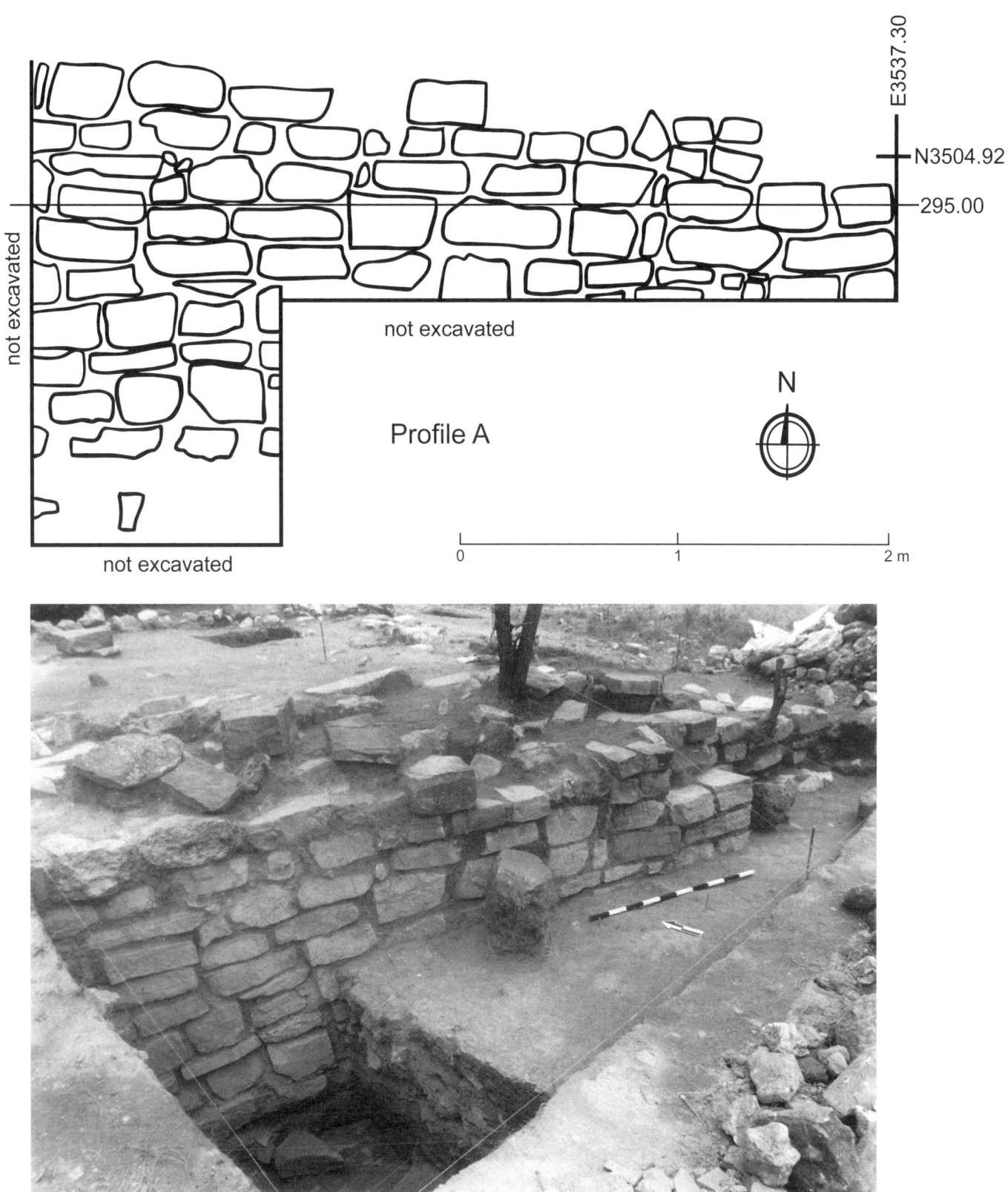

(*Upper*) Figure 4.9. Plan of the south (plaza-facing) wall of Structure 1. See Figure 4.8 for a plan of Structure 1, showing the wall's location, and Figure 4.10 for a photo of the same wall.

(*Lower*) Figure 4.10. Photo of the south (plaza-facing) wall of Structure 1. Note the plastered adobe pedestaled in front of the wall.

(*Above*) Figure 4.11. Photo of the southeast corner of Structure 1. The south and east walls meet flush but the east wall continues at a lower level. This suggests that there was a 1-2 m wide platform that ran along the east side of the building. Note the plastered adobe. (See Fig. 4.8 for a plan of Structure 1.)

(*Left*) Figure 4.12. Modeled gray-paste ceramic ornament from the fill of Room 2 in Structure 1, showing a deceased individual. Similar objects recovered in the valley are dated to Monte Albán I and this object may be an heirloom. Sherd is 9.5 cm at its widest point.

Figure 4.13. Plan of Structure 3, Area C, a residential palace. The terrace drops off sharply east of E3576 and the platform retaining walls were used to support the eastern end of the structure. Floors were not preserved, but the structure had three to four rooms around a possible open patio in the southeast.

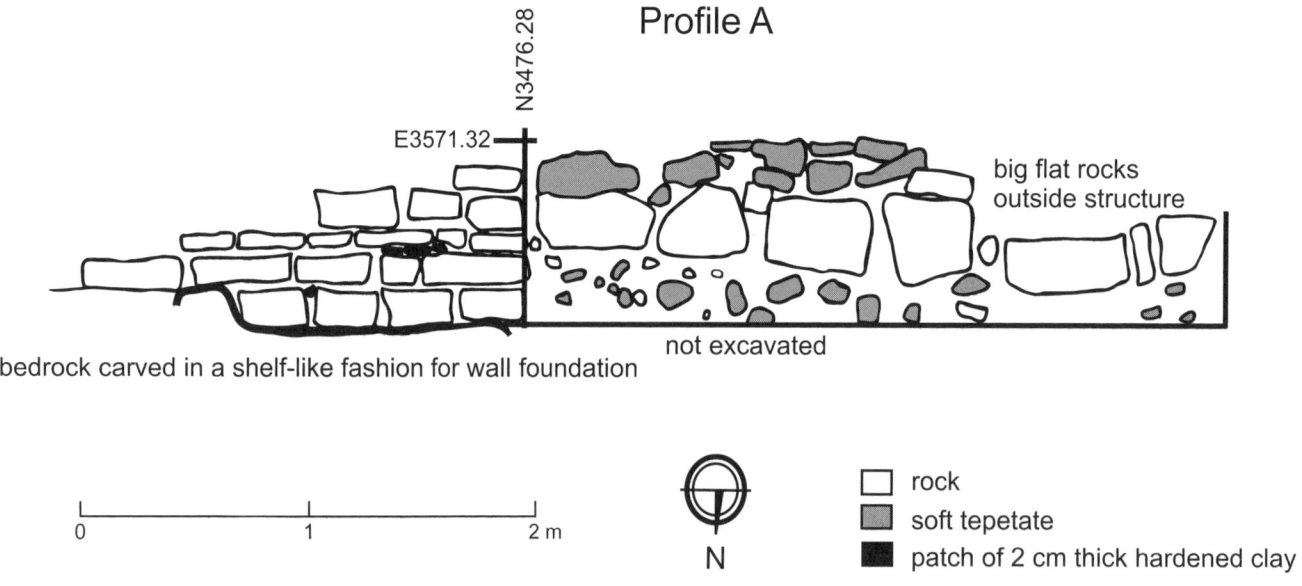

Figure 4.14. North profile of Structure 3, Area C (see Fig. 4.13 for location of the profile).

of this room were 80 cm thick and made of nicely faced stone (Fig. 4.15). My best determination is that this structure consisted of three to four rooms, partially enclosing an open patio set at the southeast corner of the house.

I made several soundings under rooms and into probable patio areas. It appears that like Structure 1, Structure 3 did not have any integrated mortuary features. I did find fragments of an infant and an adolescent in Test Pit 1 and fragments of an adolescent in Test Pit 4. In both cases, the human remains are mixed with the trash used to create the fill of the platform supporting Structure 3 (Appendix B).

Just beyond the eastern wall of Structure 3, and on the slope of the terrace, I found a midden—Feature 1—atop a level of sterile, very hard-packed soil and bedrock (Figs. 4.16-4.17). I excavated an area of 1.47 m² in this midden to a depth of 1.33 m (recovering an estimated volume of 1.96 m³), saving all material. The Feature 1 sample included nearly 2000 large sherds in addition to worked sherds, figurines, mica, chipped stone, polished stone, a metate fragment, bone, shell, carbon, daub, and plaster. An infant had been buried in the midden, which also contained fragments of an adult and a child (Appendix B).

Structure 4

Structure 4, located on a terrace on the southeastern slope of the site, the location of Collection Square 147, is an example of a low-status residence (Fig. 4.18). Excavations exposed 88.5 m² and uncovered four burials, two hearths, a storage area full of whole and restorable vessels, and a drain. The house was modified over its lifespan but during its last stage it covered 38.4 m² and took on the form of an L or C, partially dug into the hillside. The west room was built up as much as 78 cm above the patio surface and had a stucco floor. Unfortunately, time constraints did not permit a complete excavation of the north or west rooms.

The east room was attached to a massive wall (60-80 cm thick and made of large, irregularly shaped stones) that also served as a retaining wall for the east side of the terrace. The tiny east room may have been built as a burial structure. Inside I found two burials, a child and an adult (Appendix B). Both individuals were buried extended, face up, and oriented to the structure's walls (Fig. 4.19 and Table 4.6). The child (Burial 1) was stratigraphically above and slightly west of the adult and was accompanied by three offerings: a plain gray-paste bowl placed upside down on the child's face; a gray-paste rattle/whistle in the shape of a turkey (the stomach contains rattles and the tail is the whistle blow) (Fig. 4.20); and a string of 46 tiny shells (2 cm long) perforated for suspension on a necklace. The adult (Burial 2) was accompanied by two offerings: an orange-paste bowl with designs painted in red (illustrated in Fig. 3.5), placed upside down on the pelvis, and a greenstone pendant placed near the head.

The fill of the small room also produced three broken or partially complete ceramic objects, a metate fragment and two mano fragments. It is not clear if these were offerings or were simply included in the room fill. The first object is the head and

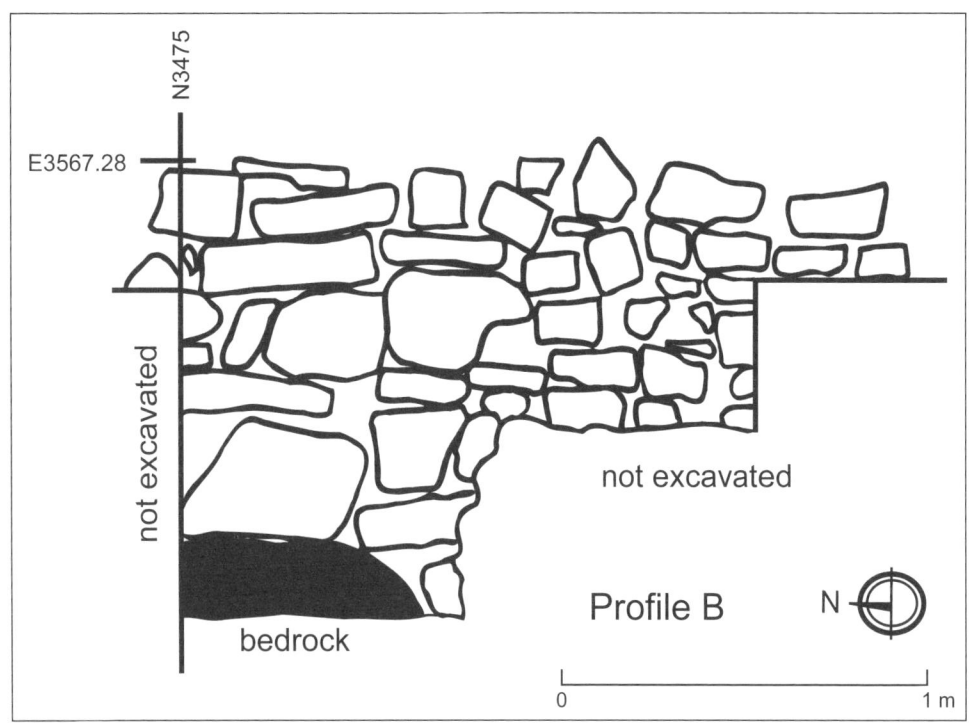

Figure 4.15. West profile of Structure 3, Area C (see Fig. 4.13 for location of the profile).

(*Left*) Figure 4.16. West profile of Feature 1, Structure 3. The feature sits in the east slope of the terrace and abuts the east wall of Structure 3.

(*Right*) Figure 4.17. Plan of Feature 1, Structure 3, Area C. The north side of the feature is a retaining wall of the terrace, built with stone and with adobes made from earth with different soil compositions. The south side of the feature is a retaining wall of the terrace, made primarily of stone.

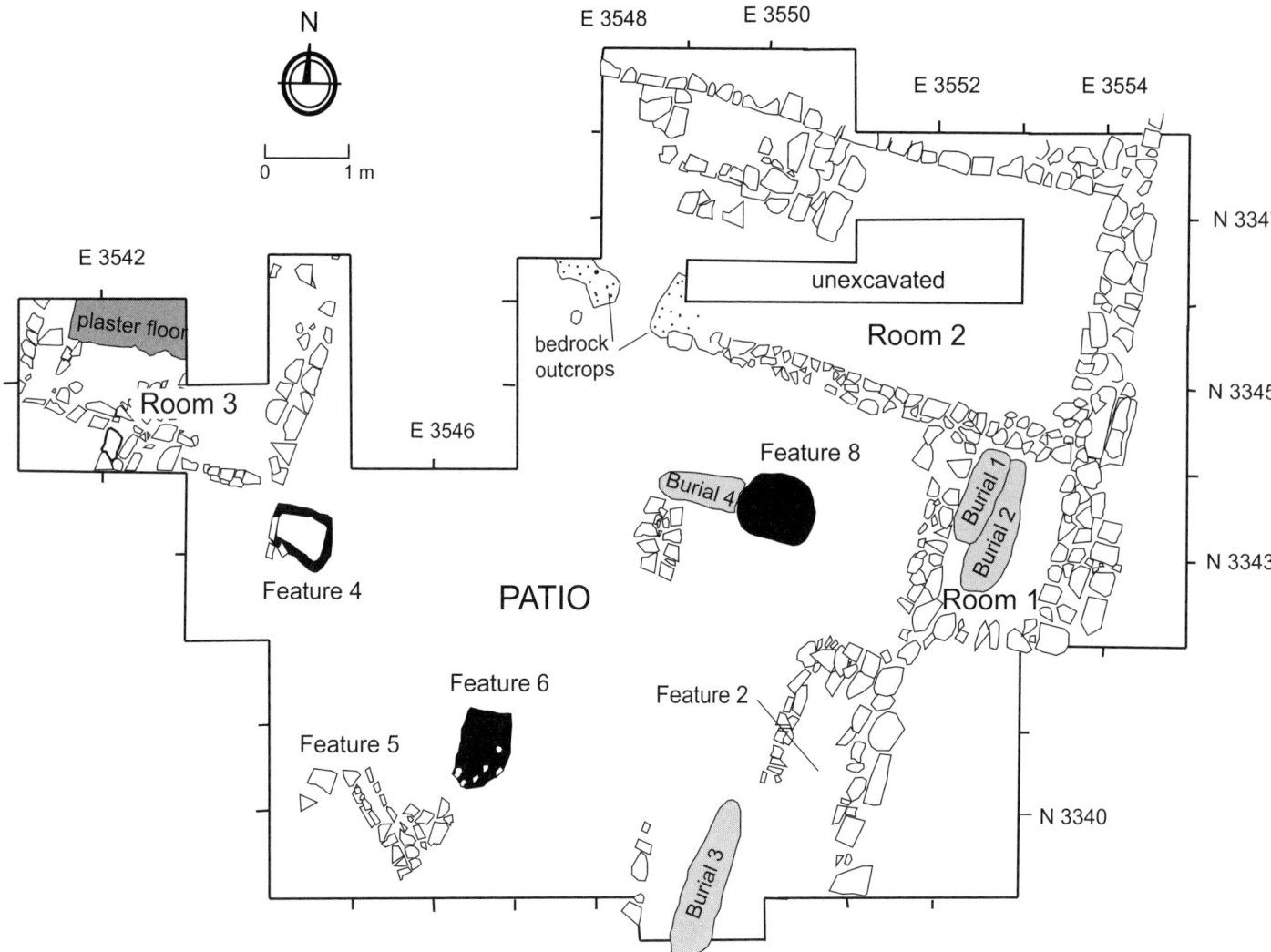

Figure 4.18. Plan of Structure 4, a lower-status residence. The L-shaped house has three or four rooms around a central patio. Room 1 may have been specially built to house Burials 1 and 2.

torso of an orange-paste figurine depicting a man wearing an elaborate headdress (Fig. 4.21). The second, found in many pieces throughout the fill, is an orange-paste figure of a man with an elaborate headdress; it functioned as a whistle (Fig. 4.22). The third object was half of a red-painted and incised cream-paste bowl with broken supports.

Two more burials had been dug into the patio, which had a simple surface of packed earth, small stones, sherds, and ashy earth. On the north side of the patio we found Burial 4, placed in a simple grave dug into sterile, hard-packed earth (Fig. 4.23). Burial 4 was partially destroyed by an intrusive hearth. Interestingly, it contained the remains of a child and the partial remains of one adult. Two offerings accompanied these individuals: a gray-paste bowl with a "pie crust" rim, placed over the child's pelvis (see Fig. 4.23), and a figurine representing a human with an elaborate headdress or hairdo, and extended arms and legs; this figure could have been suspended from a loop on its back (Fig. 4.24).

A fourth individual, Burial 3, was buried at the southeastern edge of the patio; this was a child, placed in the extended position in a simple grave. The remains were not well preserved and the skull was eroded and almost completely destroyed. Burial 3 was accompanied by at least three vessels: a partially complete gray-paste flat-bottomed bowl with mammiform supports and no decoration; a very fragmentary café-paste jar; and a partially reconstructible, thin-walled café-paste bowl with a nicely burnished exterior displaying an incised step-fret motif and a pinched rim reminiscent of a gourd (Fig. 4.25). I discuss these offerings further in the section on mortuary ritual.

The patio produced several features that provided data on subsistence and other activities. Feature 2, a rectangular, stone-

Figure 4.19. Photo of Burial 2, Structure 4. The bowl, an orange-paste bowl with designs painted in red, is illustrated in Figure 3.5. A broken cream-paste bowl with red paint and incised designs is visible in the upper right area of the burial. See Figure 4.18 for the structure's plan.

Table 4.6. Offerings with Structure 4 burials at Cerro Tilcajete.

Burial	Offering	Object	Paste/Decoration	Height/Length (cm)	Width (cm)	Depth (cm)	Dm. (cm)
1	3	bowl, straight rim, slightly outleaned wall	gray	5.25			13
1	5	46 shells made into beads		2			
1	2	turkey rattle/whistle	gray with red paint	7.5	7.5	8	
1, 2	4	standing human figure	orange	19	9		8
1, 2	1	human head and torso	orange	10.25	7.6	3	
1, 2	8	bowl, incomplete	cream (C.12)	10			22
2	6	greenstone bead		1.75	0.25		
2	7	bowl, straight rim, slightly outleaned wall	orange (A.9)	6.5			22
3	1	bowl w/ mammiform feet, outflared rim, incomplete	gray	9.75			22
3	2	bowl, pinched ovate rim, incomplete	café with incising	12	22	12	
4	1	human "flying" figure	gray	4.5	10	5.5	
4	2	bowl, "pie crust" rim	gray	4			21

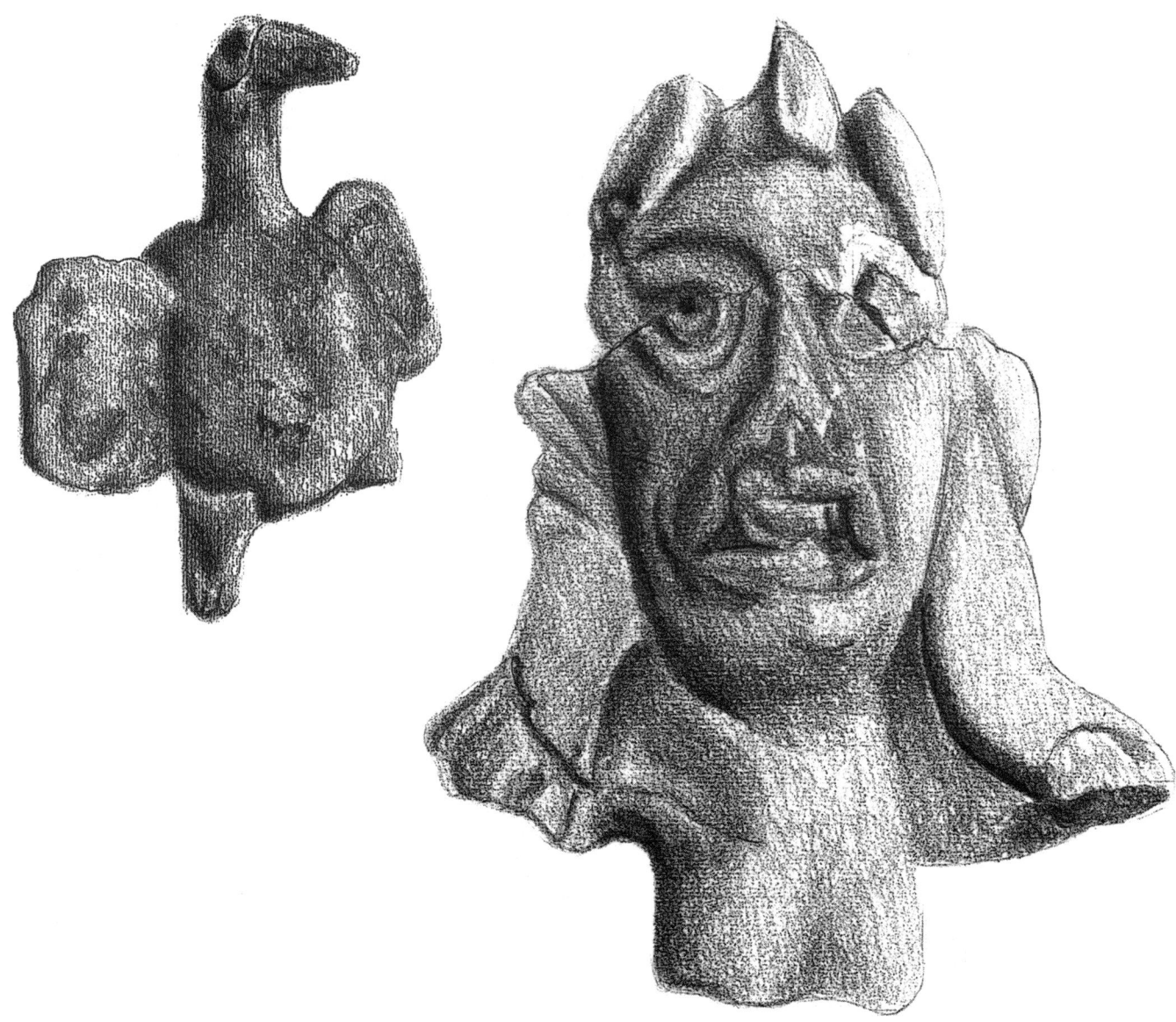

(*Left*) Figure 4.20. The turkey figurine (7.5 cm tall), made in gray paste, is both a rattle and a whistle. It was placed with Burial 1, a child, in Structure 4. See Figure 4.18 for the burial's location (drawing by Miriam Vallesteros).

(*Right*) Figure 4.21. Orange-paste figurine (10.25 cm tall) of a person with an elaborate headdress. This partially complete figurine was placed as an offering for Burial 1, a child, or Burial 2, an adult. See Figure 4.18 for the burials' locations (drawing by Miriam Vallesteros).

lined structure attached to the eastern edge of the terrace, was filled with large pieces of restorable utilitarian vessels (Fig. 4.26). There was no evidence of burning (such as chunks of carbon or burned stones) inside the feature, so I interpret it as a storage area. I saved all material from Feature 2 (see discussion of subsistence activities, below).

The west side of the patio produced Feature 4, a roughly rectangular adobe- and stone-lined hearth measuring 76 × 64 cm. The hearth was dug into the patio surface and was filled with 7 to 9 cm of ash, carbon, bone, and a few burned pottery fragments, including the rim-to-base section of a G.21 bowl (Figs. 4.27, A3*c*). Just to the south of Feature 4, excavations exposed a section of a drain (Feature 5) constructed of small flagstones set upright on a flagstone surface. Feature 5 was associated with a dense scatter of sherds and an ashy patch of earth (Feature 6). Feature 6 was either a midden or a concentration of refuse that washed downslope into this area after the house was abandoned. Besides ceramic material, the feature produced a mano and some bone.

Figure 4.22. Front and side views of an orange-paste figure of a man with an elaborate headdress and walking stick. This figure (19 cm tall) has been reconstructed from numerous pieces found in the fill of Burial 1. It functioned as a whistle (drawing by Miriam Vallesteros).

Pottery Types Believed to Reflect Status

In Oaxaca, not many of the gray- and café-paste pottery types were confined to a single chronological time period. More often, pottery changes are *frequency shifts* that can be detected only when one has large assemblages of excavated sherds; these reveal the changing popularity of each type over time. Appendix A documents the Monte Albán II ceramic assemblage excavated at Cerro Tilcajete and compares it with the Monte Albán II ceramic assemblage excavated at Monte Albán.

In this section, I focus on several categories of general ceramic information, including the frequency of elite serving vessels versus more utilitarian vessels and the distribution of several decorated types. Overall, relative to other periods, Monte Albán II pottery is quite elegant in terms of its production time and effort. It is generally assumed that elegant wares are of limited access and that elite households at administrative sites (that is, those in the upper tiers of the settlement hierarchy) will have a greater diversity of vessels than will lower-status households at smaller sites (Kowalewski et al. 1989:165, 173). To evaluate the diversity of each household's ceramic assemblage at Cerro Tilcajete, I classified identifiable rims by form and then grouped them into more general categories. In each residential structure, upwards of 50% of the diagnostics were rims, and I was able to classify at least 75% of these by form.

My analysis also focuses on several decorated types that I believe convey information about status. In Chapter 3, I provided evidence that cream-paste vessels may have been manufactured in the Monte Albán-Etla subregion under some degree of central authority during Monte Albán II. At Monte Albán itself, cream-paste vessels usually have a red (type C.7), brown (type C.6), or black (type C.20) exterior and occur in the form of bowls, jars, and vases. One cream-paste form that occurs almost exclusively as a red-painted (type C.11) or black-painted (type C.12) bowl, with incised step-fret or zigzag designs and three to four bulbous supports, is restricted to Monte Albán II (Caso et al. 1967: Table 7). This kind of vessel does not transport well; it is not stackable, and the supports are fragile and tend to break easily. Despite their transport problems, the acquisition and use of these bowls is probably one way that elites demonstrated their relationship with Lightning, to whom the designs refer. One possibility is that cream-paste C.11 and C.12 bowls may have been used during communal events—for example, ritual petitions for, or the celebration of, abundant harvests—and might have been obtained as gifts from nobles at Monte Albán (Elson and Sherman, in press).

While most of the gray-paste wares found at Cerro Tilcajete were probably made locally, some could have been imported. Gray ware tends to have a finer paste and better finish than other wares, and the majority of Monte Albán II gray vessels were

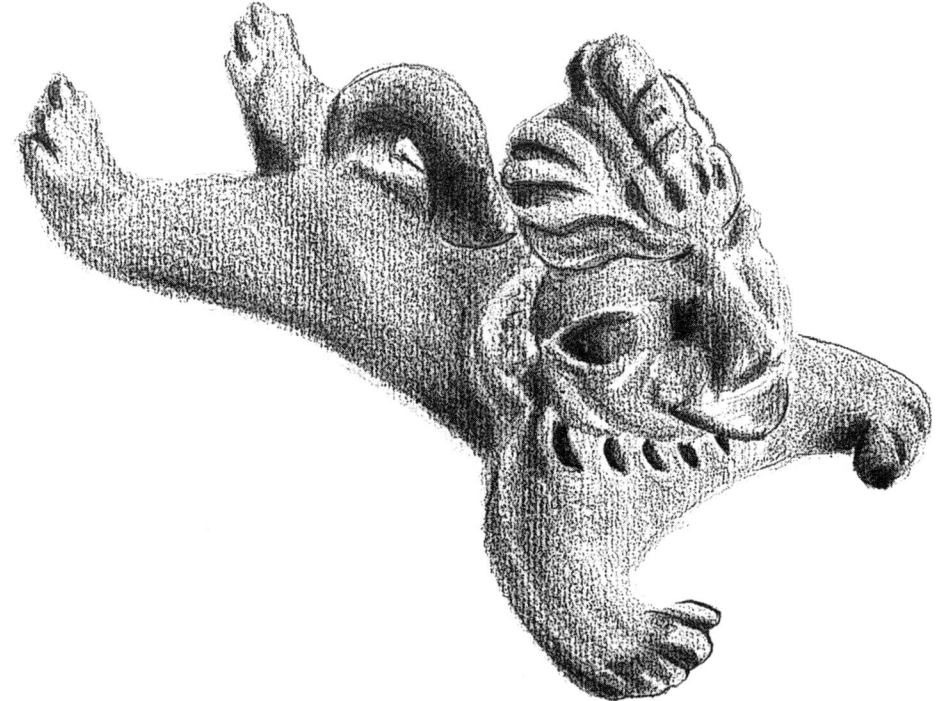

(*Upper*) Figure 4.23. Photo of Burial 4, Structure 4. Later laboratory analysis showed that the burial contained the remains of a child and the partial remains of an adult. The gray-paste bowl with a fluted "piecrust" rim is more typical of the Monte Albán I period and it may be an heirloom (see Table 4.6 for the bowl's dimensions).

(*Lower*) Figure 4.24. Gray-paste figure (10 cm from hand to toe), Burial 4, Structure 4. This gray-paste figurine was placed near the child's pelvis. It shows a flying figure with an elaborate headdress or hairdo; this figure could have been suspended from the loop on its back (see Table 4.6 for the figure's dimensions) (drawing by Miriam Vallesteros).

(*Upper*) Figure 4.25. Café-paste bowl with a pinched ovate rim and incised step-fret motif, Burial 3, Structure 4 (see Table 4.6 for the bowl's dimensions) (drawing by Miriam Vallesteros).

(*Lower*) Figure 4.26. Photo of Feature 2, Structure 4, a storage room filled with large sherds of restorable utilitarian vessels (see Fig. 4.18 for the feature's location).

Figure 4.27. Photo of Feature 4, a hearth in Structure 4. See Figure A3c for an illustration of the G.21 bowl sherd found in the hearth.

manufactured for use as serving dishes. Excavations at Cerro Tilcajete isolated one type, called G.29, which was locally made, but which was often designed to imitate C.7 cream-paste vessels by adding red paint (see Appendix A). Similar G.29 vessels have been excavated at Monte Albán II sites in the Valle Grande or Zimatlán subregion (Sherman et al. 2004; Sherman 2005:108-10). At Cerro Tilcajete, the G.29 vessels that imitate C.7 vessels are usually gray-paste bowls given a brownish slip, a painted red line on the interior of the rim, and splotchy red strokes elsewhere on the vessel.

In contrast to the gray-paste ceramics, the vast majority of café wares were utilitarian (cooking/storage) jars, bowls, and *comales*. At Cerro Tilcajete, excavations isolated one café type called K.17, which occurs in low frequencies but seems often to have been given a darkly burnished exterior similar to the C.20 type of cream-paste vessels. K.17 was also found in small quantities at Monte Albán, where it has been interpreted as a café-paste regional variant of C.20 (Caso et al. 1967:53). At Monte Albán, K.17 vessels occur as bowls; at Cerro Tilcajete, they occur as both bowls and vases. The bowl illustrated in Figure 4.25 is a K.17 bowl with incised designs on the exterior; these designs are similar to those on C.12 bowls, showing that café paste was sometimes employed to make significant decorated wares. I do not know whether K.17 pottery was manufactured in many locations or only a few.

My expectation is that because cream wares had to be imported to Cerro Tilcajete, their acquisition and use were likely restricted to higher-status residents. True cream-paste vessels with bulbous supports and incised designs should be particularly limited in their distribution. On the other hand, G.29 and K.17 vessels were most likely local variants of some of the most sought-after cream-paste vessels; these imitative types may be found more evenly distributed across the site, or even concentrated in lower-status households.

Before examining the distribution of true cream-paste vessels, and the G.29 and K.17 imitations, I will consider two additional types. The first is orange-paste wares. Orange-paste wares are often just gray-paste ceramics fired in an oxidized environment. They made up a small portion of most excavated Monte Albán II ceramic assemblages at Monte Albán (Caso et al. 1967: Table 1). Many orange wares were undecorated, but one decorated type, described in Chapter 3 and Appendix A and referred to as

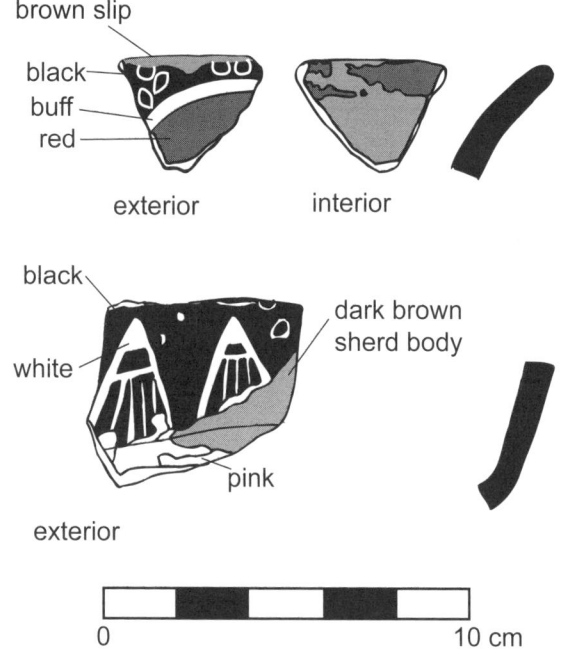

Figure 4.28. Fragments from stuccoed and painted vessels. Both vessels were recovered in excavations on Mound A at Cerro Tilcajete.

A.9, was restricted to Monte Albán II. A.9 was often slipped or burnished and had a shiny surface painted with step-frets and other kinds of geometric motifs.

The production network for A.9 vessels is not clear, but regional surveys have found that this type was concentrated in the Tlacolula and Valle Grande-Ocotlán subregions. At Cerro Tilcajete, most A.9 vessels were bowls, a few of which had supports similar to the bulbous supports on some cream-paste vessels, albeit smaller. It can be difficult to determine a vessel's motif from individual sherds; however, I detected a much wider range of decoration on A.9 vessels than the decoration on C.11 and C.12 vessels, which was restricted to step-fret/zigzag motifs. I suspect that A.9 ceramics would rank below cream-paste ceramics in desirability, in the sense that they were accessible to a wider number of people. They do, however, occur in a limited range of forms and probably functioned exclusively as serving ware.

Finally, one Monte Albán II type—elaborately decorated bowls with stuccoed and painted designs—occurred so rarely at Cerro Tilcajete that we can discuss it only in terms of its presence or absence in excavation units. Because these vessels were very limited in manufacture and distribution, their presence has been interpreted as a marker of elite contexts (Caso et al. 1967:61-67). At Monte Albán, this ceramic type was found in Tombs 77, 78, and 96 in the El Pitahayo zone, and in Tomb 103 in the Mound of the Carved Stone. Some of these vessels were stuccoed in panels of colors; others were stuccoed and then had designs carved into the stucco. Such vessels preserve poorly; nevertheless, excavations at Cerro Tilcajete produced four sherds with stucco from Structure 1 and three from Structure 3 (Fig. 4.28).

Ceramic Types and Forms Found in Residences

Tables 4.7 and 4.8 provide data on the ceramic types and forms found in residences. It is immediately evident that gray-paste wares predominated and that all three structures showed roughly the same percentages of café wares. There were significant differences in cream and orange wares: the two residences on Plaza II (Structures 1 and 3) had twice as many cream wares, and many times fewer orange wares, than Structure 4.

I suspected that elite residences would contain more cream wares. Structure 1 has 27.48% cream wares and Structure 4 has 11.66% cream wares as a percentage of all diagnostics coded in each structure. In particular, combined C.12 and C.20 cream wares with dark-colored exteriors occur much more frequently in Structure 1 than in Structure 4 (10.16% versus 1.65%). Combined C.7 and C.11 cream wares with red-colored exteriors also occur more frequently in Structure 1 than in Structure 4 (9.70% versus 6.39%). It is important to note that C.7 and C.20 sherds can come from undecorated zones of bowls with scratched designs and bulbous feet or from non-incised bowls. This makes it difficult to determine the prevalence of incised versus non-incised cream wares at the site. The reason to combine C.7 and C.11, and C.12 and C.20, is to illustrate preferences for red and black cream wares, and to show the overall ability of elites and non-elites to obtain red and black cream wares.

In contrast to the cream-paste vessels, orange wares made up a relatively small amount of the decorated pottery in the residences. Even in the low-status residence, A.9s occurred less frequently than cream wares (although they were a bit more common than incised cream-paste bowls, combined C.11 and C.12). Orange wares, probably locally made, could have a variety of motifs and likely had less cachet than cream wares.

All residences contain K.17 and G.29 pottery, two types often designed to imitate black and red cream-paste vessels. K.17 vessels, which usually have a dark brown to black exterior, and still have a poorly defined production network, occur more frequently in Structure 1, while G.29s, which usually have a greenish-brown or red-painted exterior, and were probably locally made, occur more frequently in Structure 4. This pattern does not lend itself to easy interpretation. K.17 vessels could be very well made and even take the shape of two vessels with strong elite connotations: bowls with incised step-fret designs (some with supports) and straight-walled vases (some with lids). Vases did occur in earlier time periods, and by Monte Albán II, they were fairly uniform in manufacture, with straight walls and simple rims. Vases with lids, however, were a type novel to Monte Albán II (Caso et al. 1967:243). At Monte Albán, they appeared in tombs and burials and were predominantly made in cream paste (Caso et al. 1967:240; Martínez López 1998; Winter et al. 1995). It is not clear what these vessels were used for, but the fact that they had lids and occurred in low numbers suggests a specialized function. One rim form (Fig. 4.29) seems to have belonged exclusively to vases with lids, while vases in general could have several rim forms. In the future it will be important to define the production and distribution network of K.17 vessels to better assess how they might have functioned as elite goods.

Another way to compare residences is to examine vessel form. In my analysis, identifiable rims were sorted as originating from jars, bowls, vases, vases with lids, plates, *apaxtles* or *comales*, then were further divided into serving vessels or cooking/storage vessels, regardless of paste type (Figs. 4.30-4.31). I found differences between residences as regards serving and cooking/storage vessels: there were fewer serving wares and more cooking/storage wares as one moved from higher-status to lower-status residences. The frequency of specific vessel types within these two groups suggests that lower-status residents had access to the same kinds of serving vessels, but had fewer of them. In contrast, cooking/storage wares were not utilized in the same proportions; I will address why this may be when I examine subsistence activities. Overall, the data on vessel form add support to the impression that gradations of status existed among the occupants of Structures 1, 3, and 4.

Ceramic Types and Forms Found in Middens

An examination of data from two middens at Cerro Tilcajete, Feature 1 in Structure 3 and Feature 6 in Structure 4, provides a final point of comparison among residences (Tables 4.9-4.10). Feature 1 (from a high-status residence) contained at least 108 different kinds of serving and cooking/storage vessels, as well as a café-paste incense burner; these vessels exhibited a minimum of 49 different rim forms. In contrast, while Feature 6 (in a low-status residence) contained many of the same types of vessels, the assemblage exhibited only 24 different rim forms and lacked two relatively rare ceramic types: orange-paste vessels with incised designs (A.11) and well-finished, thin-walled café-paste vessels (K.17). As often happens, the differences between the higher- and lower-status residences were not sharply defined, but indicated graduated access to serving wares and elegant decorated or imported pottery.

Subsistence Activities

Maize was the staple of the ancient Mesoamerican diet. Recent literature on the diet of Mexican peasants in Oaxaca's Sierra Norte and other regions suggests that even after the introduction of Old World animals, maize still makes up 75% of the calories consumed daily (González 2001:155; see also Ghindelli 1971;

Table 4.7. Ceramics in residential structures by paste, diagnostic form, and type.

	Str. 1 n = 2165	Str. 3 n = 1794	Str. 4 n = 1518
Paste (as %)			
orange	4.11	3.90	13.77
café	22.31	17.45	19.04
cream	27.48	22.85	11.66
gray	45.87	55.69	54.94
other	0.23	0.11	0.59
Diagnostic Form (as %)			
base	18.85	23.21	21.74
body	20.60	12.98	19.04
rim-to-base	1.34	0.34	0.66
hollow foot	1.66	1.03	0.07
other	2.31	3.37	0.99
rim	55.24	61.64	57.51
*Type (as % of all diagnostics coded)**			
A.9	1.85	1.43	2.90
A.11	0.37	0.46	0.13
C.5	0.05	0.00	0.00
C.6	5.59	6.75	2.96
C.7	7.85	8.12	4.22
C.11	1.85	1.49	2.17
C.12	2.54	2.17	0.20
C.20	7.62	4.52	1.45
G.11	0.14	0.17	0.00
G.12 b, d**	4.53	5.15	6.06
G.12 r**	7.81	7.38	7.58
G.15	0.00	1.14	0.13
G.16	0.00	0.17	0.07
G.21	0.97	0.63	0.07
G.25	0.09	0.17	0.00
G.26	0.55	0.69	0.00
G.29	1.02	3.89	7.44
G.34	1.71	0.57	0.00
K.2	0.00	0.00	0.13
K.3	0.97	0.11	0.26
K.4	0.18	0.23	1.38
K.17	5.31	2.12	0.53

*Not all diagnostic sherds coded were assigned a type.
**b = base; d = rim-to-base; r = rim

Table 4.8. Ceramics in residential structures, by vessel form.

Vessel Form	Str. 1	Str. 3	Str. 4
number of identifiable rims	914	882	670
% of identifiable rims that are:			
serving wares	83.81	79.25	71.19
cooking/storage wares	16.19	20.75	28.81
% of coded cooking/storage rims that are:			
apaxtles	0.44	1.94	2.38
bowls	0.11	1.83	2.94
braziers	0.00	0.11	0.14
comales	10.67	10.62	8.95
jars	5.06	6.39	12.59

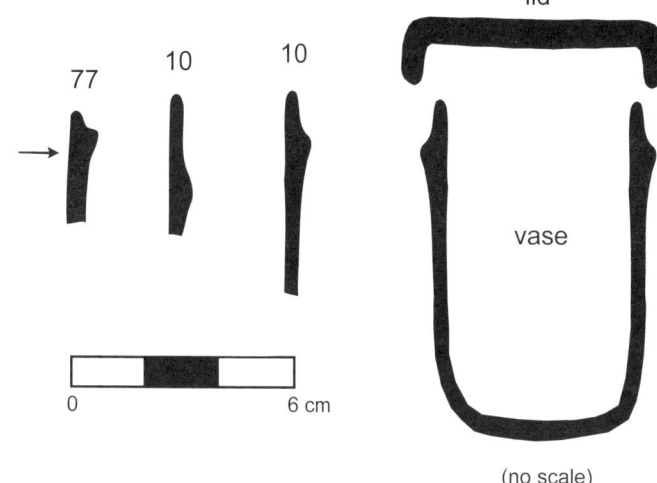

Figure 4.29. Rim forms of vases with lids recovered at Cerro Tilcajete. The arrow points to the vessel's interior. No whole or reconstructable vessels were recovered. The whole vessel illustration is adapted from that recovered at Monte Albán, illustrated in Caso et al. (1967: Fig. 219).

Lipp 1991; Williams 1973). Subsistence farmers in the Sierra Norte may consume 3500-4000 calories a day, which they easily expend working (González 2001:172). Other estimates for the number of calories consumed a day by peasants at the time of Spanish contact are around 2200 calories, of which at least 75% came from maize (Ortiz de Montellano 1990:119). These data allow me to suggest that maize provided a pre-Hispanic adult with some 1650-3000 calories a day.

I noted that the *comal* first appeared at Monte Albán about 500 B.C., possibly associated with the mass production of food for urban laborers (Marcus and Flannery 1996:146). Preparing maize for tortillas is a daily and time-consuming process. Stored kernels have to be soaked in lime, often overnight. They then are boiled over a low fire to remove the pericarp, rinsed with clean water in a large bowl, and ground (using more water) into *masa* or dough. Without preservatives, fresh *masa* does not keep for long periods of time; it sours and loses flavor. Tortillas are quick to cook and easy to stack and carry. Today, a farming family of two adults and three children in the Sierra Norte would consume 17-20 tortillas a day (each weighing 0.17 kg) (González 2001:155). *Masa* also can be processed into *pozole* (a thick drink) and tamales.

The equipment for making tortillas—a *comal*—is quite portable, while the equipment for preparing the *masa*—large bowls to soak, boil, and wash the maize, and stone implements to grind it—is less so. Archaeologically, *apaxtles* (thick-walled vessels with a diameter of more than 30 cm) could have had many purposes, but one of their primary functions likely was for soaking and rinsing maize. Large jars also can have many purposes, but many presumably functioned as receptacles for holding dried maize and for carrying and storing the water needed for soaking, rinsing, and grinding the maize. Thus, analyses of the frequencies of *comales*, *apaxtles*, and utilitarian jars (as well as metates and manos) tell us something about a household's involvement in food production.

Food storage is a related, and not well understood, issue in Oaxaca. Few architecturally identifiable storage structures have been found at archaeological sites, and there is little sixteenth-century ethnohistoric data on food storage in Oaxaca.

Ethnographic studies of the way modern Maya subsistence farmers store maize provide some data for thinking about household storage (Smyth 1991). When storing maize for human consumption, the modern Maya prefer to build rooms that are not necessarily attached to the main dwelling, but are made from wattle-and-daub and have well-sealed walls. These rooms frequently have flagstone or plaster floors (and may be the only room in the house to have such a floor). In addition to maize, Maya storage rooms often contain provisionally discarded objects and household utilities (Smyth 1991:87, 95-97).

Inside these rooms, maize is stored in wooden bins raised above the floor by large stones. The bins may hold shelled maize or maize on the ear packed vertically. Properly dried shelled maize can be stored for up to a year in the warm Yucatán climate, while packed ears can last for three years (Smyth 1991:24-25). Smyth (1991:39) estimates that a family of five consumes 3.0 kg of maize a day, or 1095 kg a year. Data from the Sierra Norte of Oaxaca are similar: a family of five consumes 2.89-3.40 kg of corn a day or 1054-1241 kg a year. If 155 kg of shelled maize take up a volume of 1 m^3, then a family of five could store a year's worth of shelled maize in 6.8-8.0 m^3 of space.

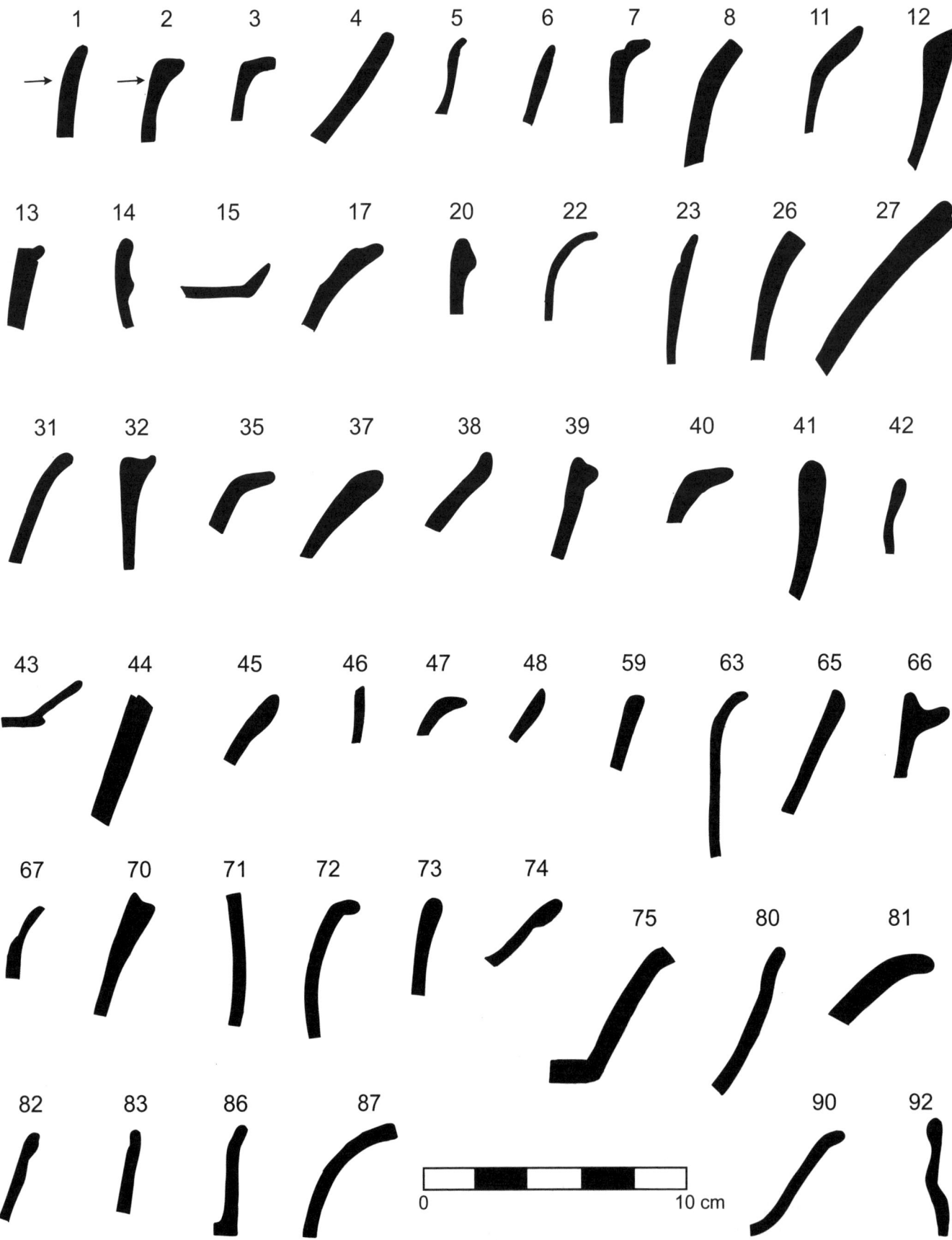

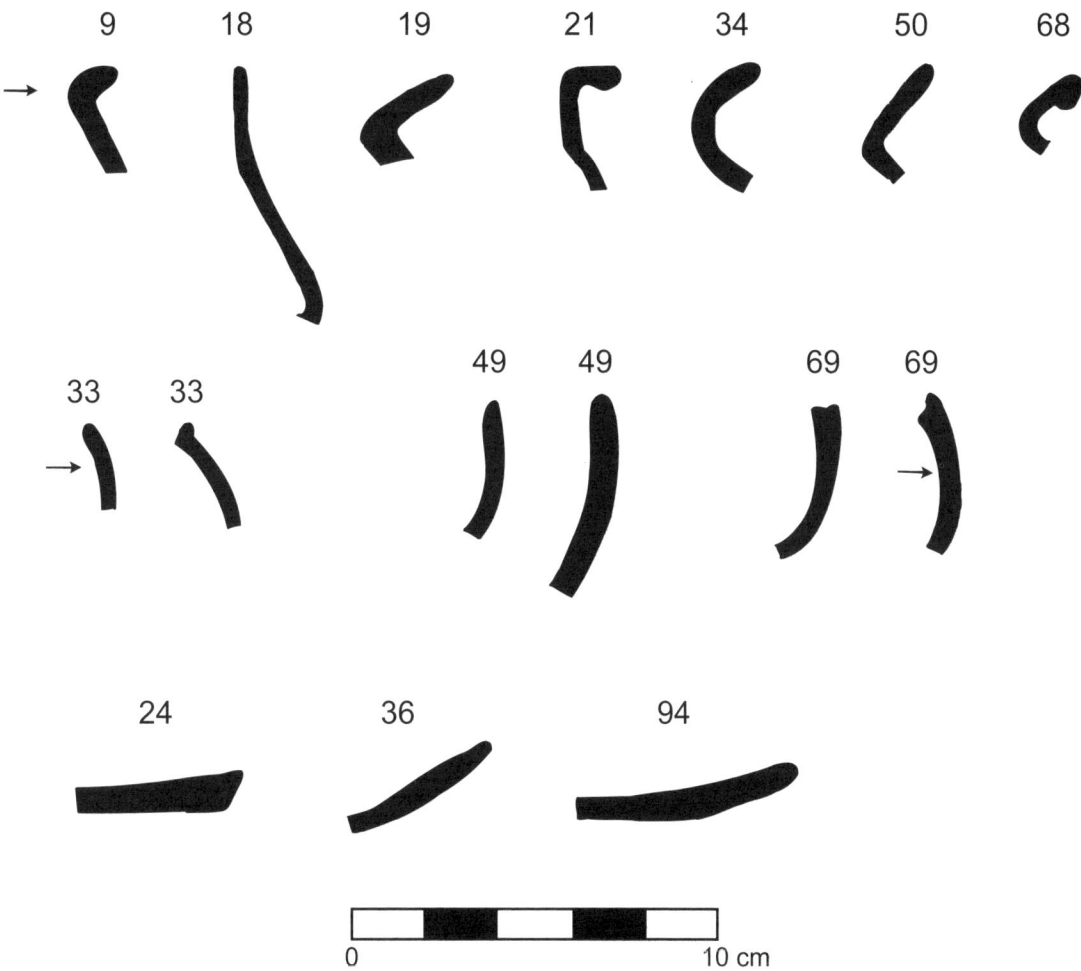

(*Facing page*) Figure 4.30a. Rim forms of serving bowls recovered at Cerro Tilcajete. Arrows point to vessel interior.

(*This page*) Figure 4.30b. Rim forms of serving vessels recovered at Cerro Tilcajete. *top row*, jars; *middle row*, vessel number 33 is a *tecomate*, and vessel numbers 49 and 69 are incurving bowls; *bottom row*, plates. Arrows point to vessel interior.

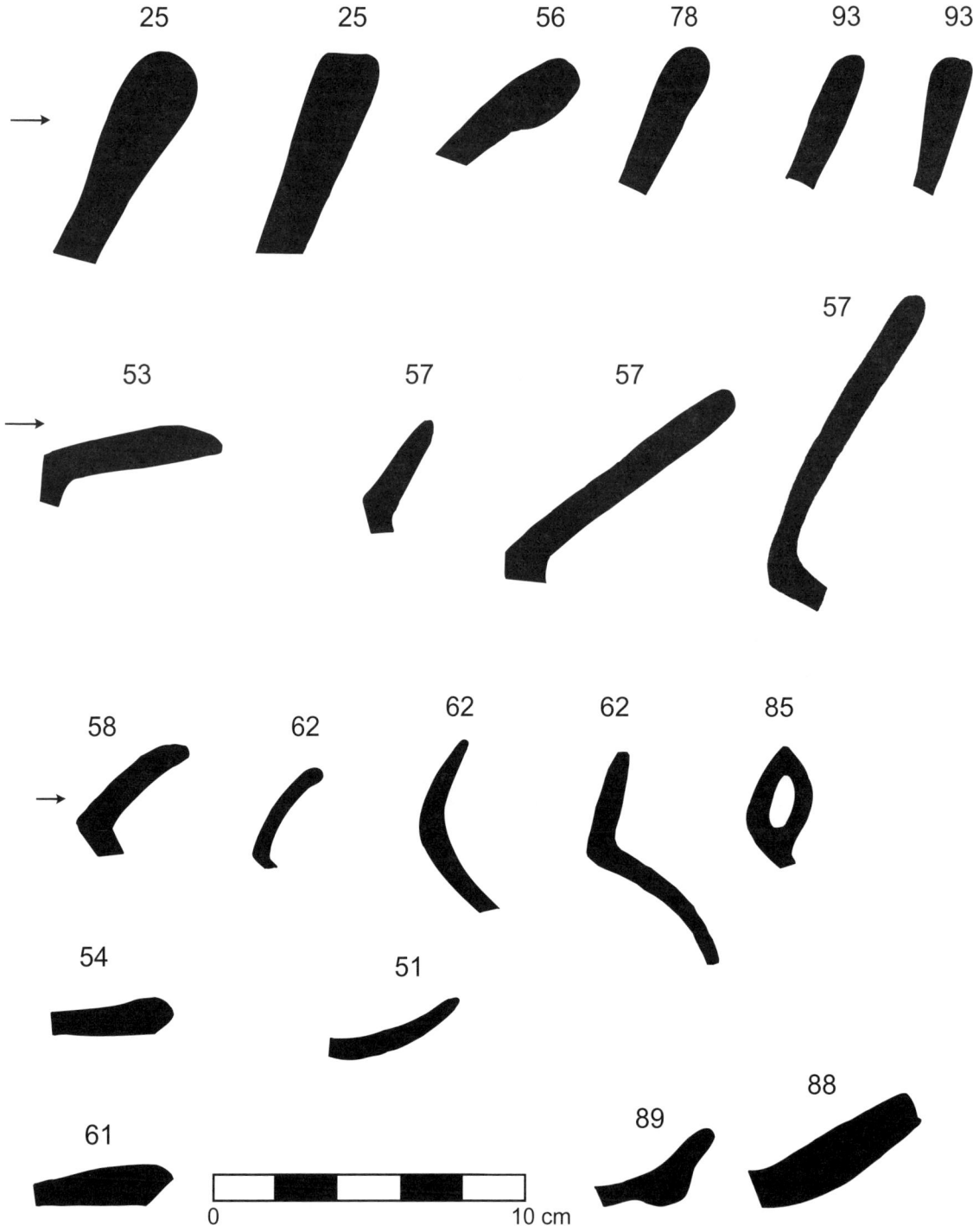

Figure 4.31. Rim forms of cooking/storage wares recovered at Cerro Tilcajete. *top row*, *apaxtles*; *second and third rows*, jars; *fourth and fifth rows*, rim forms 54, 51, and 61 are *comales*, and rim forms 89 and 88 are braziers. The arrows point to vessel interior.

Table 4.9. Minimum number of vessels in Feature 1, Structure 3, Cerro Tilcajete.

Vessel No.	Rim No.*	Paste	Vessel Type	Description
1	2	orange	serving	A.9 bowl, red rim and exterior line design
2	6	orange	serving	A.9 bowl, red rim and interior line design
3	71	orange	serving	straight-walled bowl slipped on both sides
4	72	orange	serving	bowl slipped on both sides
5	73	orange	serving	straight-walled bowl slipped on both sides
6	73	orange	serving	A.9 straight-walled bowl, interior line design, no slipping
7	75	orange	serving	A.9 straight-walled bowl, red rim and exterior line design
8	87	orange	serving	bowl, flared wall slipped on both sides
9	none	orange	serving	A.9 jar, red line design on exterior
10	none	orange	serving	A.11 jar, incised exterior lines
11	none	orange	serving	A.11 bowl, incised exterior
12	1	cream	serving	C.12 bowl
13	1	cream	serving	C.20 bowl
14	1	cream	serving	C.7 bowl, specular red rim and exterior
15	1	cream	serving	C.7 bowl, red/orange interior
16	2	cream	serving	C.7 bowl
17	2	cream	serving	C.20 bowl
18	2	cream	serving	C.12 bowl
19	3	cream	serving	C.7 bowl, specular red on rim interior
20	3	cream	serving	C.7 bowl, specular red rim and vessel exterior
21	4	cream	serving	C.6 bowl
22	4	cream	serving	C.7 bowl
23	4	cream	serving	C.20 bowl
24	6	cream	serving	C.6 bowl
25	6	cream	serving	C.7 bowl
26	6	cream	serving	C.20 bowl
27	31	cream	serving	C.20 bowl
28	49	cream	serving	C.20 incurving bowl
29	59	cream	serving	C.20 straight-walled bowl
30	71	cream	serving	C.20 straight-walled bowl
32	1	gray	serving	bowl, burnished interior and two incised lines at rim interior
33	1	gray	serving	bowl, not burnished with two incised lines at rim interior
34	1	gray	serving	G.29 bowl
35	1	gray	serving	bowl, single incised line at rim interior
36	1	gray	serving	undecorated bowl
37	3	gray	serving	incurving bowl, two incised lines at rim interior
38	4	gray	serving	bowl, two incised lines at rim interior
39	4	gray	serving	bowl, single incised line at rim interior
40	4	gray	serving	undecorated bowl
41	6	gray	serving	G.29 bowl
42	6	gray	serving	G.29 bowl, red on rim interior
43	9	gray	serving	jar
44	10	gray	serving	G.29 vase with lid
45	12	gray	serving	bowl
46	14	gray	serving	composite wall bowl
47	15	gray	serving	shallow bowl
48	18	gray	serving	jar
49	19	gray	serving	jar
50	24	gray	serving	plate, single incised line on rim interior
51	25	gray	cooking/storage	*apaxtle*
52	26	gray	serving	G.15, incised lines on vessel exterior
53	27	gray	serving	bowl, single incised line at rim interior
54	31	gray	serving	bowl
55	33	gray	serving	bowl
56	34	gray	serving	jar
57	35	gray	serving	bowl, two incised lines at rim interior
58	37	gray	serving	bowl with two incised lines at rim interior
59	37	gray	serving	bowl
60	38	gray	serving	bowl
61	38	gray	serving	bowl

Table 4.9. cont.

Vessel No.	Rim No.*	Paste	Vessel Type	Description
62	40	gray	serving	bowl
63	42	gray	serving	bowl
64	44	gray	serving	bowl
65	45	gray	serving	bowl, two incised lines at rim interior
66	45	gray	serving	bowl
67	46	gray	serving	G.15, incised lines on vessel exterior
68	46	gray	serving	G.29 bowl, red on rim interior
69	46	gray	serving	G.29 bowl
70	46	gray	serving	incised line on rim exterior
71	46	gray	serving	bowl, two incised lines at rim interior
72	46	gray	serving	highly burnished blackish bowl
73	46	gray	serving	bowl
74	49	gray	serving	incurving bowl, two incised lines at rim interior
75	49	gray	serving	incurving bowl
76	50	gray	serving	jar incised with red pigment
77	50	gray	serving	jar
78	62	gray	cooking/storage	jar, incised
79	62	gray	cooking/storage	jar
80	70	gray	serving	bowl, incised line on rim interior
81	70	gray	serving	bowl, incised wavy line on rim flange
82	none	gray	serving	potstand
83	80	gray	serving	bowl, pinched rim and incised line on rim interior
84	1	café	serving	K.17 bowl
85	2	café	serving	K.17 bowl
87	4	café	serving	K.17 bowl
88	6	café	serving	K.17 bowl
89	6	café	serving	K.3 bowl, red rim interior
90	7	café	serving	bowl
91	10	café	serving	K.17 vase with lid
92	15	café	serving	K.3 shallow bowl, red rim interior
93	17	café	serving	K.17 bowl
94	33	café	serving	K.17 incurving bowl
95	40	café	serving	K.17 bowl
96	46	café	serving	K.17 bowl, scratched exterior
97	47	café	serving	K.17 bowl
98	54	café	cooking/storage	*comal*
99	54	café	cooking/storage	*comal*, burnished interior
100	57	café	cooking/storage	jar
101	57	café	cooking/storage	jar (long lip)
102	58	café	cooking/storage	jar
103	61	café	cooking/storage	*comal*
104	62	café	cooking/storage	jar
105	none	café	ritual	incense burner
106	78	café	cooking/storage	bowl
108	88	café	cooking/storage	cooking bowl

*See Figures 4.30-4.31.

Table 4.10. Minimum number of vessels in Feature 6, Structure 4, Cerro Tilcajete.

Vessel No.	Rim No.*	Paste	Vessel Type	Description
1	6	orange	serving	A.9 bowl, red on interior of rim
2	1	cream	serving	C.20 bowl, black interior and exterior
3	1	cream	serving	C.6 bowl, coffee-colored slip
4	3	cream	serving	C.11 bowl, specular red
5	4	cream	serving	C.6 bowl, coffee-colored slip
6	5	cream	serving	C.7 bowl, specular red
7	6	cream	serving	C.6 bowl, coffee-colored slip
8	1	gray	serving	bowl, two incised lines at rim interior
9	4	gray	serving	straight-walled undecorated bowl
10	9	gray	serving	miniature jar
11	14	gray	serving	straight-walled bowl, exterior flange and incised line
12	19	gray	serving	jar
13	22	gray	serving	bowl, flared wall and two incised lines at rim interior
14	31	gray	serving	bowl, slightly flared rim and two incised lines at rim interior
15	31	gray	serving	undecorated bowl, slightly flared rim
16	33	gray	serving	*tecomate*
17	34	gray	serving	jar
18	35	gray	serving	bowl, flared rim and two incised lines at rim interior
19	35	gray	serving	bowl, flared rim
20	37	gray	serving	bowl, thickened rim and two incised lines at rim interior
21	38	gray	serving	bowl, two incised lines at rim interior
22	39	gray	serving	G.29 paste bowl slipped like a C.6
23	40	gray	serving	bowl, thickened and outflared rim, two incised lines at rim interior
24	6	café	serving	straight-walled bowl
25	10	café	serving	vase with lid
26	54	café	cooking/storage	*comal*
27	57	café	cooking/storage	jar
28	58	café	cooking/storage	jar
27	62	café	cooking/storage	jar
30	78	café	cooking/storage	large bowl
31	92	café	serving	composite wall bowl

*See Figures 4.30-4.31.

Table 4.11. Minimum number of vessels in Feature 2, Structure 4, Cerro Tilcajete.

Vessel No.	Rim No.*	Paste	Vessel Type	Description
1	25	gray	cooking/storage	*apaxtle*
2	78	gray	cooking/storage	*apaxtle*
3	93	gray	cooking/storage	*apaxtle*
4	27	gray	serving	outcurving wall bowl
5	12	gray	serving	straight-walled bowl, thickened lip
6	19	gray	serving	jar
7	35	gray	serving	bowl, flared lip, double line incising
8	57	gray	cooking/storage	jar
9	54	café	cooking/storage	*comal*
10	56	café	cooking/storage	*apaxtle*, bolstered rim
11	57	café	cooking/storage	jar (long rim)
12	57	café	cooking/storage	jar
13	59	café	serving	straight-walled bowl, exterior scratching
14	62	café	cooking/storage	jar
15	78	café	cooking/storage	*apaxtle*
16	93	café	cooking/storage	*apaxtle*
17	31	cream	serving	bowl, slightly flared lip
18	none	gray	serving	G.21 bowl base
19	none	café	cooking/storage	brazier

*See Figures 4.30-4.31.

It is not clear if the pre-Hispanic Oaxacans stored maize in a way similar to the modern Maya, or how much maize they stored at a time. Today, over 80% of agricultural production in Oaxaca relies solely on rainfall farming, and the valley experiences some level of drought and crop failure as frequently as one out of every four years (Feinman 2006; Flannery et al. 1967). Storage must have been important, and it is likely that families seeking to store maize beyond their immediate or short-term needs would prefer a well-sealed room in which maize could be placed in bins or large jars. Such a structure would not necessarily be easy to identify archaeologically. In many higher-status houses, a 7 × 7 m room with a plaster floor would not stand out, particularly if the storage area also contained utilitarian or provisionally discarded items. Archaeologically, however, a room that had stone foundations and a well-packed plaster or flagstone floor surface, and was associated with, but detached from, the main residence could potentially be considered a storage room.

Excavations at San José Mogote have uncovered a 1.4 × 2.2 m stone-and-adobe structure dating to the Rosario phase (700-500 B.C.) with a storage room that closely fits this description. The room contained bowls, jars, plates, and an effigy incense burner (Flannery and Marcus 2005:417-25).

At Cerro Tilcajete, the stone structure designated Feature 2 in Structure 4 is likely to have been a storage structure. We should, therefore, look more closely at what the vessels deposited here can tell us about food production activities (Tables 4.11-4.12). I will assess the form and variety of utilitarian vessels by looking at the minimum number of vessels found inside this probable storage unit. A total of 78 diagnostic and 243 non-diagnostic sherds (totaling 22,510 g) were tabulated from the feature. These sherds represent a minimum of 17 vessels, predominantly utilitarian bowls and jars. There were no orange-paste vessels and only one fragment from a cream-paste serving bowl. The feature contained several forms of jars, large bowls, *apaxtles*, and *comales* made in both gray and café paste. Most of these vessels were used for preparing and storing food.

The cooking/storage vessel forms found here were similar to the cooking/storage vessel forms found in other Structure 4 contexts. However, some data suggest that cooking/storage vessels were used differently in Structure 4 as compared with those in Structure 1 (Table 4.8). In Structure 1, almost all of the cooking/storage vessels were *comales* and jars. In Structure 4 (and to a similar extent, in Structure 3) many more *apaxtles* and bowls were present in the cooking/storage assemblage. Why

Table 4.12. Ceramics by weight and number in Feature 2, Structure 4, Cerro Tilcajete.

Type	No.	Frequency by Paste	Weight (g)	Frequency by Weight
gray	102	31.78	5570	24.74
café	203	63.24	14,060	62.46
cream	8	2.49	500	2.22
café brazier fragments	8	2.49	2380	10.57
Total	321	100.00	22,510	100.00

were so many *comales* used in Structures 1 and 3? One possible explanation is that higher-status households devoted more energy to preparing large quantities of tortillas for consumption in feasting, or for communal labor events incorporating large numbers of people, while the production needs of lower-status households were more focused on the needs of the immediate family. To be sure, higher-status families might have been able to draw on the stored maize resources of client lower-status families and enlisted their assistance in preparing the *masa* for tortillas consumed during community labor activities and elite-sponsored feasts. If this is the case, it is less likely that centralized or elite-controlled storage areas exist at sites such as Cerro Tilcajete. Most ethnohistoric or ethnographic cases of such feasting, however, make it appear that elites wanted to look generous, and thus drew on the obligations of relatives and affines to feed large numbers of guests.

Household Ritual

I have already discussed some of the aspects of Zapotec religion and worldview that can be gleaned from studies of sixteenth-century documents. Recent studies of Formative period ritual have contributed greatly to what is known about household ritual in the pre-state period (Marcus 1998). Comparative settlement pattern data and architectural evidence from Monte Albán and its secondary administrative centers show Monte Albán II as a period during which a valley-wide state hierarchy had been cemented in place. The political changes associated with state formation undoubtedly affected the way ritual activities were carried out at the household level. Although this is not an easy topic to address with archaeological data, I will look at three classes of evidence allowing suggestions about ritual behavior and religious beliefs.

Figurines and Urns

Marcus (1983g, 1998) has suggested that the small ceramic figurines abundant in Early and Middle Formative domestic contexts were used in rituals conducted primarily by women engaged in ancestor veneration. Other researchers propose alternate uses for Formative figurines found in neighboring regions of Mesoamerica (Cyphers 1993; Lesure 1997). In Oaxaca, small handmade figurines gradually disappear from the archaeological record after 500 B.C. (Marcus 1998:282-83). Such figurines disappear from elite contexts as anthropomorphic urns become more prevalent (Marcus 1983g:144-48).

Prior to A.D. 100, most urns are made of gray paste, are relatively simple in manufacture, and should probably be considered jars with effigy faces rather than true urns (Marcus 1983g:144). By Monte Albán II, there are more convincing urns, such as the very elaborate example (previously discussed) found in a tomb in the El Pitahayo zone at Monte Albán, which depicts an individual wearing a raptorial bird headdress.

Initially, most gray-paste urns are thought to represent either deceased noble ancestors or *Cociyo* (see Fig. 2.1). In Monte Albán III (that is, after A.D. 200), urns become very elaborate and are constructed from moldmade pieces attached to a receptacle that serves as the figure's central core. Tombs and burials at Monte Albán often contain urns, and some of these have been interpreted as depicting nobles dressed in the guise of *Cociyo* (Caso 1935: Figs. 47-48; Caso and Bernal 1952:150; Marcus and Flannery 1996:19). Others, such as the urn from Monte Albán's Tomb 104, show headdresses with *Cociyo* iconography (see Fig. 3.9).

When found *in situ*, urns are almost always empty. It is not clear if they held an organic substance that decomposed or if they had a poorly understood ritual purpose—such as acting as receptacles for something non-tangible (Caso and Bernal 1952:10). Urn fragments also show up in residences, so it is clear that at least some were used in elite households and served a purpose in family ritual.

Because urns are strongly associated with elite identity and *Cociyo*, in Monte Albán II, I would expect that higher-status households would employ more urns than would lower-status households. It is not clear whether small figurines continued to be used in women's ritual into these later periods. Marcus (1998), in fact, stresses that her interpretation applies only to the small handmade figurines of Early and Middle Formative (pre-state) times, not to the moldmade figurines of the Monte Albán state.

At Cerro Tilcajete, some urns do appear in households, but more in domestic contexts are figurine fragments. Most urn fragments are of gray paste (the rest are orange ware) and depict human faces: eyes, ears, hair and headdresses. If most Cerro Tilcajete urns were locally made to depict ancestors, the headdresses suggest elite ancestors.

Figurines also tended to be made of gray paste (Fig. 4.32 and Table 4.13). Some represent animals, such as dogs, deer, and turkeys—but particularly frogs, which some have associated with rain and fertility ceremonies (Martínez López and Winter

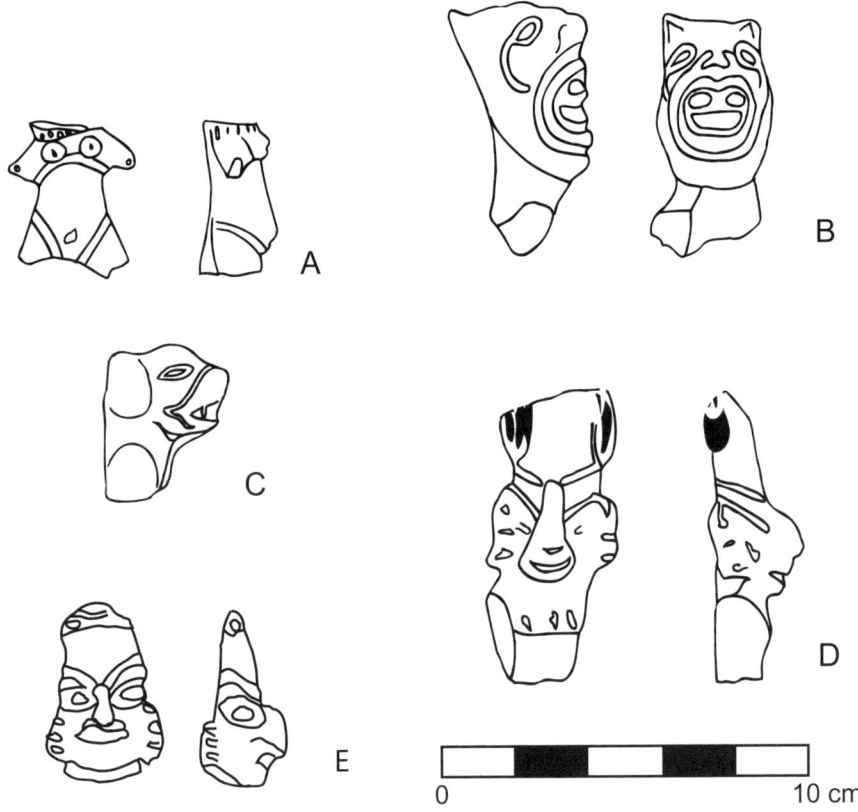

Figure 4.32. Examples of figurines found in residential excavations at Cerro Tilcajete. *A*, pregnant female torso; *B*, man with feline headdress; *C*, feline head; *D, E*, individuals, probably female.

1994). The majority, however, are solid human figures with the almond eyes and "coffee bean" mouths typical of Monte Albán II. Figurines also can have headgear, jewelry, or body incisions (see Martínez López and Winter 1994).

Eleven figurines found in Structures 1 and 3 at Cerro Tilcajete were female and at least two of these appear to be representations of pregnant women (Fig. 4.32*A*). These figures are similar enough to earlier specimens to suggest that household members, probably women, still were responsible for conducting curing and fertility ceremonies.

At the same time, two of our figurines have feline imagery, and several depict individuals dressed in elaborate costumes. Two figurines found near the surface in Area C (not associated with a structure) feature feline imagery: the figure of a jaguar or puma (Fig. 4.32*C*), and a man with a feline headdress (Fig. 4.32*B*). Three more figurines, placed with burials in Structure 4, depict individuals with elaborate headgear: (1) the head and torso of a man with elaborate headgear (see Fig. 4.21); (2) a figure with a large fanlike headdress and a "walking stick" (see Fig. 4.22); and (3) a small gray-paste figure with extended arms and legs and an elaborate hairdo or headdress (see Fig. 4.24). This latter figure is reminiscent of (although less elaborate than) a "flying" figurine found in a Monte Albán II temple at San José Mogote, which may depict the transition of a noble into a "cloud person" (Marcus and Flannery 1996:187).

Cerro Tilcajete's figurine and urn assemblage suggests that some of the site's occupants did use urns depicting noble ancestors as an important part of household ritual, but these activities were combined with traditional practices, related to honoring a family's ancestors. Burials did not include urns, but did contain figurines with elaborate headgear.

Incense Burners

Ethnohistoric descriptions of Mesoamerican society reveal that incense burners were used in temple and household ceremonies to burn copal, a fragrant resin. In Oaxaca, *incensarios* came in many shapes, from the hourglass-shaped effigy braziers of Monte Albán II and IIIa to the frying pan-shaped incense burners of Monte Albán IIIb-IV and V.

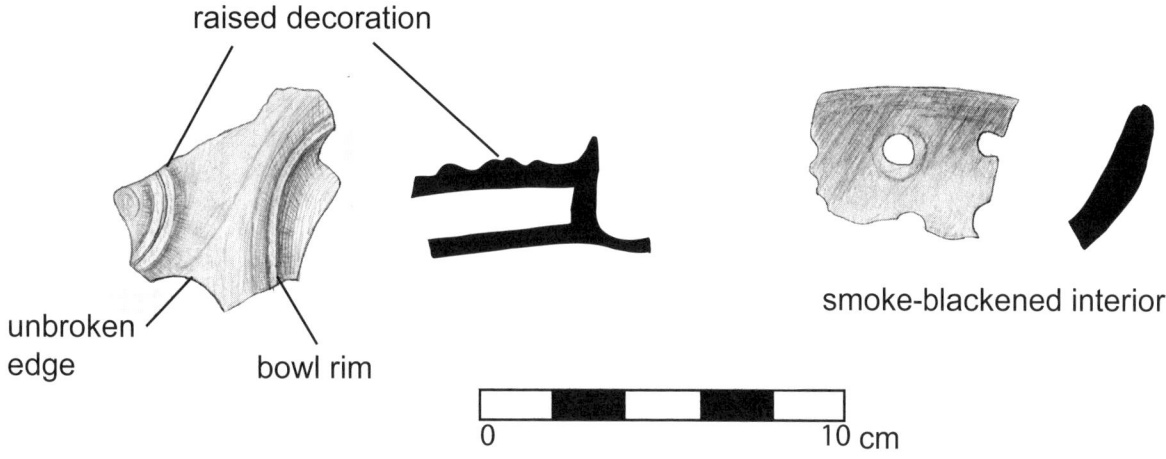

Figure 4.33. Incense burner fragments from Cerro Tilcajete. *left*, gray-paste hollow handle incense burner with modeled decoration more typical of Monte Albán I, found in Structure 1; *right*, café-paste fragment of a frying pan incense burner bowl, found in Structure 3.

Incense burners were relatively infrequent during Monte Albán I, showing up primarily as burial offerings. Monte Albán I incense burners were usually made of gray paste and had solid receptacles with elaborately carved or modeled designs. According to Caso et al., some of these incense burners depicted a realistic serpent (Caso et al. 1967: Fig. 163, pp. 196-97).

During Monte Albán II, temple floors were often heavily burned from the use of hourglass-shaped *incensarios*, while frying pan incense burners were less common. The latter occurred in both gray and café paste and, unlike their Monte Albán I counterparts, most were undecorated (Caso et al. 1967:249). Frying pan *incensarios*, especially if undecorated, would have required little effort to manufacture and could have been produced in the average pottery workshop. In the Ejutla Valley during Monte Albán III, such incense burners were mass produced in household workshops and were found to be common in domestic contexts (Feinman and Nicholas 1999:90).

At Cerro Tilcajete, two decorated Monte Albán I style gray-paste frying pan incense burners (one similar to the illustration in Caso et al. 1967:196) were found in Structure 1. Since this was a Monte Albán II context, it is possible that these objects were heirlooms curated by the high-status residents (Fig. 4.33). Structure 1 also contained a café-paste handle from a frying pan incense burner. Fragments from another café-paste incense burner (with punctations on the pan) and one more café-paste *incensario* handle were recovered in Structure 3. The evidence thus suggests that while frying pan incense burners were utilized in elite domestic contexts, they were not very common at Cerro Tilcajete.

Table 4.13. Figurines and urns in residential excavations at Cerro Tilcajete.

	Str. 1	Str. 3	Str. 4
Figurines by paste			
gray	56	66	31
café	18	11	8
orange	6	6	13
Figurines by form			
Human	35	58	39
solid	22	35	36
hollow	10	13	3
body incisions	9	4	3
headgear, clothing, or jewelry	6	12	6
female	5	6	1
Animal	14	5	4
frogs	6	2	2
dogs/deer	2	2	0
birds	1	1	1
Urns	20	16	5
Vessel appliqués	2	2	1
Fragments	9	2	3

Table 4.14. Obsidian in Structures 1-4, Cerro Tilcajete.

	Blades			Flakes		
	Number		Weight (g)	Number		Weight (g)
	gray	*green*	*gray & green*	*gray*	*green*	*gray & green*
Structure 1	7	5	13	264	2	134
Structure 2	3	2	4	18	0	8.5
Structure 3	16	16	19	163	2	66.5
Structure 4	1	3	3	35	7	23

Mortuary Ritual

The custom of interring family members below the floors of residences was widespread in Oaxaca by Monte Albán I. Formal masonry tombs, probably reserved for the highest-ranking members of society, appear both at Monte Albán and its dependencies by Late Monte Albán I; burials in simple pits were also found under floors or in patios (Whalen 1981).

I expected to find tombs and multiple burials in elite residences at Cerro Tilcajete, and was surprised when I did not find them in Structures 1 and 3. One surface collection made at the southwest corner of Plaza II, of an eroded and looted elite burial or offering, did produce a worked human maxilla that may have served as a war trophy (see Appendix B).

Why did Structures 1 and 3 not contain tombs? I can only speculate. It is possible that the individuals who occupied these elite residences were representatives of the Monte Albán state who had been sent to administer Cerro Tilcajete, and did not necessarily have familial attachments to the location. At death, these individuals and their families might have been returned to their original place of residence—possibly even at Monte Albán, although there is no way to test this possibility.

Structure 4, a lower-status residence, produced the remains of five individuals. An adult and a young child were interred together in what may be a specially constructed room (although this room does not conform to the plan of typical residential tombs found at Monte Albán). Two children were buried in simple pits in the patio, and one of these contexts also contained the partial remains of an adult. I do not know whether the adult's remains were disturbed by the intrusive pit or had been transferred to this location from elsewhere. Archaeologists do occasionally find empty, reopened tombs in residences, suggesting that households carried their family members with them when they moved from place to place (see Flannery and Marcus 2005:425).

Obsidian

Obsidian, known to be an imported commodity, does not appear in large quantities in Monte Albán II contexts at Cerro Tilcajete (Table 4.14). Obsidian blades are known to have had both domestic and ritual uses. Most obsidian at Cerro Tilcajete occurs in the form of flakes that average less than a gram in weight and could have been produced from reworking exhausted blades. My excavations uncovered both gray and green blades. Gray obsidian was mined in several sources in the states of Veracruz and Mexico and as far away as Guatemala. Green obsidian likely comes from a source at Pachuca, Hidalgo, a town in Central Mexico located 260 miles (as the crow flies) from Oaxaca.

Cerro Tilcajete's Structure 3 stands out because it had many more blades (and more total weight of obsidian) than virtually all other Monte Albán II contexts at the site (for example, Structure 3 yielded 32 of the 53 blades I recovered). The blades in Structure 3 were evenly divided between gray and green. One possible explanation for the high number of blades in Structure 3 might be the close affiliation between this residence and the two-room temple nearby; perhaps some of the blades had been acquired for ritual use.

The obsidian data from Cerro Tilcajete can be compared with those from the Monte Albán II excavations at San José Mogote (Parry 1987). At the latter site, excavations uncovered 80 obsidian artifacts that took the form of blades, lancets, bifaces, bipolar flakes and cores. Previously I noted that Structure 35, a two-room Monte Albán II temple with well-preserved plaster floors, had not been swept clean upon its abandonment and still contained an abundance of green obsidian blades that probably were used in bloodletting and then discarded on the temple floor. The Monte Albán II temples were the only locations at San José Mogote where obsidian bifaces and lancets were found. Little obsidian appeared in the site's administrative palace. A Monte Albán II elite residence and a less elegant Monte Albán II residence at San José Mogote both produced primarily green blades.

There was a clear preference for green obsidian at San José Mogote (76% of the Monte Albán II artifacts tabulated) and there is no evidence (in the form of cores or bipolar flakes) that green obsidian tools were produced at that site (Parry 1987:111-17). Cerro Tilcajete's residents also used green obsidian (49% of the Monte Albán II artifacts tabulated were green blades), and the lack of green cores or bipolar flakes suggests that most green obsidian showed up at the site in the form of prepared blades. In contrast, some gray obsidian (from imported chunks) was worked at San José Mogote, although not into prismatic blades. Gray obsidian might have been worked (or at least reworked) at Cerro Tilcajete. Monte Albán may have controlled access to green obsidian and regulated its distribution to secondary centers.

Shell

The shell was identified and analyzed by Feinman and Nicholas who suggest shell working at Cerro Tilcajete was probably for local use (see Appendix C).

Structure 1 contained the greatest amount of shell (31 pieces); the majority of these pieces ($n = 22$) had been worked into small flat ornament pieces or placas. Nine *Olivella?* shells had been drilled, either to be strung on a necklace or sewn onto clothing. Burial 1 of Structure 4 contained 46 tiny *Marginella* shells, perforated and evidently strung on a necklace.

Summary

This chapter has synthesized data from intensive surface collection, mapping, and excavation to discuss the Monte Albán II occupation of Cerro Tilcajete. This hilltop administrative center was newly built after the Ocotlán subregion's incorporation by Monte Albán circa 100 B.C.; at 24.5 ha, Cerro Tilcajete is one-third the size of the Late Monte Albán I site of El Palenque, which preceded it. Numerous points can be made about the nature of the Monte Albán II occupation and the activities of its inhabitants.

A great deal of labor was employed in building the site's structures, terraces, and plazas. Cerro Tilcajete was situated in a place that allowed its administrators to maintain visual contact with Monte Albán. At the same time, the layout of Cerro Tilcajete is not at all like that of Monte Albán or, for that matter, the secondary Monte Albán II center of San José Mogote. Cerro Tilcajete had three mound groups, and most of the site's elite residences and administrative buildings were placed within a ceremonial core with limited access.

One mound group, placed along a road linking Ocotlán to the central Valley of Oaxaca, lay near an important point of access to the ceremonial core of the site. Surface evidence suggests some items, such as cream-paste ceramics and marine shell, might have arrived here before being distributed to the rest of the site. This might suggest that the administrators living in this mound group monitored the movement of traffic (and presumably tribute) along the road.

Two mound groups and fifteen to twenty smaller residential house mounds were situated inside the ceremonial core. On the surface of this area, cream-paste pottery was more concentrated, supporting my contention that the ceremonial core was also a zone of elite residences. I excavated one elite residence (Structure 1) and a small two-room temple (Structure 2) on the north and east mounds of Plaza II, respectively, and a second elite residence (Structure 3) on a terrace closely associated with the east mound of Plaza II.

Plaza I was a third area with administrative architecture; on Mound E there, I excavated a structure (or complex of structures) totaling just under 100 m^2 and made of cut stone with plaster floors. The overall lack of ceramics and the building's size and layout lead me to interpret its function as either a temple or a civic-ceremonial structure.

Residences could have either a closed or a semi-open (L-shaped) plan, and all three of those excavated incorporated stone, adobe, and plaster in their construction. The ceramic data show gradations of access to prestige goods. Both the architecture and the artifacts are believed to reflect the social status of the families occupying the residences. Structure 1, considered the residence of a high-ranking family, had a closed plan, sat on a platform of nicely faced cut stone blocks, and had stone foundations. It yielded our highest amount of cream-paste ceramics and other serving wares. Structure 3, also thought to house high-status residents, appears to have been L-shaped. This structure sat atop a stone platform partially made with well faced stone blocks. Structure 4, considered a lower-status residence, was L- or C-shaped. It contained the smallest quantity of cream-paste ceramics and other serving wares.

While Structure 4 had burials, neither of the two high-status residences did, perhaps because the occupants were administrators sent to Cerro Tilcajete by the Monte Albán state, and later carried home for burial.

The distribution of serving vessels versus cooking and food preparation artifacts, combined with storage facilities, supports the conclusion that while lower-status people were more directly concerned with growing maize than were elite families, the latter were involved in feeding tortillas to large numbers of people, perhaps at public feasts or to laborers in the service of the state.

Perhaps the most valued vessels at Cerro Tilcajete were made in cream-paste pottery, many probably imported from the Monte Albán area as bowls, some with large hollow supports. These vessels were presumably costly to transport, but played a role as sumptuary goods for Cerro Tilcajete's most important families.

Obsidian, and in particular green obsidian blades, was another commodity the elite obtained in larger quantities, given their ties to Monte Albán. Ritual artifacts such as urns, figurines, and incense burners show interesting patterns of distribution. For example, I found frying pan incense burners only in the two elite residences on Plaza II, while figurines and urn fragments occurred in all three residences. I have suggested that while Monte Albán II households still used small solid figurines in family-oriented rituals related to ancestor veneration, the elite of Cerro Tilcajete were motivated to demonstrate ties to Lightning and noble ancestors they shared with important families at Monte Albán. They thus adopted urns and cream-paste bowls with Lightning designs as essential ritual equipment that demonstrated their supra-local political position.

There are also a few hints that the people who came to Cerro Tilcajete around 100 B.C. might have had heirloom artifacts with them, or curated those as relics of earlier time periods. Two objects found in Structure 1—one an incense burner and one the fragment of a vessel modeled to depict a deceased ancestor or sacrificed individual—appear to be ritual artifacts manufactured in Late Monte Albán I rather than in Monte Albán II. One burial in Structure 4 contained the partial remains of an adult, perhaps brought from elsewhere. The other individual in this burial was provided with a bowl whose form is more characteristic of Monte Albán I than Monte Albán II.

Obviously, I cannot specify which of the residents at Cerro Tilcajete had local roots and which might have been sent in from elsewhere by the state. I suspect that some high-status families came to Cerro Tilcajete to monitor local activities on behalf of Monte Albán's rulers; however, some local elite families from the Ocotlán subregion may also have been resettled at Cerro Tilcajete. The estimated fifteen to twenty noble families living in the ceremonial precinct and presumably charged with overseeing local politics and religion might therefore have been of multiple ethnic identities. Lower-ranking families seem to have lived outside the ceremonial precinct and probably were engaged more directly in production activities and in supporting the demands of the elites. If this is the case, Cerro Tilcajete's initial administration would seem more comparable to that of La Coyotera in the Cuicatlán Cañada than that of San José Mogote in Etla.

It is interesting that Cerro Tilcajete has no I-shaped ballcourt, particularly in light of theories that such ballcourts may have played a role in settling local disputes or defusing potential military situations. This could mean that the presence of representatives from Monte Albán was sufficient.

Cerro Tilcajete was abandoned about A.D. 200. As will be discussed in Chapter 5, several factors might have played into the site's demise. If Cerro Tilcajete was set up originally to administer an initially "hostile" conquered territory, its overall utility may have declined once that territory was well incorporated into the Zapotec state. We will see, however, that other factors—such as a fourfold increase in the population of the Valle Grande and Ocotlán during the Classic period—also may have affected the subregion, and necessitated changes in the way it was administered.

Chapter 5

Cerro Tilcajete and the Decline of the Zapotec State

This chapter examines Monte Albán and the Valle Grande-Ocotlán subregion during the Late Classic (A.D. 500-700) and Epiclassic (A.D. 700-1000) to determine why Cerro Tilcajete was abandoned for 300 years, then modestly reoccupied after A.D. 500. Chapter 6 summarizes research at Cerro Tilcajete and considers how it sheds light on the social, political, and economic structure of the Zapotec state.

Monte Albán

Much of the consolidated architecture a visitor sees today around Monte Albán's Main Plaza dates to A.D. 200-700. At its maximum extent, Monte Albán covered 6.5 km^2, including settlement on the adjacent hills of Atzompa, El Gallo, and Monte Albán Chico, areas first colonized between A.D. 200 and 500, the Early Classic period (Blanton 1978:57-100). In Monte Albán II, there was at least one major mound group, El Pitahayo, outside the Main Plaza. By Monte Albán IIIb-IV (A.D. 500-700), there were fourteen such mound groups.

The proliferation of these "neighborhood" groups is an interesting development in the Classic period, possibly reflecting the need to reorganize the city as its population grew. The elite continued to build residential palaces north and east of the Main Plaza. In Chapter 3, I proposed this zone as an area associated with urban elites, while the Mound of the Carved Stone—set at the northwest corner of the Main Plaza—was a possible location for the residence of the Zapotec ruler and his family. By Monte Albán III, there were more similarities than differences in the architecture and iconography of these areas, which may reflect increasing competition among elites. An example would be Tomb 104, which dates to this period, whose entryway contained an urn showing a young lord with *Cociyo* and jaguar imagery; the tomb murals showed the noble lineage of its occupants.

To the northwest of the North Platform lay Tomb 105, located in a palace set atop a large platform with an attached I-shaped ballcourt (Fig. 5.1). The palace covered 453 m^2 and took the form of four main rooms around a central patio. Under the floor of the palace's west room, excavations revealed offerings such as a *Cociyo* urn and a female figurine, carved out of jade in a Central Mexican style (Caso 1938:83-92). Tomb 105, beneath the east room, was cruciform in shape, partially cut into bedrock, and roofed over with enormous stone slabs. The tomb's walls were covered with well-preserved mural paintings; the tomb itself, however, contained only the partial remains of one skeleton. It is unlikely that the tomb had been looted, so the paucity of offerings when compared to the elegance of the murals makes an interesting contrast. The murals depict pairs of royal men and women, possibly the ancestors of the tomb's occupant. At least one man wears a turban with jaguar symbolism. Another man is conducting a divination, similar to some depictions of priests found in Teotihuacán frescos (Marcus 1983f:143; see also Miller 1973, 1995:84-106).

Both Tombs 104 (Caso 1938; Marcus 1983f:140) and 105 display pairs of named persons, probably noble ancestors, and a concern for establishing genealogical credentials. Both locations feature *Cociyo* and jaguar imagery. Additionally, Tomb 105 has offerings suggesting its occupants wanted to demonstrate a familiarity with Central Mexican or Teotihuacán-style iconography.

Classic period public architecture shows that nobles employed writing and iconography in the service of elite expression. One of the best examples of this behavior is the South Platform, the

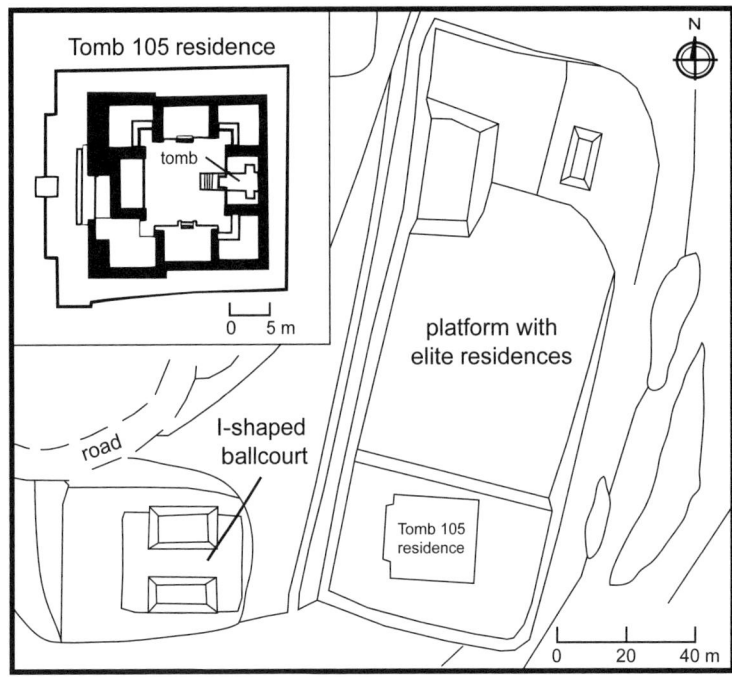

Figure 5.1. The Tomb 105 residence at Monte Albán (redrawn from Caso 1938: Plan 18; Blanton 1978: Appendix VI).

dedication of which may have coincided with the inauguration of a Zapotec king (Marcus 1992b). A series of carved stone monuments (some 2 m tall) are set into the South Platform as orthostats. Six of these slabs depict bound, high-status captives standing on different hill glyphs (probably named places), while two others depict Zapotec lords with lances. One of these lords is named 12 Jaguar, and the slabs may have been created as part of his inauguration ceremony. The ruler 12 Jaguar is shown seated on a jaguar cushion, wearing a jaguar or puma costume, and holding a lance. Beneath his throne are two heads of Lightning (Marcus 1983f:137-38, 1992:400-409; Marcus and Flannery 1996:216-21).

In addition to these depictions of Zapotec nobles and military captives, Stelae 1, 7, 8, and the "Estela Lisa" in the same platform depict named Teotihuacano visitors, perhaps ambassadors showing support for the new ruler. Interestingly, these slabs were placed so that some carvings were hidden from view.

The carved stones of the South Platform show the Zapotec ruling elite claiming to undertake military conquests, commissioning massive constructions, and consulting with powerful foreign elites. It may be that this iconography was employed because the new ruler was concerned with legitimizing his inauguration. The public placement of the carved stone slabs meant that 12 Jaguar's message could be read by elites and commoners alike; the message on the hidden slabs, however, would have been grasped only by other elites attending the dedicatory rites (Marcus 1992b).

I have evaluated the use of *Cociyo* iconography during Monte Albán II and found that one prime medium for its expression was the imagery on cream-paste vessels with bulbous feet. During Monte Albán III, these vessels disappeared from the archaeological record. Gray-paste urns with imagery linking nobles to *Cociyo* became common, and the use of feline imagery—particularly nobles dressed in feline costumes—became more explicit. The "jaws of the sky" glyph was used to indicate noble descent (Marcus 1992b). A few examples of this iconography painted in private tomb murals and carved on the hidden sides of stones indicate that some high-ranking elites wished to demonstrate their knowledge of, or ties with, Central Mexico—namely, Teotihuacán. This is an interesting point, as recent analyses of Teotihuacán posit that the city declined dramatically as early as A.D. 550 (and certainly by A.D. 650), when many temples and palaces in the city's ceremonial core were burned and destroyed (Evans 2004; López Luján et al. 2006; Millon 1995:156-57). After this point, it is unlikely that Teotihuacán's rulers would have been able to invest the same effort in establishing and maintaining relations with foreign powers. Thus, it is no surprise that at Monte Albán, Teotihuacán-style iconography is largely confined to Monte Albán IIIa (A.D. 200-500).

Overall, the data from Monte Albán show that over the course of the Classic period, iconography became more complex in the sense that it consisted of more elements. While in Monte Albán II jaguar warrior and *Cociyo* imagery were sometimes used in the same context, during Monte Albán IIIa various iconographic elements—the jaws of the sky or "noble descent," jaguar warriors, and *Cociyo*, consistently used together—indicated noble rank. This iconography reinforced the idea that noble power stemmed from an ability to access supernatural realms and, by portraying ritual and military prowess, demonstrated the legitimacy of that power.

Why were Monte Albán's ruling elite investing such effort in reinforcing the dominant social and political ideology? Monumental architecture was a kind of conspicuous consumption, and rulers often felt compelled to refresh its message from time to time. However, the events taking place at Monte Albán cannot really be understood without reference to changes taking place in the valley. On the one hand, it may be that a proliferation of elite families at Monte Albán meant increased internal competition to demonstrate rank and position. On the other hand, it could be that social and political relationships between the capital and its secondary centers were changing, and Monte Albán's elites were striving to reinforce their place at the top of the political hierarchy. There is some evidence that up until Teotihuacán's decline, Monte Albán's rulers had ties with Central Mexico (Flannery and Marcus 1983d), but during Monte Albán IIIa, the Zapotec were already withdrawing from areas on the route to Central Mexico (such as the Cuicatlán Cañada) that they previously had administered as conquest territories (Redmond 1983).

The Oaxaca Valley in the Classic Period

One interpretation of Oaxaca Valley history is that there was a "latent instability" in the Zapotec state that provided a "potential for within-valley conflict" during the Early Classic (A.D. 200-500) (Balkansky 1998:475). At the very least, events taking place outside Monte Albán suggest that Zapotec elites were developing the kinds of resources that would eventually allow them to assert greater autonomy from the capital. After A.D. 200, two very large urban centers—one in the Tlacolula subregion called the Dainzú-Macuilxochitl-Tlacochahuaya-Guadalupe (DMTG) settlement cluster and one in the Ocotlán subregion, called Jalieza—appear on the landscape (Fig. 5.2). By the end of Monte Albán IIIa, these centers had populations of approximately 12,000 and 13,000 persons, respectively (Kowalewski et al. 1989: Fig. 8.1, Table 8.3).

The entire Valle Grande-Ocotlán subregion, not just the site of Jalieza, experienced enormous population growth during Monte Albán IIIa. Based on regional survey data, the population of the Valle Grande-Ocotlán subregion may have quadrupled, from 19,995 to 43,475 persons (Kowalewski et al. 1989). In part, this dramatic increase could have been stimulated by a Zapotec state policy designed to shift the agricultural labor force until it was more effective at exploiting agricultural land (Spencer 1982:252; see also Blanton et al. 1979:383). On the other hand, large regional secondary centers such as Jalieza might have been encouraged by Monte Albán to be as self-sufficient as possible, a policy that could have created new opportunities for local elites.

The Chronology of the Late Classic and Epiclassic

A great deal of construction continued at Monte Albán during the Late Classic, or Monte Albán IIIb, period (A.D. 500-700). After A.D. 700, public construction declined but the site was not completely abandoned; some offerings and burials continued to be placed in earlier buildings. Initially, Caso et al. (1967) hoped to use the ceramic assemblage to distinguish what they considered the apogee of the site (A.D. 500-700) from the period of its decline (Monte Albán IV, A.D. 700-1000). They eventually realized that the site's abandonment did not coincide with an abrupt change in ceramic style; rather, there was a slow shift in the frequency of certain traits over time. Caso et al. therefore created one long period called Monte Albán IIIb-IV. As a result, there are difficulties involved in using pottery to interpret chronological change during the period A.D. 500-1000 (Kowalewski et al. 1989:251-52; Marcus and Flannery 1990).

Recent work at Monte Albán has described and analyzed the vessels found in tombs, burials, and offerings (see Martínez López et al. 2000). On the basis of these data, scholars now suggest that Monte Albán may have significantly declined by A.D. 600, and that (at least at Monte Albán itself) Monte Albán IIIb-IV style pottery tends not to be found after about A.D. 800 (Martínez López et al. 2000: Table 2). If Monte Albán did decline earlier than previously thought, and did go through a more prolonged period of decline, it is likely that we will have to examine other sites in the valley to fully understand Late Classic period social and political changes.

One way to evaluate the relationship between the decline of Monte Albán and the rise of large population centers on the valley floor is to use excavated ceramic samples and obtain radiocarbon dates from different contexts at different kinds of sites throughout the valley. For example, seven radiocarbon dates from the site of Lambityeco—an area of the Tlacolula-area site of Yegüih, with a single phase of occupation and some very elaborate elite residences—suggest that "Monte Albán IV" began there soon after A.D. 600 (Drennan 1983). It may be that the elaborate residential and ritual architecture at Lambityeco was actually built after Monte Albán had begun to decline (Paddock 1983). As for the Ocotlán subregion, until recently, the only ceramic data available (excluding regional survey data) consisted of fewer than a dozen whole vessels from salvage work near Ocotlán (Martínez López et al. 2000: Table 58) and several hundred diagnostic sherds from intensive surface collections at Jalieza (Finsten 1995: Table 2).

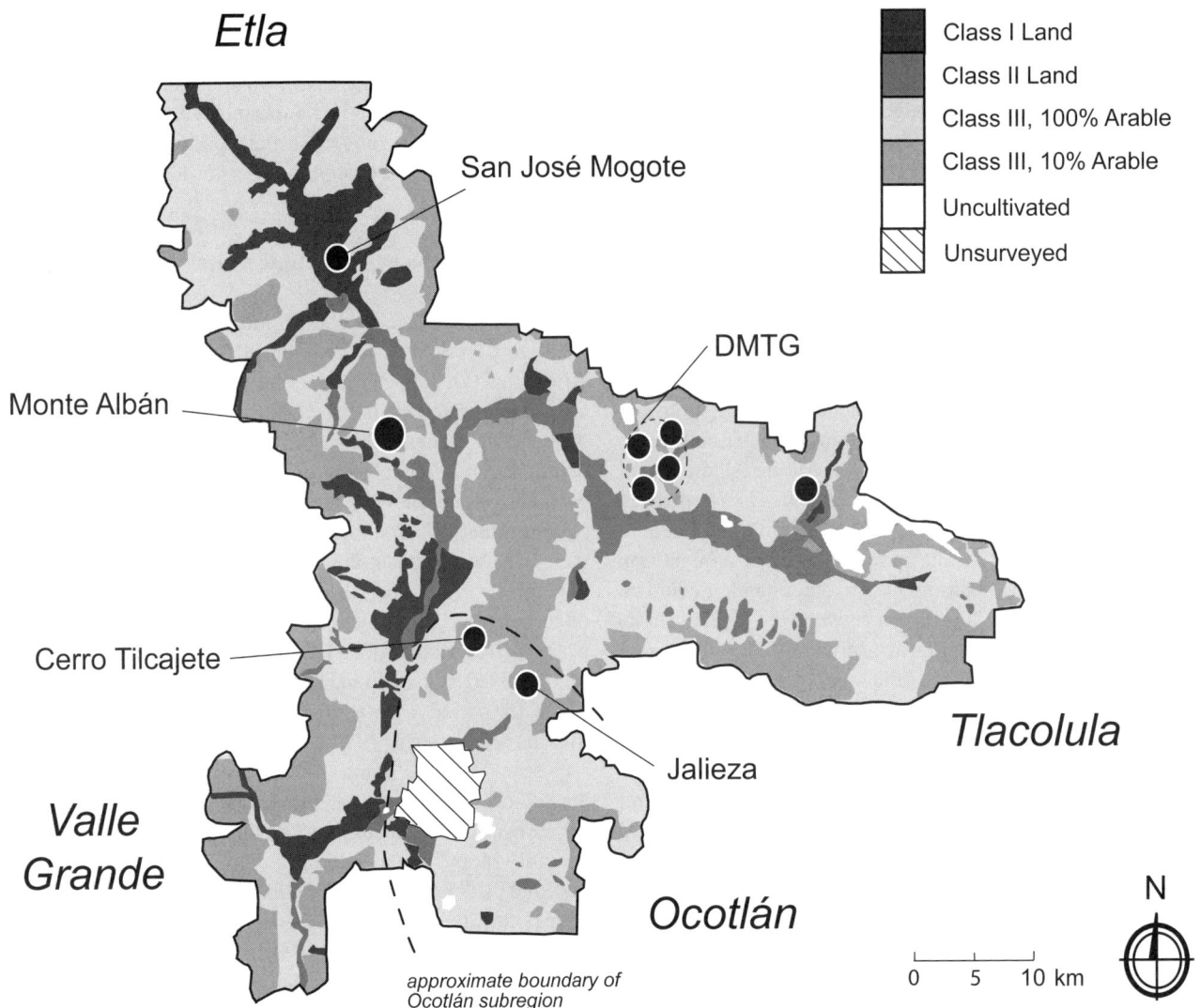

Figure 5.2. The Oaxaca Valley showing major Classic and Epiclassic sites (agricultural land-use map adapted from Marcus and Flannery 1996).

Jalieza

At this writing, Luca Casparis and I are working at the urban center of Jalieza, aiming to clarify the chronological and cultural sequence of the Ocotlán subregion after A.D. 200. So far, excavations at Cerro Tilcajete allow me to suggest several scenarios to describe the relationship between Ocotlán and the Central Valley after A.D. 500. I stress that these scenarios are preliminary and will be confirmed or modified in the future; they already, however, provide a context in which to conceptualize the reoccupation of Cerro Tilcajete in Monte Albán IIIb-IV. Examining what we know so far about the appearance of Jalieza, it appears that when Cerro Tilcajete was abandoned around A.D. 200, its entire population may have moved to nearby Jalieza (Fig. 5.3).

In 1988, Laura Finsten conducted a program of systematic intensive surface collection and mapping on selected terraces and mounds at Jalieza. She proposed that Jalieza was made up of two contiguous sites: a western occupation that dates to the Early Classic, and an eastern occupation that dates to the Late Classic-Epiclassic (Fig. 4.1). The rapid and enormous growth of Jalieza—from a few scattered hamlets in Monte Albán II to a site covering 4 km² by the end of Monte Albán IIIa—reflects important local processes in the Ocotlán subregion (Casparis 2005; Finsten 1995:3). Jalieza is an enormous archaeological site covering some 9 km², larger than Monte Albán at its peak. It includes two main ceremonial centers, set atop distinct ridges whose slopes are extensively terraced. Isolated mound groups can also be found along the bases of these hills. Casparis (2005)

Figure 5.3. Photo of the Early Classic Jalieza site from the Late Classic-Epiclassic site (see Fig. 4.1 for a map showing the relationship between the two sites) (photo by Kevin DeVorsey).

has mapped and excavated the Early Classic site, and he and I mapped the Late Classic-Epiclassic site and are currently excavating there (our work at Jalieza will be described in forthcoming publications). Here, I consider how Casparis' and my work has shed light on (1) the chronology of Jalieza, and (2) the relationship between Jalieza and Cerro Tilcajete.

The Monte Albán IIIa ceremonial center at Jalieza is set atop a peak that has good sightlines to Monte Albán. The slopes of this hill are extensively terraced, and four separate areas with mounds are distributed around the base of the hill. The ceremonial core of the site has a layout similar to Monte Albán's: a four-mound group with a sunken patio at the north end of the Main Plaza, and a large platform at the south end. The northernmost building has not been excavated, but its similarities to Monte Albán's North Platform and San José Mogote's Mound 8 allow us to hypothesize that it is an administrative palace. Casparis directed excavations of a residential palace attached to the South Platform. This building—made of stone, adobe, and plaster—has three adjoining patios surrounded by rooms. Excavations uncovered a kitchen area and a tomb containing two individuals. The pottery and burial offerings are typical of Monte Albán IIIa, and the radiocarbon dates indicate that the palace was abandoned at the end of Monte Albán IIIa (Casparis 2005).

A central feature of the eastern part of Jalieza is a road that climbs up from nearby Ocotlán, traverses one mound group, and continues in a northeast direction toward the Tlacolula subregion of the valley (Fig. 5.4). Mounds and plazas can be found on high points on the ridge line along the road. The largest mound group at the site, Mound Group 1-4, is on a high ridge north of the road. Our recently completed map of Mound Group 1-4 shows that the four mounds cover a total of 950 m^2, while the patio or plaza in the middle of those mounds is 625 m^2. Elites living on this ridge had a view of both Tlacolula and Ocotlán, but not of Monte Albán.

Our program of mapping and intensive surface collecting of the eastern part of Jalieza, recently completed, uncovered ceramics in the ceremonial core that can be dated to Monte Albán IIIb. Our current thinking is that the ceremonial core of eastern Jalieza was built in Monte Albán IIIb (A.D. 500-700), accompanied by a slow shift of population from the western sector to the eastern sector. Surface evidence further suggests that after A.D. 1000-1200, Jalieza was largely abandoned (Elson and Casparis

Figure 5.4. Photo looking west along the ridge line supporting the ceremonial core of the Late Classic-Epiclassic Jalieza site (photo by Kevin DeVorsey).

2006). In general, the Postclassic period that followed was one of more dispersed population throughout the Valley of Oaxaca, but sites appear to be aggregated within the boundaries of many small polities or petty kingdoms.

Cerro Tilcajete

Let us turn now to the reoccupation of Cerro Tilcajete during Monte Albán IIIb-IV. This reoccupation centered on Plaza I, four of whose six mounds had been occupied in some form during Monte Albán II. Based on surface evidence, a generous estimate for the number of Monte Albán IIIb-IV households associated with this mound group would be in the vicinity of ten to fifteen, giving us a population of no more than a few hundred people. The most important questions to address are (1) when people resettled the site and rebuilt the Plaza I mound group, and (2) what they were doing there.

The Adoratory and Mound F at Cerro Tilcajete

I excavated a Monte Albán IIIb-IV adoratory in Plaza I. This adoratory was associated with Mound H. Its east wall was situated 6.3 m from Mound H, while its west wall was 11.7 m from Mound I (Fig. 5.5). The structure atop Mound H was probably a temple. It is important to note that Mound H was closely tied to the complex of mounds on the north side of Plaza I by an elevated terrace.

The adoratory measured approximately 5 × 5 m and was no more than a meter tall. Modern plowing had removed much of the north and south walls, but the east and west walls were well preserved, as were the platform's foundations, which were made of large unshaped stones (Fig. 5.6). The top of the stone platform was located just below ground surface. At its base, excavations uncovered the 4-5 cm thick plaster floor of Plaza I.

Sherds were not abundant in the excavation, but I found several Monte Albán IIIb-IV diagnostics embedded in the plaza's plaster

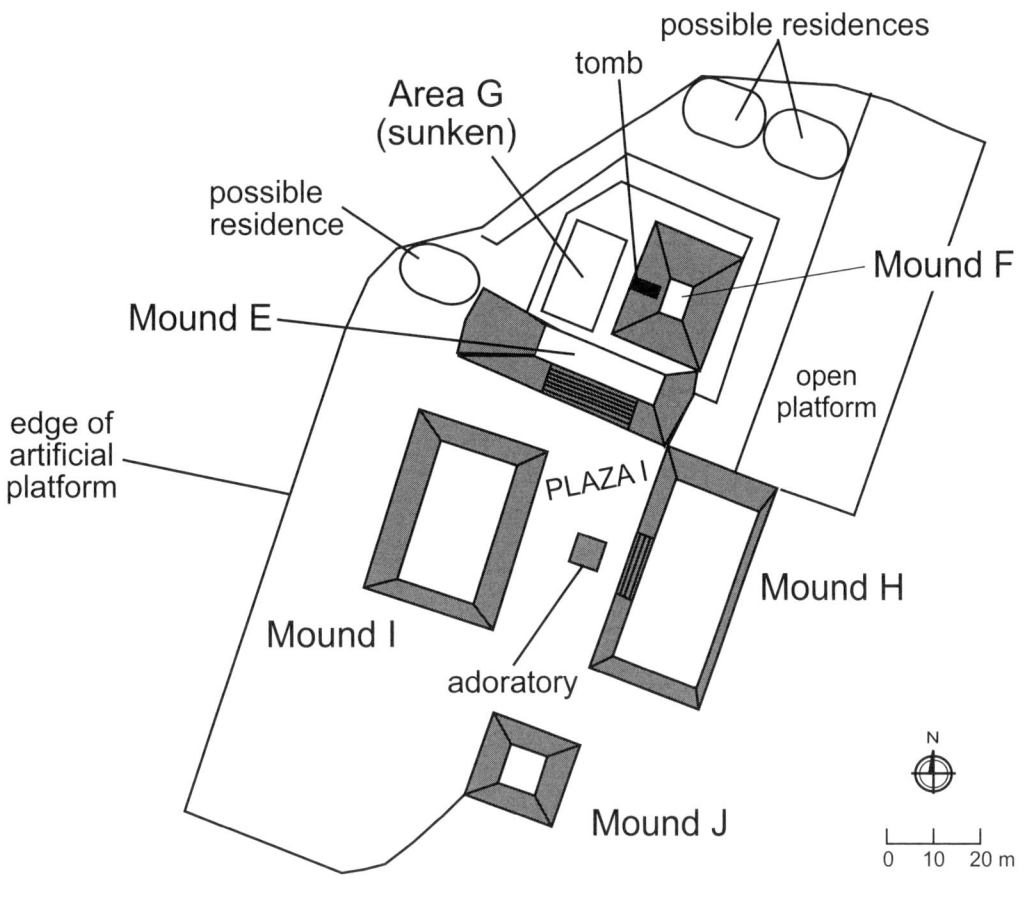

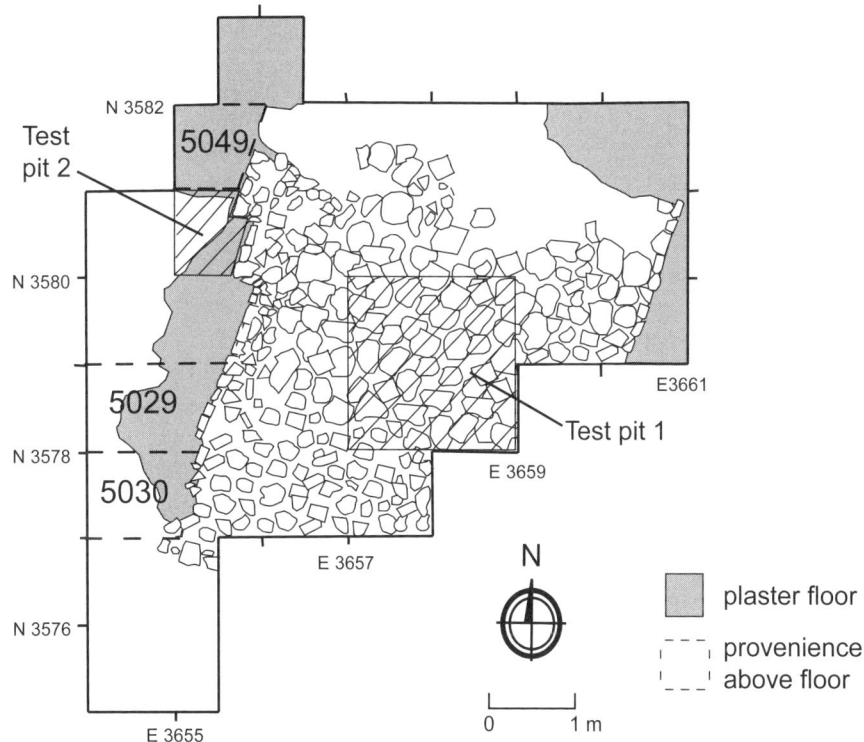

(*Above*) Figure 5.5. Schematic plan of the post A.D. 500 layout of Plaza I (also see Fig. 3.1 for the site map)

(*Right*) Figure 5.6. The Plaza I adoratory platform associated with Mound H, Plaza I's eastern mound. The plaster floors, which sat on sterile soil, are the floors of Plaza I. The zigzag of the platform's western wall may define the point of access from the plaza onto the platform. See Figure 5.5 for the relationship of the adoratory and Mound H.

Figure 5.7. A seven-centimeter-long bifacially flaked chert knife found on the adoratory, Plaza I.

floor. Provenience 5029 produced a gray-paste bowl with an incipient annular base; Provenience 5030 produced a gray-paste bowl with a pinched solid support; and Provenience 5049 produced gray-paste bowls with pattern burnishing. All these bowls belonged to the Caso, Bernal, and Acosta type G.35, which was ubiquitous in the Monte Albán IIIb and IV time periods. G.35s are gray-paste, flat-bottomed bowls that could have a variety of treatments: a thickened base, sometimes with notches; a reinforced rim; and solid or hollow supports that varied from tiny nubs to supports shaped like monkey heads. Some bowls had lightly burnished, random-line designs on the interior. Provenience 5049 produced two handles from café-paste incense burners.

The adoratory turned out to be a single phase construction built after A.D. 500. Test Pit 2's plaster floor lay on sterile soil and *tepetate* (a layer of hardpan that forms above bedrock). Test Pit 1, placed inside the adoratory, reached the same layer without uncovering any earlier construction phases.

Perhaps the most significant evidence regarding the use of the adoratory came from the chipped stone artifacts recovered in the excavations—twenty-five green and three gray obsidian blades; one chert scraper; one chert blade; a black chert biface or "sacrificial dagger" 7 cm long; and part of another black chert biface (Fig. 5.7). I therefore propose that the adoratory functioned as a ritual venue for sacrifice and autosacrifice, probably conducted for the benefit of an audience gathered on the plaza. The bifaces left behind were likely for heart sacrifice and the obsidian blades for bloodletting.

The North Mound Complex

Mounds E and F and Area G at Cerro Tilcajete had a layout superficially similar to that of Monte Albán's North Platform: a long, narrow mound leading to a sunken patio flanked on the east by a taller mound. North of this complex were terraces that could have held elite residences (Fig. 5.5). We subjected Mound E to broad, horizontal excavations that exposed 177 m². Like Mound H, Mound E had at least two major phases of construction, in Monte Albán II and again in Monte Albán IIIb-IV. (The Monte Albán II buildings were examined in Chapter 4.)

The final phase of construction on Mound E, dating to Monte Albán IIIb-IV, was generally well preserved, and I excavated it in its entirety. It consisted of a single building, Structure 5, which was on a large platform measuring 19.8 × 4.6 m. The best preserved wall of Structure 5, the south wall, was oriented 107° east of magnetic north (Figs. 5.8-5.9). Its platform foundation was at least 53 cm tall and was built of large stones; the entire surface was covered with large, irregularly shaped, fitted flagstones. There were no internal walls dividing the structure into rooms.

South of the structure, a 2 m wide flagstone floor ran the entire length of the building, some 32 cm below the level of the platform. Sections of this floor still had a thin layer of stucco covering the stones. In the middle of the building, probably where the stairway from the plaza ascended, the floor was more eroded than at either extremity. At either end of the flagstone floor were lines of stones that could indicate where pilasters stood. The pilaster at the western end would have been 2.60 m by perhaps 1 m.

Structure 5 lay within a layer of dark brown topsoil called Layer 1. Along the northern wall this earth was lighter in color, more densely packed, and had more adobe and stucco fragments (called Layer 2). Test Pit 9 uncovered a dense concentration of ceramics (designated Feature 2) just north of the platform wall and above the level of the earlier (Monte Albán II) structures. A total of 1662 sherds were found in Feature 2, along with fragments of chipped stone and figurines (described below). My interpretation of Structure 5 is that it functioned as a civic space of some kind, and had an open plan with a broad stairway leading up from Plaza I, and another stairway leading down to Area G and Mound F.

We excavated a 2 × 2 m test pit in the middle of Area G, to a depth of 80 cm below ground surface. This test pit went through three layers: a 38 cm thick level of dark brown earth (Layer 1); a 30 cm thick medium brown layer with plaster and adobes (Layer 2); and a 12 cm layer of yellow, almost sterile soil with limestone chunks. Very little material was recovered in any of the layers, and no structural remains were located.

The top of Mound F rises 9 m above the level of Plaza I. The view from the top of the mound is a 360° panorama of the Central Valley, the Valle Grande, and the Ocotlán subregion. Stone foundations and plaster are visible atop the mound's 5 × 5 m summit. Mound F contained a tomb, which had been looted sometime before 1994 (Fig. 5.10). Initially, the looters dug a hole into the western side of the mound, striking an enormous stone slab that blocked the tomb's original entrance. Unable to move this *lápida*, the looters then dug another hole from the top of the mound, striking one of several stones used to roof the tomb. Three of these stones were then removed (one of them was at least 120 cm long, 30 cm wide, and 17 cm thick), and the tomb was penetrated from the roof. Over the years the tomb had partially filled in with dirt, which we removed in order to draw its layout and find material that might help us date its use. The fill of the tomb included obsidian; human bone; several smashed but partially restorable vessels, including G.35 bowls; long handled incense burners; and a jar made of a fine orange-brown paste. This fine orange-brown paste ware does not appear in Monte Albán II contexts. Some twenty-two more sherds of the same type of

Figure 5.8. Photo of Structure 5, Mound E, a civic-ceremonial structure dating to Monte Albán IIIb-IV. The photo is looking east to west. The upper flagstone floor is visible in the center of the photo and the lower flagstone floor is visible in the upper left area of the photo. See Figure 5.9 for the structure's plan.

paste appeared in Feature 2; it may be the same type identified in surface collections at Jalieza, where Finsten (1995:12) described it as a generally underfired salmon-pink to orange-brown paste slipped inside and out in black. Unfortunately, our 2006 surface collections at Jalieza did not recover additional sherds of this type (Elson and Casparis 2006).

The tomb in Mound F was 2.20 m long and 1.20 m high, and had two niches, each about 50 cm in height. A portion of the floor and the east wall of the tomb had been dug into *tepetate*. The original entrance was in the west end and was still blocked by the enormous slab that had frustrated the looters. Figure 5.10 shows that the tomb's architecture consisted of large stone

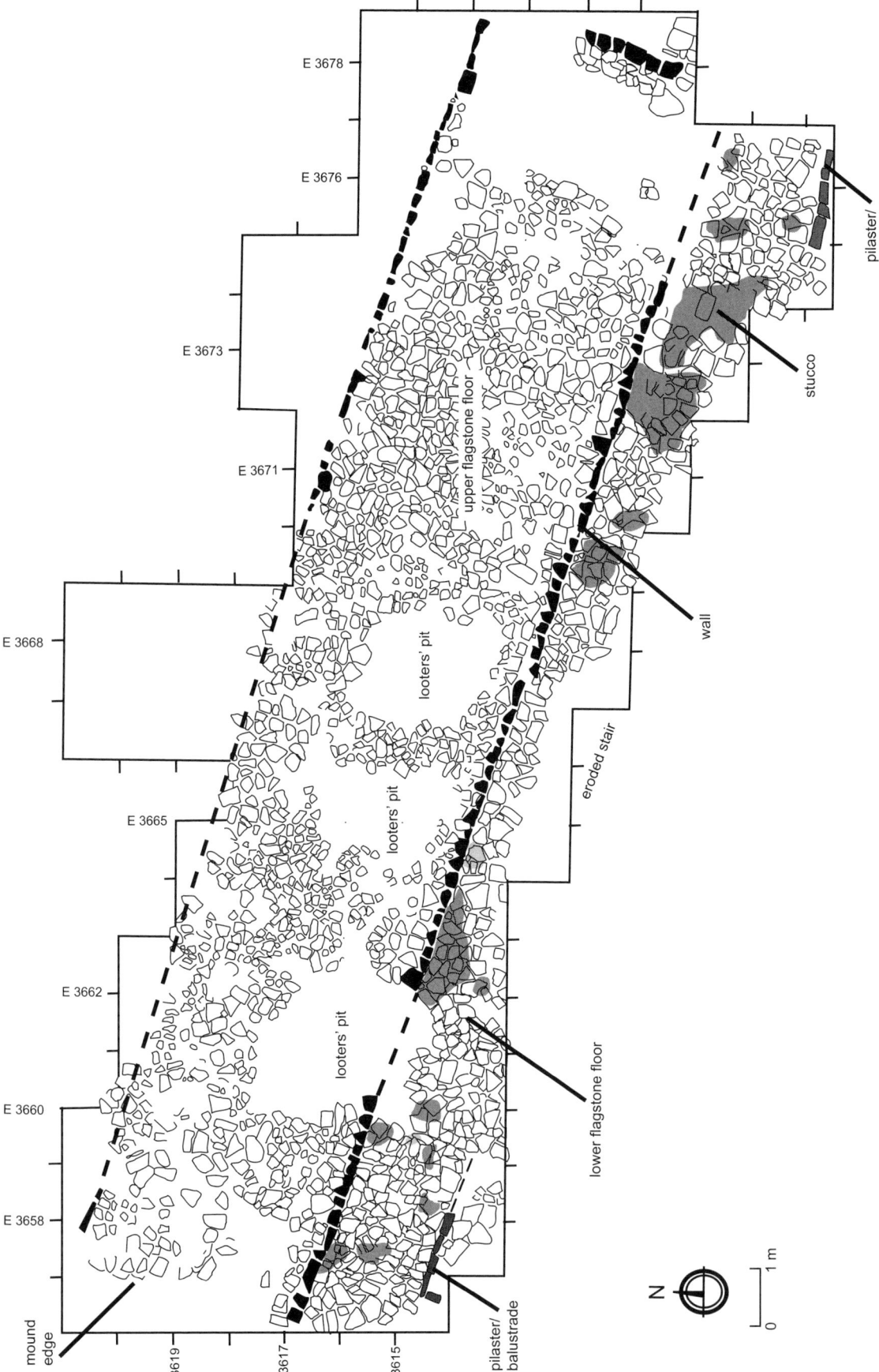

Figure 5.9. Plan of Structure 5, Mound E, a civic-ceremonial structure dating to Monte Albán IIIb-IV. The lower flagstone floor, still partially covered in stucco, was a patio area reached by a stair from Plaza I. The upper flagstone floor is the floor of the civic-ceremonial building. The blackened stones and dotted lines demarcate the building's limit. See Figure 5.8 for a photo.

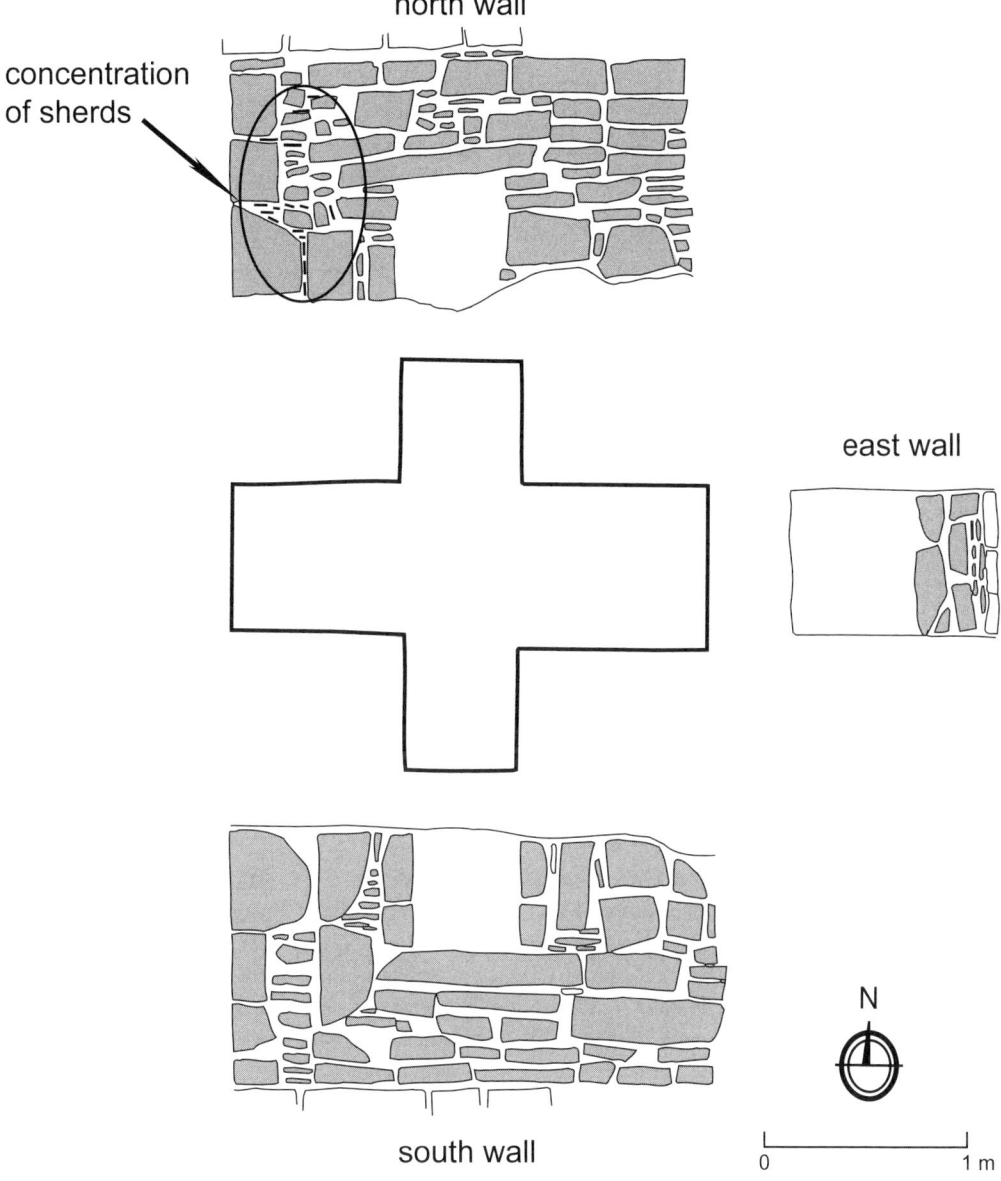

Figure 5.10. Plan of the looted Monte Albán IIIb-IV tomb in Mound F, Plaza I. The tomb was blocked on the west by an enormous stone slab. The lower section of the east wall is *tepetate*, as is the floor. Five stone slabs capped the roof.

Table 5.1. Paste and weight of sherds in Feature 2, Mound E, Cerro Tilcajete.

Type	Number of Sherds	Percentage of Total Sherds	Weight of Sherds (g)	Percentage by Weight
oxidized gray	9	0.54	230	0.88
café diagnostics	41	2.47	1660	6.33
café body sherds	123	7.40	1760	6.71
G.1 diagnostics	239	14.38	6260	23.87
G.1 body sherds	1014	61.01	12,630	48.17
gray body sherds	137	8.24	1620	6.18
gray all	50	3.01	1610	6.14
orange-brown	22	1.32	110	0.42
cream	10	0.60	230	0.88
orange	17	1.02	110	0.42
Total	1662	100.00	26,220	100.00

slabs, with small flagstones and sherds inserted into the spaces between them. Paddock (1983) identified this style of architecture as "chinking" when he found it at Lambityeco, a major Monte Albán IIIb-IV site in the Tlacolula region, and he suggested that it might be more diagnostic of Monte Albán IV (A.D. 700-1000) than IIIb. The greatest concentration of "chinking" sherds occurred in the north wall and in the niches. We removed several large sherds from the north wall and found that many of them could be refitted to form part of a burned G.35 bowl with pattern burnishing on the base.

The tomb was built on sterile soil, and its base is approximately 2 m below the lowest point we excavated on Mound E. The looters exposed no other floors or architectural remains in the platform fill. Thus, the constructions atop Mound F should be contemporaneous with, or postdate, the tomb.

Structure 5 Ceramics

Feature 2 provided a sample of sherds, which likely had been discarded as trash from the structures on Mound E. Tables 5.1 and 5.2 present the data discussed in this section. I coded 1662 sherds. The majority of these, both by weight and by number, belonged to the Caso, Bernal, and Acosta type G.1. This gray-paste ware has a sandy texture and large mineral granules; it was absent from all pure Monte Albán II deposits excavated at Cerro Tilcajete. It is likely that our G.1 was locally made during

Monte Albán IIIb-IV, and that most of the ceramics deposited in Feature 2 date to this time period. That being said, a few cream-paste Monte Albán II diagnostics had been redeposited in the trash, as frequently happens at multicomponent sites. Of the other sherds in Feature 2, many of the café- and gray-paste bowls, jars, *comales*, and incense burners did not have rim forms exclusive to a single time period.

Fifty-seven of the bowls recovered can be classed as G.35s, a type common in Monte Albán IIIb-IV. In Feature 2, I coded a sherd as G.35 only if it was possible to identify two of the following three diagnostic elements: wall/rim, base angle, or foot (Fig. 5.11). All 57 of the bowls coded as G.35 were made from the same sandy gray paste with large mineral granules described for G.1. Another 129 rims and 26 flat bases probably were from G.35 bowls. Overall, there was little variation in the shape and form of these gray-paste bowls, which are extraordinarily common in Monte Albán IIIb-IV. I did not code any supports that depicted monkey heads.

Beside the G.35 bowls, other likely Monte Albán IIIb-IV diagnostics in Feature 2 included a spouted pitcher (*cántaro*) with a strap handle, and two forms of incense burners made in gray and café pastes (Martínez López et al. 2000:131-32, 152-61, 191-97). Twenty-two sherds with dense orange-brown paste may all have come from one slipped and highly burnished incurving-rim bowl (Table 5.2 indicates only the two that are diagnostic rim sherds). Finally, one figurine head (possibly from a whistle) belonged to the type called *cara de jóven y tocado de buho* or "face of a young man with a headdress of an owl," and appears identical to figures found at Monte Albán during Period IIIb-IV (Martínez López and Winter 1994:75).

Summary

Plaza I of Cerro Tilcajete was rebuilt during Monte Albán IIIb-IV to serve as a ceremonial-ritual complex, though perhaps reoccupied only by a few dozen elite families. An adoratory was built on the plaza surface, and a temple was built on Mound H. The adoratory was littered with the kinds of obsidian blades and bifacial stone knives used to conduct ritual sacrifice.

The mounds and terraces at the north end of Plaza I functioned as a complex of civic and residential buildings. From Plaza I, one climbed a stairway to a long room atop Mound E, and passed out the other side to reach a patio (Area G) and a tall funerary mound. Associated residences appear to be on the terraces that adjoin Area G on the north and west. It is important to point out that while Mound F contained a tomb, it apparently did not support a residence (although it could have supported a very small temple); rather, it contained only a cruciform tomb, a pattern not common elsewhere in the valley.

Because of the problems with Monte Albán IIIb-IV, mentioned above, it is difficult to date these structures with much precision, given our pottery collection. If we apply comparative data from Lambityeco, where radiocarbon dates are available,

Table 5.2. Diagnostic rim and bowl base sherds in Feature 2, Mound E (by type).

Rim No.*	Paste	Vessel	Description**	No. of Sherds
1	orange	bowl	rim	1
4	orange	bowl	rim	2
33	orange-brown	neckless jar	rim	2
4	café	bowl	rim	6
7	café	bowl	rim	3
54	café	*comal*	rim	1
94	café	*comal*	rim	1
none	café	incense burner	rim, concave base	3
none	café	incense burner	rim, flat base	1
none	café	incense burner	sherd	1
57	café	jar	rim	2
58	café	jar	rim	2
62	café	jar	rim	3
1	cream	bowl	rim	3
4	cream	bowl	rim	1
6	cream	bowl	rim	1
none	G.1	bowl	G.35 base: flat bottom, unidentifiable support	3
none	G.2	bowl	G.35 base: flat bottom, nubbin support	6
none	G.3	bowl	G.35 base: flat bottom, pinched support	1
none	G.4	bowl	G.35 base: flat bottom, truncated conical support	6
none	G.5	bowl	G.35 base: flat bottom, gravel marks on exterior	1
none	G.6	bowl	G.35 base: truncated base, unidentifiable support	1
none	G.7	bowl	G.35 base: truncated base, nubbin support	2
4	G.8	bowl	G.35 rim-to-base: concave base, nubbin support	1
4	G.9	bowl	G.35 rim-to-base: flat base, nubbin support	10
4	G.10	bowl	G.35 rim-to-base: flat base, conical support	2
4	G.11	bowl	G.35 rim-to-base: flat base, unidentifiable support	2
4	G.12	bowl	G.35 rim-to-base: truncated base, pinched support	1
4	G.13	bowl	G.35 rim-to-base: truncated base, nubbin support	4
4	G.14	bowl	G.35 rim-to-base: truncated base, unidentifiable support	1
1	G.15	bowl	G.35 rim-to-base: truncated base, unidentifiable support	1
none	G.16	bowl	base, conical support	5
none	G.17	bowl	base, unidentifiable support	1
none	G.18	bowl	base, nubbin support	8
none	G.19	bowl	base, truncated support	1
4	G.20	bowl	rim-to-base: unidentifiable support	1
1	G.21	bowl	rim	15
4	G.22	bowl	rim	114
15	G.23	bowl	rim-to-base	1
65	G.24	bowl	rim	3
1	gray	bowl	rim	1
31	gray	bowl	rim	1
33	gray	bowl	rim	1
37	gray	bowl	rim	1
none	gray	incense burner	rim, concave base	2
none	gray	incense burner	rim, flat base	2
19	gray	jar	rim	3
50	gray	jar	rim	2
62	gray	jar	rim	1
none	gray	jar with a spout	rim, jar with clay strap covering the spout (*cántaro*)	9

Total 247

*See Chapter 4, Figures 4.30-4.31.
**See Figure 5.11 for illustrations of G.35 vessel bases and supports.

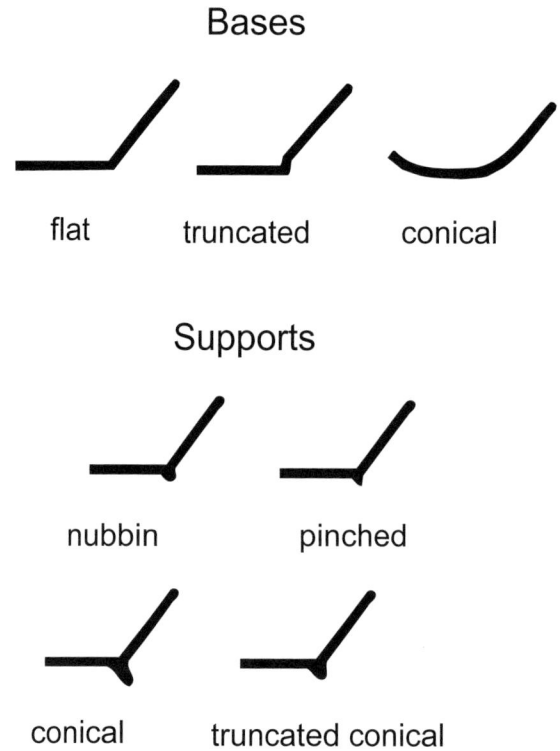

Figure 5.11. Stylized G.35 vessel forms found in Feature 2, Mound E.

we can suggest that the tomb's architecture (for example, the use of sherds for "chinking") would place its construction at about A.D. 600/700. I suspect that Cerro Tilcajete was rebuilt no more than 100 years after the civic-ceremonial core of Jalieza had shifted from west to east, an event which Casparis and I currently estimate took place at A.D. 500/600.

The evidence from Jalieza could be used to suggest two slightly different scenarios to explain the reoccupation of Cerro Tilcajete. Both scenarios take as their premise the likelihood that between A.D. 500 and 700, Monte Albán's rulers were rapidly losing their grip on the valley. At some point, Jalieza's elites decided to move the ceremonial core of their site east to a location straddling the road that connects Ocotlán with the Tlacolula subregion.

In one possible scenario, Jalieza's elites, seeking to establish themselves as the rulers of a polity independent from Monte Albán, decided to engage in boundary-marking behavior. Cerro Tilcajete in this scenario was resettled not only because it had a good view of the Valle Grande and Central Valley, but also because it would have been visible to elites engaging in similar behavior in the Central Valley and Valle Grande. In a second possible scenario, Cerro Tilcajete was resettled by populations from the Central Valley or Valle Grande—in other words, by individuals not politically connected to Jalieza.

While I expect future work to refine our chronology of events, there are three lines of evidence that support the first scenario—in other words, that Cerro Tilcajete's reoccupation was tied to the elaboration of the Late Classic-Epiclassic ceremonial center at Jalieza. First, the small size of the occupation at Cerro Tilcajete limits its effectiveness as an independent political entity. Second, the size of Plaza I at Tilcajete and its associated buildings places it in the same scale as Mound Group 1-4 at Late Classic-Epiclassic Jalieza. The similarities between these two residential-civic ceremonial mound groups make it plausible that a group of several powerful allied families politically controlled both Jalieza and Cerro Tilcajete and shared the day-to-day responsibility of monitoring thousands of people and meeting the defensive needs of the territory. Third, Cerro Tilcajete's hilltop location would not only have allowed Jalieza to monitor activities taking place in the Central Valley and Valle Grande, but also allowed it to visibly communicate the boundaries of the emerging Jalieza polity to rivals nearby. In this scenario, the re-utilization of the ancient site of Cerro Tilcajete did more than demarcate a political boundary: it symbolically validated local elite authority over the Ocotlán subregion.

Chapter 6

Conclusions

Cerro Tilcajete served as a secondary administrative center for the Valle Grande-Ocotlán subregion of the Oaxaca Valley during Monte Albán II. The data from Cerro Tilcajete allow for an assessment of the nature of Zapotec state administration.

In the Oaxaca Valley, the processes leading to state formation and regional consolidation were already detectable between 500 and 100 B.C., but it appears that Monte Albán did not control the entire valley until circa 100 B.C. As Monte Albán struggled for dominance, mortuary architecture and offerings with Lightning iconography suggest that after 500 B.C., elites across the valley were promoting an ideology that legitimized social stratification and ties to the supernatural. These elites shared a common culture, the Zapotec language, and perhaps a common ancestry that transcended Monte Albán's hegemony. Undeterred, Monte Albán's elites engaged in a power-building strategy designed to centralize and consolidate power and used their resources to subjugate other areas. Monte Albán appears to have conquered the Cuicatlán Cañada about 300 B.C., some two hundred years before its armies were finally able to subjugate Ocotlán. In this chapter, I examine several key challenges Zapotec rulers faced during Monte Albán II, and suggest ways in which they responded to the need to manage a larger territory and population.

1. The incorporation of the valley, coupled with population growth at Monte Albán, required that state administration function in a more elaborated (hierarchical) way. At Monte Albán, evidence points to an increasing hierarchy in the noble class and in the organization of the urban elite, some of whom had specific functions related to military, economic, and religious activities. While it is likely that these patterns were gradually developing during Monte Albán I, by Monte Albán II the architecture and iconography point to an effort by ruling elites to distinguish themselves clearly from lesser elites at the capital and from local elites brought into the state system.

The ruler, or *coquitào*, of Monte Albán and his family lived in stone and adobe palaces near the Mound of the Carved Stone and carried out state business in civic-ceremonial structures on the North Platform. The ruler was assisted and advised by a staff of noble relatives (*joàna*), servants, and even slaves. Ruling elites used serving vessels and urns decorated with *Cociyo* iconography to demonstrate their ability to access supernatural forces through close ties with semi-divine ancestors. Increasingly, rulers employed jaguar imagery in horizontal (elite to elite) propaganda to display their status as noble warriors or *coqui huezàquiquèche*. Large jaguar or puma statues found in offering contexts at various sites in the valley functioned as vertical (elite to non-elite or capital elite to local elite) propaganda, meant to evoke the power of Monte Albán and its rulers.

Ruling power thus stemmed not only from social position but also from military and ritual ability. Rulers were uniquely suited to influence supernatural forces and maintain cosmic order through the completion of rituals involving sacrifice (autosacrifice, human sacrifice, and animal sacrifice) and by acting as successful military leaders. After Monte Albán's incorporation of the entire valley, the ruling elite likely claimed a monopoly on the performance of some kinds of ritual activities conceptualized as benefiting the Zapotec as a people. In their role as practitioners of state-sponsored ritual, rulers came to act as the titular heads of a formalizing state religion. The distribution of standardized two-room temples—on platform mounds on Monte Albán's Main Plaza and in numerous urban neighborhoods—argues for the presence of hierarchically organized religious practitioners.

Some elite families clearly lived in neighborhoods away from the Main Plaza. The residents of the El Pitahayo Mound Group serve as an example of elites that must have occupied an important place in the social and political landscape of the capital. The El Pitahayo Mound Group is located along a major road connecting Monte Albán with the valley floor and is positioned directly behind a double defensive wall on one of the gentlest slopes of the site. Elaborate tombs excavated here contain urns with *Cociyo* imagery. One tomb also contained eagle claws made from marine shell and an urn depicting a warrior with a headdress of a bird, probably an eagle. The architecture and iconography of the El Pitahayo zone offer the possibility that these nobles acted as military leaders and headed, or were responsible for assembling and coordinating, an order of the Zapotec army.

A dense concentration of shell debris in one building with a residential and ritual component on the Main Plaza, as well as the abundance of obsidian at Monte Albán in contrast to other valley sites, are some of the lines of evidence for elite control over extra-valley resources. If Monte Albán controlled access to obsidian and dominated the production of worked shell, ruling elites would have been able to dictate who had access to these goods, and perhaps even how they were used—for example, the use of blades in temple contexts.

2. Zapotec rulers formalized architecture at Monte Albán as part of a planned visual program. An analysis of the kinds of buildings created indicates that an important component of the program was expressing a state religion and militarism. Large-scale investment in architecture included remodeling the Main Plaza, building numerous two-room temples, and renovating the North Platform. The Main Plaza was outfitted with two different types of buildings probably associated with militarism: Mound J, with its slabs of subjugated place glyphs, and an I-shaped ballcourt. Many public buildings and temples contained elaborate offerings, involving complex dedicatory rituals and reflecting state control over the disposal of sacrificial victims and exotic goods such as worked jade, whale bone, and obsidian.

Monte Albán's rulers sat at the head of a military and ritual hierarchy, yet their position may only have placed them first among noble families. Below them were the leaders of lower-ranking noble families who likely functioned in a way analogous to the *teuctli* (Nahua) or *batabob* (Maya) of other regions. For example, urban elites flourished in a dense cluster of residences northeast of the Main Plaza near System Y. These families lived in stone and adobe palaces with impressive tombs and used serving vessels and urns with *Cociyo* iconography. Not everyone living in this area belonged to the noble stratum; there are residences of lower-ranking lineages in these neighborhoods as well. The extent to which the Monte Albán II urban elite used jaguar or puma iconography to portray themselves as warriors remains to be fully documented.

3. Throughout the Valley of Oaxaca, implementation of the Zapotec state building program depended on the nature of political ties between the local and ruling/urban elite, but in general it appears that rulers were interested in creating landscapes that unified nobles as (ranked) social beings and as (ranked) ritual leaders. The Ocotlán subregion changed dramatically after it had been incorporated into the Monte Albán political system. Monte Albán's policy of subjugation included the destruction and probably forced abandonment of El Palenque, and the reorganization of some of its local population into small villages. The new hilltop center they created in Ocotlán—Cerro Tilcajete—was only half as large as San José Mogote or Dainzú, and had an estimated Monte Albán II population of 800-1600 persons, approximately one-tenth that of Monte Albán.

When we compare and contrast the history of Cerro Tilcajete (in Ocotlán) with San José Mogote (in Etla) and Dainzú (in Tlacolula) we see that, on the one hand, all three secondary centers were either built anew or extensively rebuilt in Monte Albán II. On the other hand, administrators at all three sites seem to have had different social and political relationships with Monte Albán. San José Mogote—a site that contributed much of the original founding population of Monte Albán—most closely resembles the latter. Excavations there suggest that it was deliberately rebuilt to look like Monte Albán. San José Mogote had an I-shaped ballcourt, ten two-room temples, elite residences, and a governmental palace. Local elites had access to exotic goods, including obsidian and jade, and sponsored ceremonies promoting an ideology that tied them to *Cociyo* and venerated noble ancestors. It is likely that some local elite administrators at San José Mogote were trusted nobles appointed from the capital.

In the Tlacolula region, Yegüih declined and Dainzú rose to prominence, featuring at least one two-room temple and a residential palace with tombs and other burials. Cream-paste pottery with Lightning iconography reached the site. One massive platform in the ceremonial center of Dainzú displayed a number of carved stones depicting ballplayers; another ceremonial platform displayed a carved stone representing an individual with an elaborate headdress and closed eyes, standing on a hill glyph. Ballplaying and ballgame ritual were clearly important, yet Dainzú does not have an I-shaped ballcourt. However, as suggested earlier, an I-shaped ballcourt at a small, special-purpose site only 4 km from Dainzú may have been available to the latter; this cannot be confirmed without excavation. It will be years before we can describe in detail how the relationship between Tlacolula and Monte Albán changed between Late Monte Albán I and Monte Albán II; additional excavations at both Yegüih and Dainzú will be required.

Cerro Tilcajete in Ocotlán also had residential palaces and two-room temples, but it did not have an administrative palace or an I-shaped ballcourt. Significantly, Cerro Tilcajete seems to have been laid out in such a way as to limit access to ceremonial areas. Only about 15 to 20 elite families (75 to 200 persons) lived in the ceremonial precinct, a zone that contained two mound-and-plaza groups. Mounds flanking either side of a road at Tilcajete monitored both access to the ceremonial part of the site, and the movement of traffic and tribute along the road linking Ocotlán to the Central Valley of Oaxaca.

My project excavated temples and residential palaces in the ceremonial precinct. Structure 1, a palace on the north mound, is considered the home of a local administrator. I have suggested—based on comparisons of the distribution of *comales*, large utilitarian bowls, and utilitarian jars in Structure 1, an elite residence, and Structure 4, a lower-status residence—that lower-status residents may have provided the elite family with staple goods, perhaps to support community events, host visiting dignitaries, or conduct other celebratory activities. A second residential palace at Cerro Tilcajete, Structure 3, was closely associated with a small two-room temple, and may have been inhabited by individuals affiliated with the state religion.

The data acquired at Cerro Tilcajete allow us to consider not only how local elites carried out policies set by higher-ranking administrators at Monte Albán, but also how they expressed their local authority—in essence, allowing us to evaluate where local elites fit into the valley's social hierarchy and the ways in which they participated in state ideology.

Ceramic data from the two residential palaces show an emphasis on the acquisition of cream-paste vessels produced near Monte Albán, particularly bowls with bulbous feet and Lightning motifs. I have suggested that these vessels were key objects linking nobles with their divine ancestors and *Cociyo*. Exportation of these vessels from Monte Albán to secondary centers implies that, at some level, rulers encouraged local elites to participate in what we might call "status and position affirming behavior." Local elites also incorporated urns and incense burners into their household rituals. Such objects were likely used in the veneration of state deities and noble ancestors.

Obsidian (particularly in the form of blades) did not occur in abundance at Cerro Tilcajete, nor was it worked at the site. It appears that most obsidian was acquired as blades, and that when blades became exhausted they were reworked into flakes. Structure 3 had the highest number of obsidian blades, which is perhaps not surprising since it was associated with a two-room temple. If, as many Oaxaca scholars have proposed, Monte Albán controlled access to obsidian, local elites would have depended on maintaining a good relationship with the capital in order to receive both cream-paste vessels and obsidian blades.

While Structures 1 and 3 clearly had residential functions, both may have been built for the families of administrators. Significantly, we did not find tombs in either residence. This contrasts with Monte Albán, where buildings like Structure 1 typically contained formal stone-lined tombs and multiple burials. There are several possible explanations for this contrast. One possibility is that the elite residences at Cerro Tilcajete belonged to administrators imposed from the capital, administrators who preferred to be buried at Monte Albán. An alternate possibility is that Structures 1 and 3 were owned by indigenous elites from Ocotlán, who had maintained primary residences elsewhere.

The fact that Cerro Tilcajete has no I-shaped ballcourt is interesting, but difficult to interpret given the very small number of ballcourts definitively dated to Monte Albán II by excavation. Currently, the only definite Monte Albán II I-shaped ballcourts are located in Monte Albán and San José Mogote, both larger sites than Cerro Tilcajete. Whatever the role of state ballcourts, it evidently had not been assigned to Tilcajete by the Zapotec state.

At Cerro Tilcajete, the worked human maxilla exposed by looters on the southwestern edge of Plaza II has been interpreted as a military trophy. The presence of such an object provides a fascinating glimpse of the potential result of Zapotec war and military activities, but without further data we cannot specify the source of the maxilla. We do know from Spencer and Redmond's work at the site of Loma de la Coyotera in the Cuicatlán Cañada (briefly described in Chapter 2) that the Zapotec used terror tactics—such as putting heads on racks—to subdue local populations.

4. Local groups were integral to the expansion of the Zapotec state, but might have had different political and social goals than Monte Albán's rulers. Over time, intra-elite power struggles, perhaps against a background of population growth or major regional political shifts, could have provided opportunities for a reorganization of the political hierarchy. In ethnohistorically documented premodern states, the ruling elite occasionally promoted commoners (particularly those who had achieved military success) to positions of power; low-ranking nobles also could rise to better administrative positions based on performance. Unfortunately, the kinds of data presently available for Monte Albán cannot help us determine whether or not this happened in Monte Albán II society. The anthropological literature, however, suggests that even in societies where the offices held by urban and local elites were non-hereditary, in practice the ultimate strategy of subordinate elites was to turn their individual social and economic achievement into higher status. Lower-ranking, or intermediate, elites often attempt to use their social status or achieved political position to accumulate wealth and institutionalize their positions by creating multigenerational bonds through kinship or social solidarity.

Over generations, noble and commoner groups can do this successfully so long as a coup or dynastic overthrow does not result in major restructuring of the administration. Bonds of kinship can promote loyalty between lower-level and ruling nobles, but disaffected nobles have access to many of the same resources as the ruler, and can use such resources to legitimize attempts at usurping power. I have suggested that at Monte Albán after A.D. 200, an emerging concern with elite-to-elite propaganda, including the appearance of elaborate palaces such as the one above Tomb 105, could signal increasing competition between the ruling elite and lower-ranked families who could claim noble status. Zapotec rulers began to formalize the use of *Cociyo*/jaguar/noble descent iconography, publicly and privately, to reinforce their position. Monte Albán's elite might also have sought to reinforce their position *vis-à-vis* local elite at growing secondary centers.

The appearance of large Classic urban centers at DMTG and Jalieza suggests to some scholars that Monte Albán III Zapotec state policy was designed to move the agricultural labor force around so that it was more effectively exploiting the land. The valley also may have experienced a population surge during

Monte Albán III as Zapotec control over areas such as the Cuicatlán Cañada waned and some outlying populations returned to the Oaxaca Valley. One state response to growing population could have been to reorganize valley-wide administration (Spencer 1982:252; Marcus 1992a).

The changes seen in Monte Albán IIIa left Cerro Tilcajete temporarily abandoned. As new state policies were crafted, some local elites—with or without the encouragement of Monte Albán—moved to locations that allowed them to interact more directly with the growing agricultural population. Local elites at Jalieza may have been charged with different kinds of administrative tasks than their predecessors at Cerro Tilcajete, and in the long term, the management of more people and resources could have contributed to growing local autonomy.

The excavations at Cerro Tilcajete have provided a very preliminary outline of some of the things local elites did when they pulled away from the centralized state—either reacting to problems at the capital or instigating political independence. Monte Albán's decline is not well understood. There is no evidence that Zapotec state collapse was triggered by ecological disaster, epidemic disease, or conquest by a foreign polity. One factor to consider is the pan-Mesoamerican void the fall of Teotihuacán may have created. The Zapotec did have a political relationship with Teotihuacán, and it may be that with the fall of that great polity, any external pressure on the rulers of the Oaxaca Valley to keep the region unified was alleviated. At that point, intrapolity factors, such as factional divisions in the ruling circles or the assertion of autonomy by local elites, could have triggered competition and strife, behavior that eventually disrupted the state system while not leading to endemic violence. Some scholars (for example, Kaufman 1995:224-25) consider pre-modern states inherently dysfunctional and prone to collapse.

As Monte Albán weakened between A.D. 500 and 700, Ocotlán's population shifted to more defensible ridges. The ceremonial core of Jalieza—containing several large mound groups with civic-ceremonial architecture, elite residences, and temples—shifted west. About a dozen elite families reoccupied Cerro Tilcajete, and the site was outfitted with a large plaza-mound group, similar in size to the largest mound group in the western sector of Jalieza. Once a secondary center for Monte Albán, Cerro Tilcajete had now become a secondary center for Jalieza.

On one low Monte Albán IIIb-IV platform in Plaza I, twenty-eight obsidian blades and two bifacial chert sacrificial daggers were left *in situ* as discarded artifacts from ritual sacrifice. The north mound supported a large, open civic building (Structure 5), and behind this structure sat a temple mound of Plaza I containing a stone-lined tomb with a cruciform plan. The architecture of the tomb, the sherds embedded in its wall and found broken in its fill, and the ceramics recovered in a feature associated with Structure 5 date the initial constructions at the site to after A.D. 500-600. The data allow me to suggest that this reoccupation of Cerro Tilcajete was directed by elites from Jalieza and was intended to create a very visible hilltop boundary for an emerging Late Classic-Epiclassic Jalieza polity. Both Late Classic-Epiclassic Jalieza and Cerro Tilcajete were placed at important, visible features on the landscape. From Jalieza, local Ocotlán elites could monitor the road from Ocotlán to Tlacolula and the massive Dainzú-Macuilxochitl-Tlacochahuaya-Guadalupe (DMTG) settlement cluster. From Cerro Tilcajete, those same elites could monitor both the Central Valley and the Valle Grande.

Whether interested in pre-modern, prehistoric, or protohistoric states, many archaeologists want to go beyond addressing questions of scale and structure, and consider instead how people interacted and shaped their society. In Oaxaca, it is now possible to begin to examine these questions because (1) a century of archaeological research has provided a wealth of data from many different sites and time periods, and (2) there is demonstrable cultural continuity in Zapotec society from the prehistoric to historic period. Beyond this continuity, I have found that when addressing the early periods of the Zapotec state, it is fruitful to use ethnographic analogy to identify patterns in elite behavior and to consider how those patterns would be manifested in the archaeological record.

Survey and excavation over the last thirty-five years show that Monte Albán II is the first time period for which there is conclusive evidence that the entire Oaxaca Valley was politically unified under Monte Albán's leadership. This unification affected how Monte Albán interacted with newly incorporated but ethnically homogeneous populations in different regions of the valley.

The primary goal of the present work is to present detailed data from a secondary center in the Ocotlán subregion and show how the patterns found at that site can be interpreted within a valley-wide framework. I hope that this Memoir will be considered a case study that other researchers can use when considering prehistoric state societies. Researchers are beginning to realize that primary states such as that of the Zapotec state may function, at least initially, in an *ad hoc* fashion as new ways of administering land and people are worked out. These new ways of doing things eventually become regularized, standardized, and embedded over time, often serving as models for neighboring areas.

The Monte Albán II state exhibits some indications that the growing social hierarchy was encouraging the development of bureaucracy—the creation of positions such as priest or military leader, tied more to specialized activities than to social status. This was at best an "incipient bureaucracy," but many of the roles created survived the political collapse of primary states and reemerged clearly in second- and third-generation states. More elaborate bureaucracies grew out of generations of elite competition; competitive elites are so successful at creating and perpetuating offices and privileges that often not even the cleverest of rulers can find ways to restructure the system.

This is not the last my colleagues and I will have to say on Cerro Tilcajete, Jalieza, and other sites in the important Ocotlán subregion. I trust that future research will add more detail to the preliminary picture I have sketched, and that complementary work elsewhere in Mesoamerica will lead to a more comprehensive picture of how elites at the capital and elites at secondary centers negotiated power over the lifetime of a state.

Appendix A

Ceramic Terms, Analysis, and Illustrations

The definitive volume on Oaxaca ceramics for time periods after 500 B.C. is *La Cerámica de Monte Albán*, published in 1967 by Alfonso Caso, Ignacio Bernal, and Jorge Acosta. Since that volume is out of print and difficult to obtain, the goal of this appendix is twofold: to provide the reader with some information on major ceramic types, and to describe how the excavations at Cerro Tilcajete shed new light on the Monte Albán II time period.

Caso and his colleagues based their ceramic classification on three criteria: (1) the color and texture of the clay body, (2) vessel form, and (3) vessel decoration. Some "types" are specific combinations of these three criteria. For example, the "G.26" type combines attributes from all three criteria: after firing, the vessels have a gray color; the vessels all have an exterior flange near the rim; and most have exterior incised designs near the rim or on the flange. Other types, in contrast, are very general categories that include some variation in paste and a range of vessel forms. For example, the "G.3" type is defined as a thin to medium-thick walled, well-fired vessel, tempered with sand or diorite, that appears in both domestic and ceremonial contexts. Only some kinds of whole vessels made of G.3 paste can be used as diagnostics because G.3 paste is used during *all* periods. Therefore, G.3 body sherds by themselves cannot be used as chronological markers.

It is important to keep in mind that very few types defined in *La Cerámica de Monte Albán* begin and end a chronological time period. Most often, the shifts are *frequency* shifts that can be detected only with very large assemblages of excavated sherds.

Large ceramic assemblages reveal the popularity of each type and reveal how the percentages of a type fluctuate over time. Caso and his colleagues discussed assemblages from stratigraphic excavations and other deposits at Monte Albán, the capital; nevertheless, we should expect the ceramic assemblages at other sites in the valley to vary from the capital's. During Monte Albán II, four general paste types predominate: gray (*gris*), café (*café*), orange (*amarillo*), and cream (*crema*). I will discuss each paste in turn. Note that the rim forms described in this appendix are illustrated in Figures 4.30-4.31 of Chapter 4.

Gray-Paste Wares

The most common pottery is made from sand (or occasionally diorite-tempered) clay and fires to a light gray color. Given its abundance, I would expect that most gray-paste vessels were made with locally available clays. A few gray-paste types are particularly important in this study.

G.2 (Fig. 4.31: rims 25, 56, 78, 93). This type is a very large (up to 76.5 cm in diameter), thick-rimmed utilitarian bowl called an *apaxtle*. At Monte Albán, the term *apaxtle* was used to describe only gray-paste vessels, but at Cerro Tilcajete, rim form 78, which occurs only on café-paste vessels, has also been classified as an *apaxtle*. This type is not limited to Monte Albán II. Caso et al. (1967:24) did not find any whole *apaxtles* in tombs or offerings. They noted that these kinds of bowls were used in the modern era for washing clothes. I have suggested, based on an analysis of houses at Cerro Tilcajete, that they also were used for soaking corn and preparing *masa* or corn dough.

G.12 and G.21 (Figs. A1-A5). The G.12 is a straight- to outleaned-wall serving bowl with two distinct co-occurring attributes: (1) two parallel lines on the interior of the vessel near the rim (Fig. A2), and (2) parallel lines incised in a variety of patterns on the interior base or bottom of the bowl. (Caso et al. [1967:25-26] recognized that these attributes co-occurred because they were working with a large number of whole vessels from tombs and burials.) This type of decoration is referred to as "combing" because many of the parallel designs look like they were made with an instrument containing from three to ten or more equidistantly spaced points, like that of a comb, that was drawn across the vessel bottom (Fig. A1). G.12 vessels are more common in Monte Albán I, but they continue to be made in Monte Albán II.

Several aspects of G.12 vessels should be discussed because these diagnostic features may help distinguish Monte Albán II contexts from Monte Albán I contexts (Table A1). In Monte Albán II contexts at Cerro Tilcajete, most G.12 bowls are decorated with scalloped or parallel concentric lines (see Fig. A4 for G.12 motifs). Across the site, rim forms 1, 31, 37, and 40 dominate the assemblage (see Fig. 4.30a). I coded the occurrence of certain motifs illustrated in Figure A4. Most of these are variations of scalloped or parallel concentric lines. In addition, I assigned a value to the quality of motif decoration: sloppy, non-sloppy, or indeterminate. Figure A1*a-f* shows examples of non-sloppy G.12 bowl bases while A1*g-j* shows examples of sloppy G.12 bowl bases. As indicated in Table A1, between 21% and 32% of the bases had decoration that was sloppily or hurriedly achieved (that is, when it was possible to determine the quality of decoration applied to the base). This means that the design was not completely or uniformly carried out, or that design elements overlapped or ran over one another. Obviously, quality of design is a somewhat subjective category.

In contrast to the G.12 vessels made during Monte Albán II, those made in Monte Albán I are usually very finely made serving vessels and the designs on the base are neatly and carefully applied. At Cerro Tilcajete, the sloppy G.12 vessels occur more frequently in the lower-status Structure 4. These data may suggest that Monte Albán II potters invested less effort than their Monte Albán I counterparts in making G.12 bowls. In Monte Albán II, these gray bowls may have been in less demand by the elites who wanted to use wares such as fancy cream-paste and orange-paste ceramics.

Caso et al. (1967:67) considered the G.21 as the "devolution" of the G.12. The G.21 is defined by its form. It is a medium to thick outleaned-wall bowl that sometimes has crudely scratched lines around the interior rim (Fig. A.3). The base is decorated with a random pattern of scratched lines.

G.21s occur in low frequencies at Cerro Tilcajete. They tend to be thicker and less well made than G.12s, but there is not enough information to evaluate the chronological relationship between the two types.

G.15 and G.16 (Fig. A6). G.15 vessels occur most frequently as thin to medium-thick walled serving bowls decorated with various kinds of incised lines—swirling, wavy, or straight (often parallel) (Caso et al. 1967:32). Outleaned-wall bowls tend to have the decoration on the inside rim, while incurving or straight-wall bowls tend to have the decoration on the exterior of the vessel. Some sherds still have vestiges of red pigment rubbed into the incisions after firing.

G.16 vessels occur as serving bowls and jars and are decorated with zones of "hatching." Some vessels probably have zones of both G.15 and G.16 decoration. G.15 and G.16 vessels are very common in Monte Albán I offerings, tombs, and burials, and these types continue to be used in small quantities in Monte Albán II. Except for Structure 3 at Cerro Tilcajete, G.15s and G.16s (combined) make up less than 1% of diagnostic ceramics.

G.25 and G.26 (Fig. A6). The G.26 is a serving bowl with flanged rim, often with incised decoration on the rim or flange. The G.25 is a serving bowl with a basal flange that can have incised decoration. Caso et al. (1967:37-41) state that these types do not appear until late in Monte Albán I and that the basal flange may be more common in Monte Albán II than it is in Monte Albán I. G.25 and G.26 vessels make up less than 1% of the diagnostics in residences at Cerro Tilcajete.

G.34 (Fig. A7). This type is defined as a very thin-wall jar, darkly burnished on the exterior except for a thin line where the natural color of the fired clay appears (Caso et al. 1967:67). At Cerro Tilcajete, the treatment of several gray-paste jars with rim form 50 (Fig. 4.30b) leads me to suspect that G.34 vessels occur with this rim type; however, I did not find whole or nearly whole vessels, so this suggestion is tentative since they may occur with other or additional rim forms. G.34s occur more frequently in Structure 1 at Cerro Tilacajete and it is possible that these nicely made serving jars were used in elite contexts. However, data from other sites must also be evaluated. G.34 vessels appear to be limited to the Monte Albán II period.

G.29 (Fig. A8). Caso et al. (1967:67) suggested that the G.29 was an "intrusive" type at Monte Albán, where it takes the form of a serving bowl. In Chapter 4, I evaluated the possibility that this paste type was manufactured in the Valle Grande-Ocotlán subregion. The G.29 appears at Cerro Tilcajete and at the Valle Grande site of Yaasuchi; sherds from both sites cluster in terms of their trace elements. Therefore, it is likely that the paste used to make these vessels comes from one source or just a few sources. The G.29 paste is sand-tempered and contains opaline inclusions in spicules or "clumps" of slate. Many have a painted red line on the inside rim and some also have splotchy red strokes on the body. At Cerro Tilcajete, G.29s almost always occur as bowls, but a few vessels are straight-wall vessels (Table A2).

Appendix A: Ceramic Terms, Analysis, and Illustrations 101

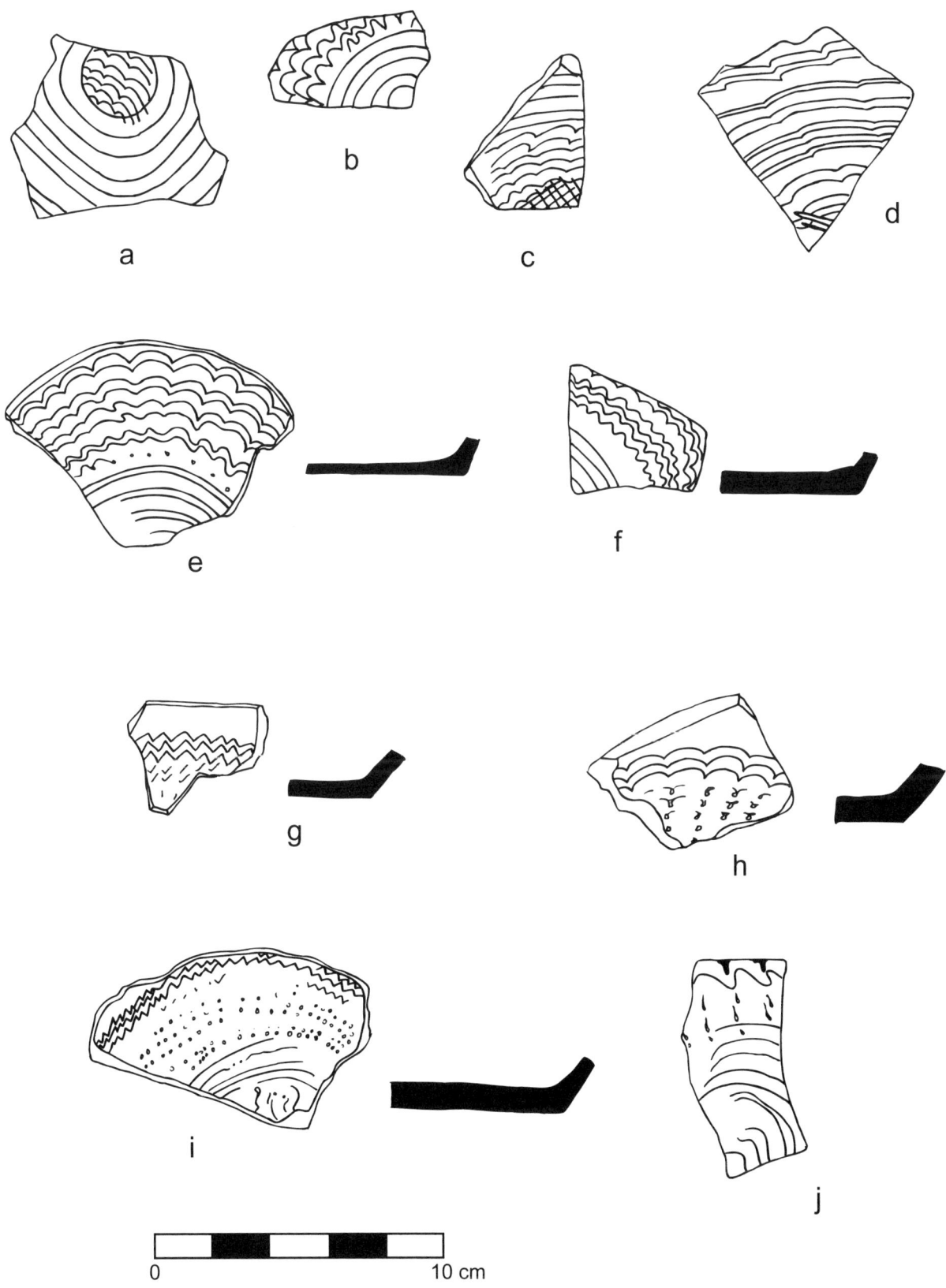

Figure A1. Examples of G.12 bowl base decoration found on vessels at Cerro Tilcajete. *a-f*, non-sloppy G.12 designs; *g-j*, sloppy G.12 designs.

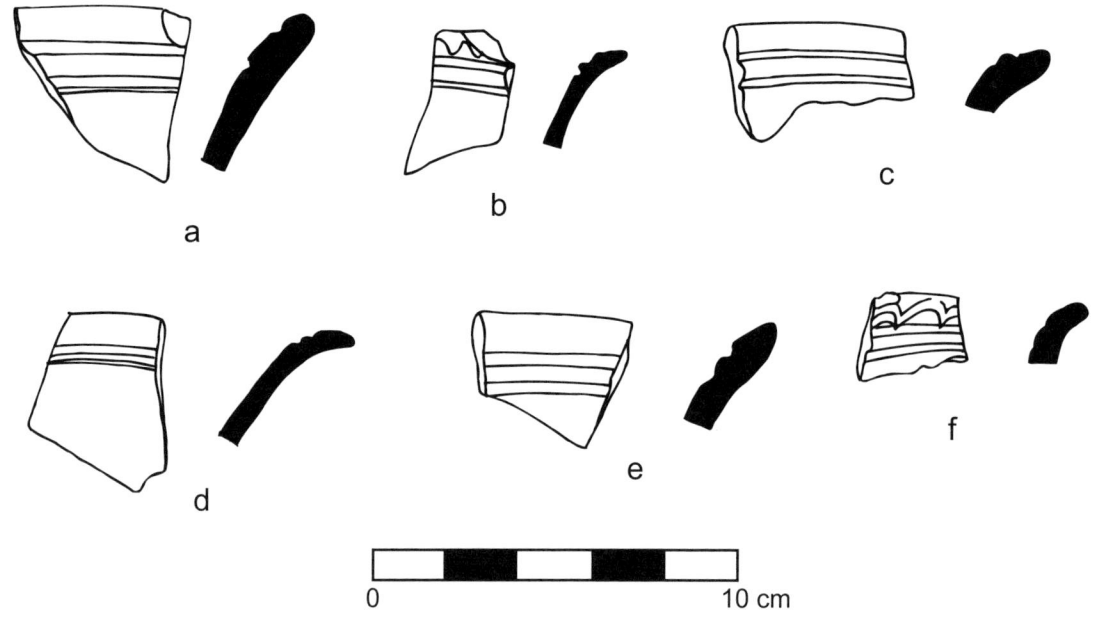

Figure A2. Examples of G.12 rim forms and rim decoration found on vessels at Cerro Tilcajete.

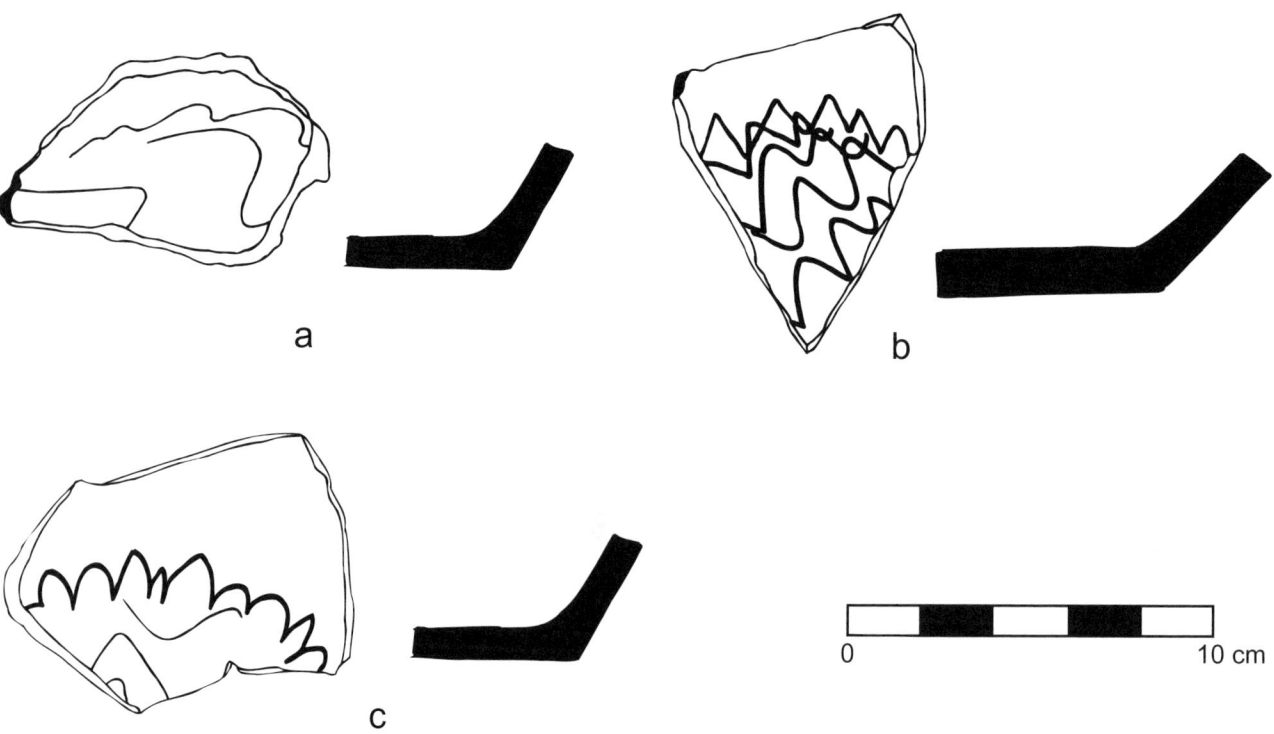

Figure A3. Examples of G.21 bowl base decoration found on vessels at Cerro Tilcajete (*c* from Feature 4, Structure 4).

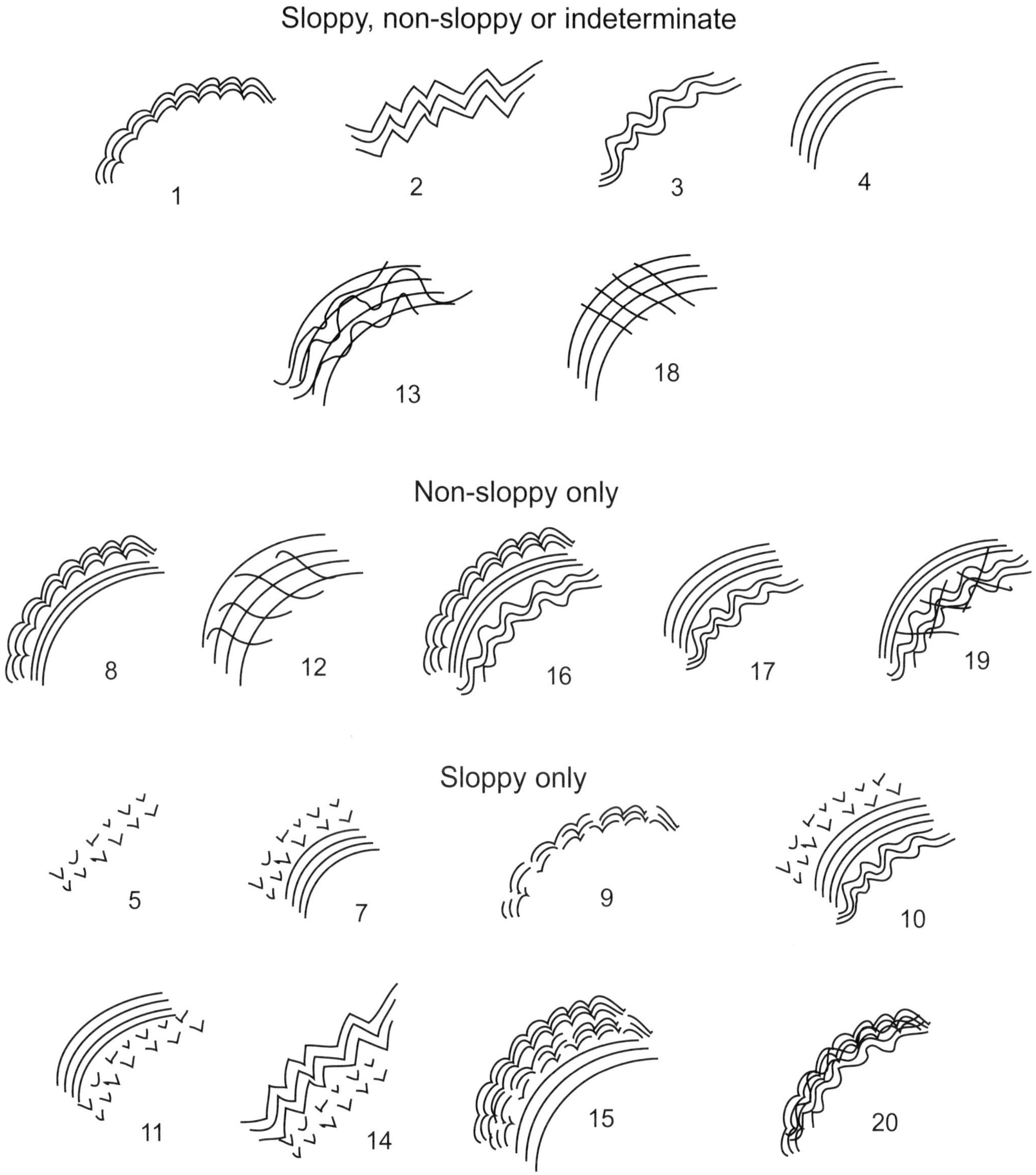
Sloppy, non-sloppy or indeterminate
1
2
3
4
13
18
Non-sloppy only
8
12
16
17
19
Sloppy only
5
7
9
10
11
14
15
20

Figure A4. G.12 bowl base motifs. *0*, none; *1*, scallops; *2*, zigzags; *3*, undulating lines; *4*, parallel concentric lines; *5*, punctation; *6*, random patterns (not shown); *7*, parallel concentric lines and punctation; *8*, parallel concentric lines and scallops; *9*, skipping scallops; *10*, punctation, parallel concentric lines, and undulating lines; *11*, parallel concentric lines and punctation; *12*, parallel concentric lines and squiggles; *13*, undulating lines and parallel concentric lines; *14*, zigzags and punctations; *15*, scallops, skipping scallops, and parallel concentric lines; *16*, scallops, parallel concentric lines, and undulating lines; *17*, undulating lines and parallel concentric lines; *18*, parallel concentric lines intersected by parallel lines; *19*, parallel concentric lines with cross hatching; *20*, scallops and undulations that intersect.

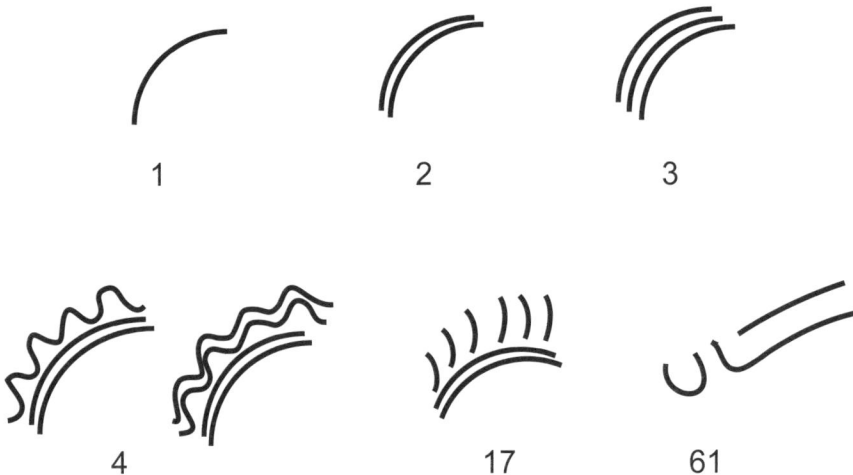

Figure A5. G.12 rim motifs. *1*, a single line on the interior of the rim; *2*, double lines on the interior of the rim; *3*, triple lines on the interior of the rim; *4*, double lines with one or two wavy lines on the interior of the rim; *6*, a single line on both the interior and exterior of the rim (not shown); *17*, double lines incised on the interior of the rim with stroke marks; *61*, breaking lines on the interior of the rim.

Appendix A: Ceramic Terms, Analysis, and Illustrations 105

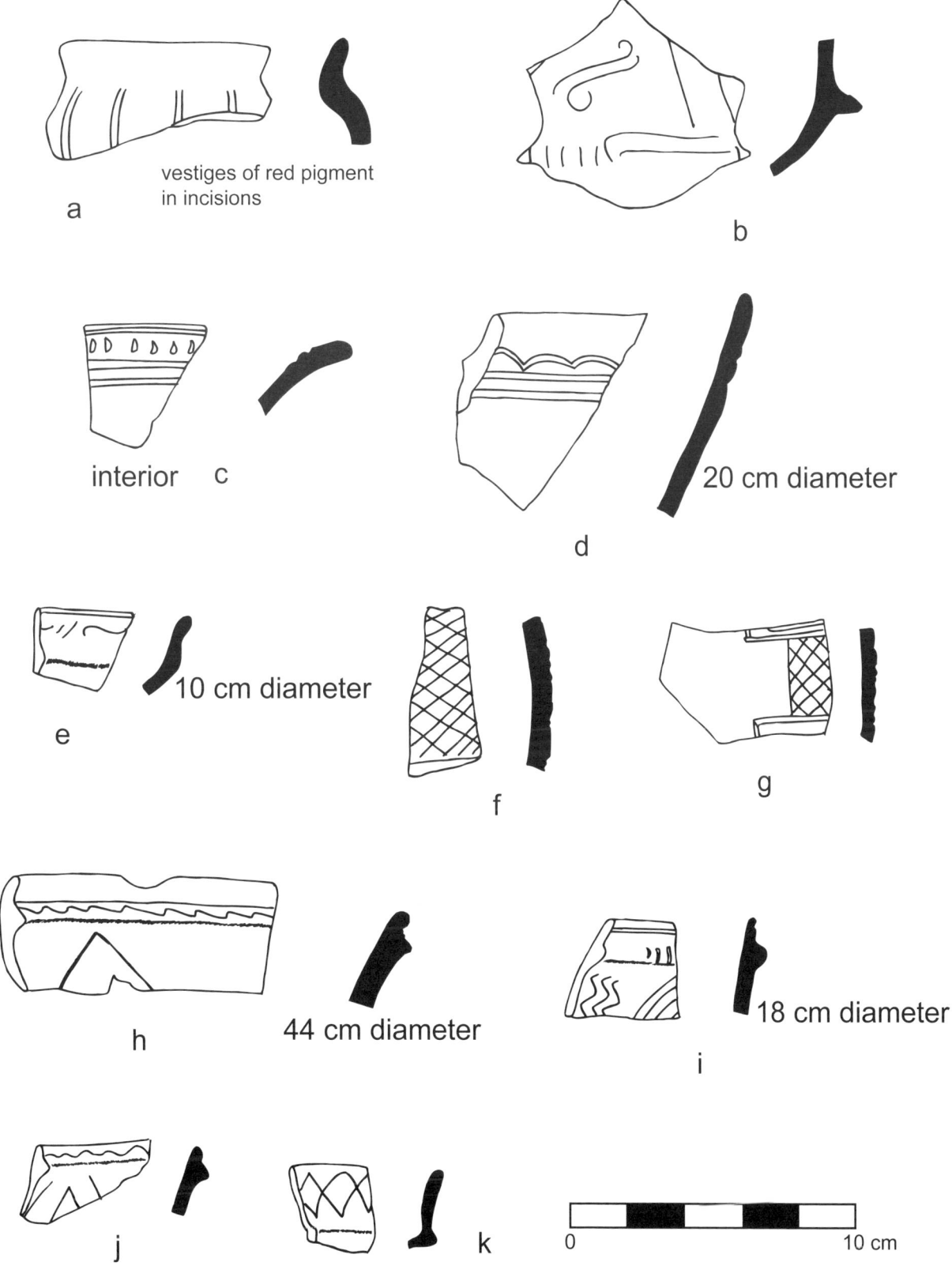

Figure A6. Examples of G.15, G.16, G.25, and G.26 rim forms and vessel decoration. *a-e*, G.15; *f-g*, G.16; *h-j*, G.25; *k*, G.26.

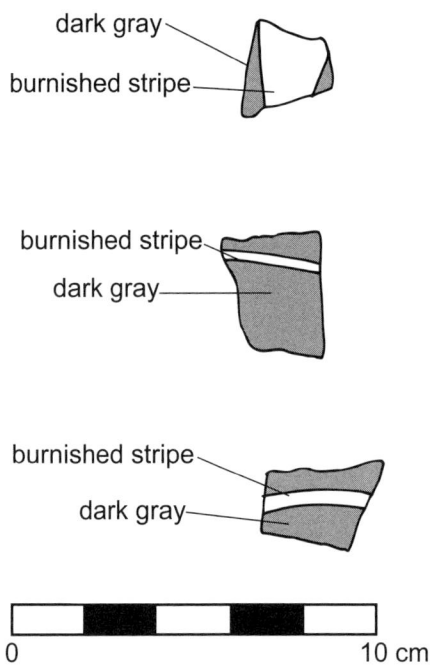

Figure A7. Examples of G.34 jars from Cerro Tilcajete. These thin-walled serving jars may occur with rim form 50 (illustrated in Fig. 4.30b).

(*Facing page*) Figure A8. Examples of G.29 rim and base forms and vessel decoration from Cerro Tilcajete. *a*, bowl covered with splotchy red paint; *b*, bowl with a burnished dark black exterior and interior; *c*, bowl with a brownish color; *d-k*, bowls that are a brownish to greenish-brown color with red-painted rims.

Appendix A: Ceramic Terms, Analysis, and Illustrations

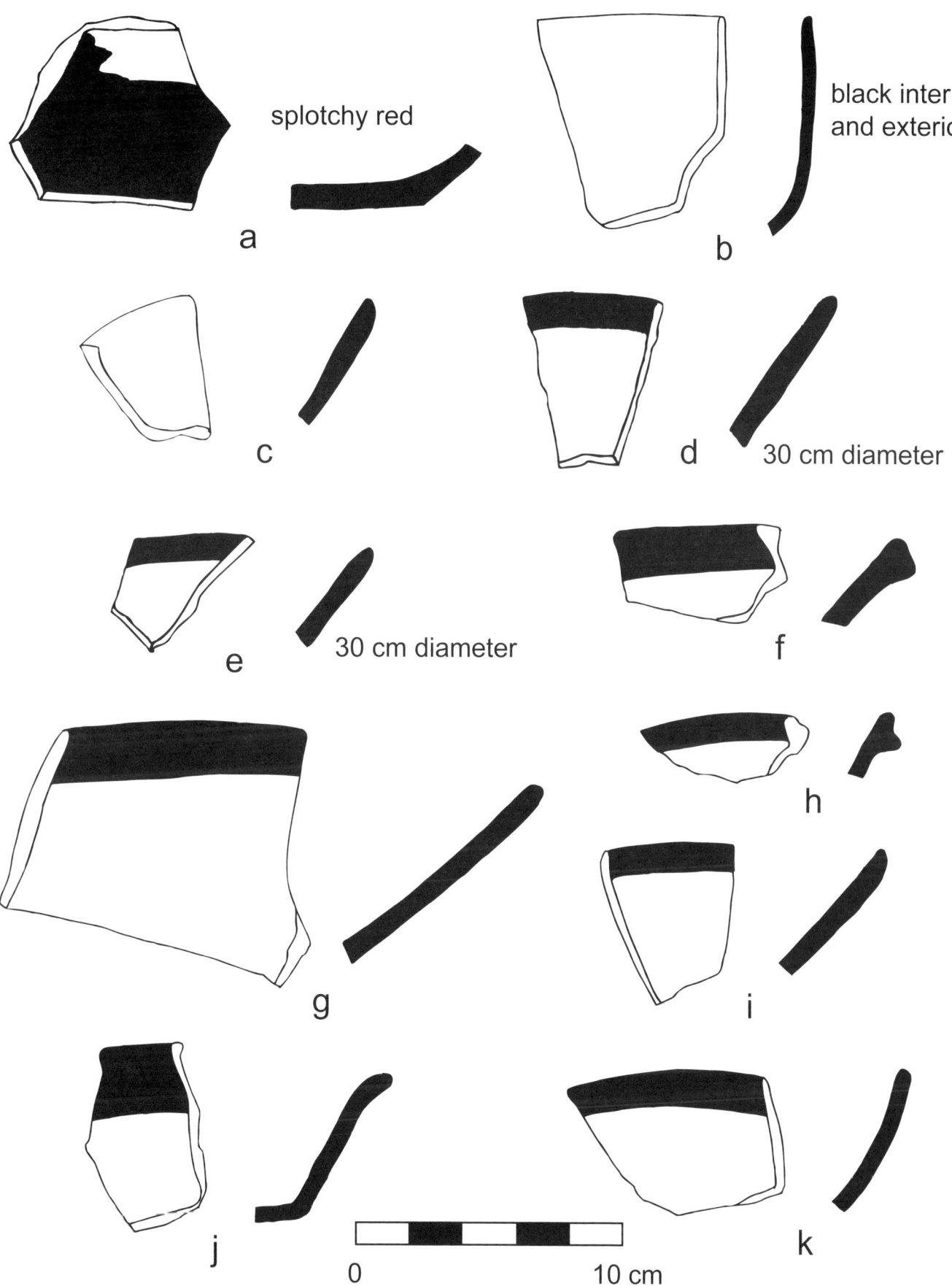

Table A1. Data on G.12 motifs and rim forms from residential structures at Cerro Tilcajete.

	Str. 1 n = 98 (%)	Str. 3 n = 90 (%)	Str. 4 n = 92 (%)		Str. 1 n = 173 (%)	Str. 3 n = 130 (%)	Str. 4 n = 118 (%)
G.12 Base Motif*				*G.12 Rim Motif***			
indeterminate	5.10	2.22	1.09	indeterminate	0.58	0.00	3.39
1	45.92	34.44	54.35	1	2.31	3.85	0.00
2	8.16	11.11	8.70	2	91.91	96.15	96.61
3	3.06	8.89	3.26	3	0.58	0.00	0.00
4	12.24	13.33	6.52	4	1.16	0.00	0.00
5	0.00	2.22	1.09	6	3.47	0.00	0.00
7	2.04	2.22	5.43	17	0.00	0.00	0.85
8	8.16	3.33	5.43	61	0.00	0.00	1.69
9	6.12	7.78	4.35	*G.12 Rim Form****			
10	0.00	2.22	0.00	indeterminate	6.94	3.85	2.54
11	2.04	0.00	0.00	1	22.54	38.46	33.90
12	3.06	0.00	0.00	3	1.73	1.54	0.00
13	1.02	0.00	2.17	4	3.47	7.69	6.78
14	0.00	1.11	1.09	11	1.16	0.00	0.00
15	1.02	4.44	2.17	12	0.00	0.00	0.85
16	1.02	0.00	1.09	27	0.00	0.77	0.00
17	1.02	5.56	2.17	31	29.48	10.77	11.86
19	0.00	1.11	0.00	35	3.47	7.69	3.39
20	0.00	0.00	1.09	36	0.00	0.77	0.00
G.12 Base Quality*				37	17.92	14.62	16.10
sloppy	21.43	26.67	31.52	38	0.58	1.54	6.78
non-sloppy	50.00	48.89	36.96	40	10.40	7.69	10.17
indeterminate	28.57	24.44	31.52	45	0.58	0.77	4.24
				46	1.16	0.77	0.85
				47	0.58	0.77	2.54
				48	0.00	0.77	0.00
				49	0.00	0.77	0.00
				70	0.00	0.77	0.00

*See Figure A4.
**See Figure A5.
***See Chapter 4, Figures 4.30-4.31.

Table A2. Diagnostic elements of G.29 vessels in residential structures.

	Str. 1 n = 22 (%)	Str. 3 n = 68 (%)	Str. 4 n = 113 (%)
Exterior Surface Color			
orange/red paint	68.18	50.00	21.24
black	0.00	2.94	0.88
brownish	31.82	47.06	77.88
*Rim Form**			
1	0.00	4.41	3.54
4	0.00	13.24	11.50
6	63.64	29.41	10.62
10	0.00	1.47	0.00
20	4.55	0.00	0.00
32	0.00	0.00	0.88
38	0.00	0.00	1.77
39	0.00	0.00	1.77
46	0.00	0.00	0.88
48	0.00	2.94	0.00
49	0.00	1.47	1.77
65	0.00	0.00	3.54

*See Chapter 4, Figures 4.30-4.31.

G.29 vessels appear less frequently in high-status residences at Cerro Tilcajete (Table 4.7). Table A2 indicates several characteristics of G.29 vessels. In higher-status residences (Structures 1 and 3), most G.29s are decorated with red paint and the vessels themselves have a limited number of rim forms. In contrast, in Structure 4 at Cerro Tilcajete, most G.29s are undecorated—they have a greenish-brown color—and the vessels exhibit a wider variety of rim forms. In part, these vessels may have been produced because they imitated the form and decoration of some types of red-painted cream-paste vessels manufactured near Monte Albán.

Orange Wares

The orange-paste ware actually encompasses a wide variety of paste color and texture. Orange pastes range from rose to orange to brick-colored. Almost all are sand-tempered and many are simply oxidized gray-paste vessels (Caso et al. 1967:55-57), so they could have been made at many locations throughout the valley.

A.9 (Fig. A9, Table A3). This type has a sand-tempered paste with a very hard consistency. The A.9, one of the most diagnostic of the Monte Albán II vessel types, does appear to begin and end with the Monte Albán II period. Some vessels are slipped or burnished with a shiny surface, and all have painted designs in a red to reddish-brown color. Many A.9s have step-fret motifs, but unlike cream-paste vessels with incising and bulbous feet (C.11 and C.12), they also have geometric and other line designs. The majority of A.9 vessels are bowls; some have supports that are smaller than, but otherwise similar to, the bulbous supports found on C.11 and C.12 vessels (Caso et al. 1967: Plate 11 and Figs. 207-208 illustrate vessels from Monte Albán).

In Chapter 3, I noted that during the mapping and survey of Monte Albán, A.9 pottery was found primarily around the Main Plaza and on an eastern spur of the site. On the valley-wide regional survey, A.9 pottery was heavily concentrated in the Valle Grande-Ocotlán and Tlacolula branches, and was largely absent from Etla (Kowalewski et al. 1989:168-79). These data may suggest that A.9s were produced in the Valle Grande-Ocotlán or Tlacolula; however, at Cerro Tilcajete, A.9s are much less popular in the two elite residences (Structures 1 and 3) than are incised red and black cream wares (combined C.11 and C.12) (Table 4.7). It is probable that even if A.9 vessels were made in the Valle Grande-Ocotlán, they did not convey the same status information as cream wares.

Nevertheless, the frequency of A.9 vessels as a proportion of all orange ware is higher in higher-status residences (in Structure 1 it is 44.94%) and lower in lower-status residences (in Structure 4 it is 21.05%) (Table A3). So, A.9 vessels probably do convey something about a household's relative position at a site, while cream-paste vessels tell us more about a household's participation in the valley-wide elite economy.

A.9 vessels occur primarily as outleaned-wall bowls. A few hollow feet (five total) were coded in the three structures at Cerro Tilcajete and some bowls clearly had hollow supports (Fig. A9k). A few body sherds are from jars, but it is not clear what rim forms these vessels had (see Fig. A9b, c).

A.11 (Fig. A10, Table A3). This type has a yellow to rose paste with designs carved or scratched into the exterior surface. At Monte Albán, A.11s occur as bowls and jars (Caso et al. 1967:78). At Cerro Tilcajete, the few examples I have occur as bowls and one odd example of an upturned plate. These vessels probably are fancy versions of simple orange-paste bowls, but more study of the production and distribution of decorated A.9 and A.11 ceramics remains to be done.

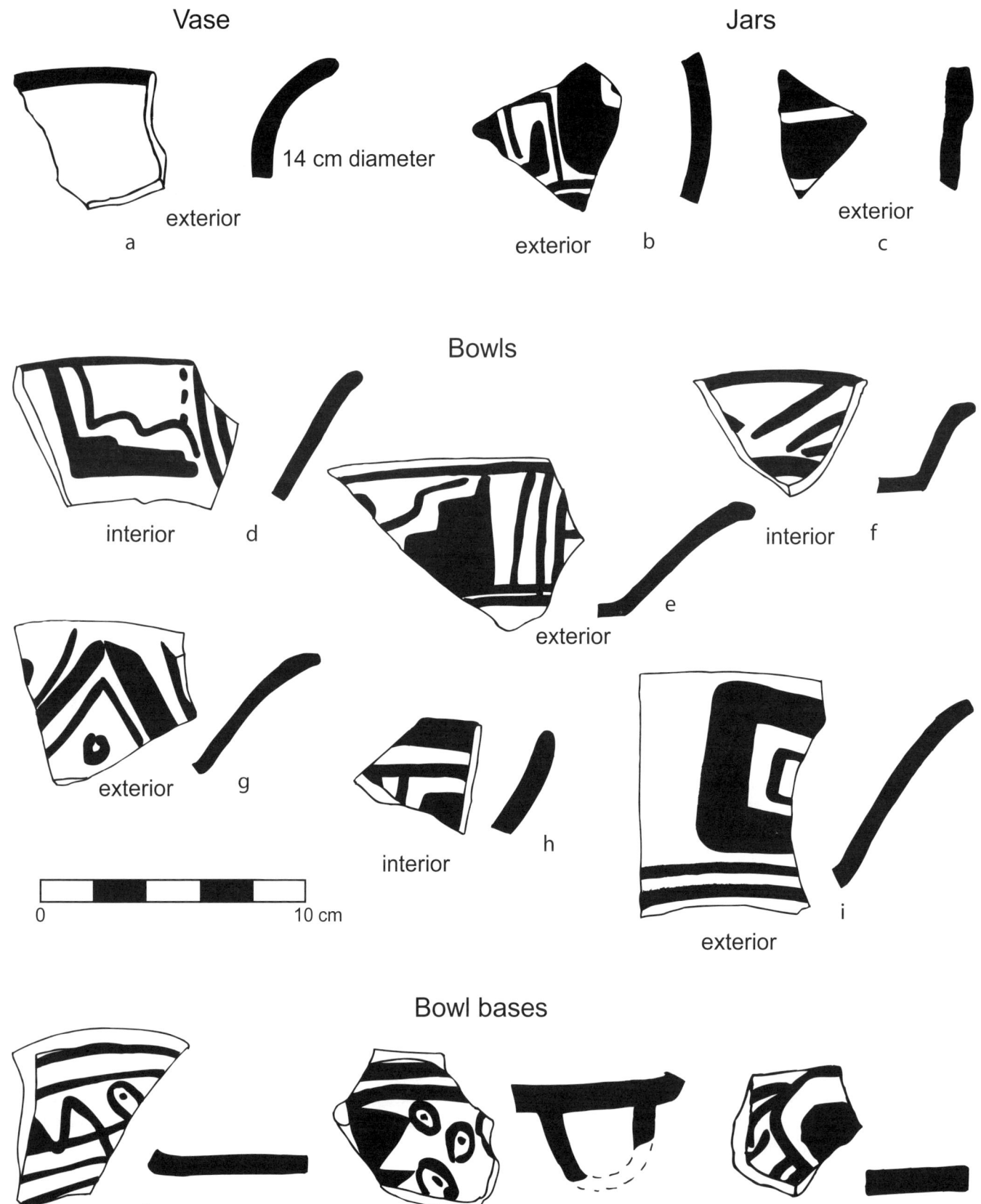

Appendix A: Ceramic Terms, Analysis, and Illustrations

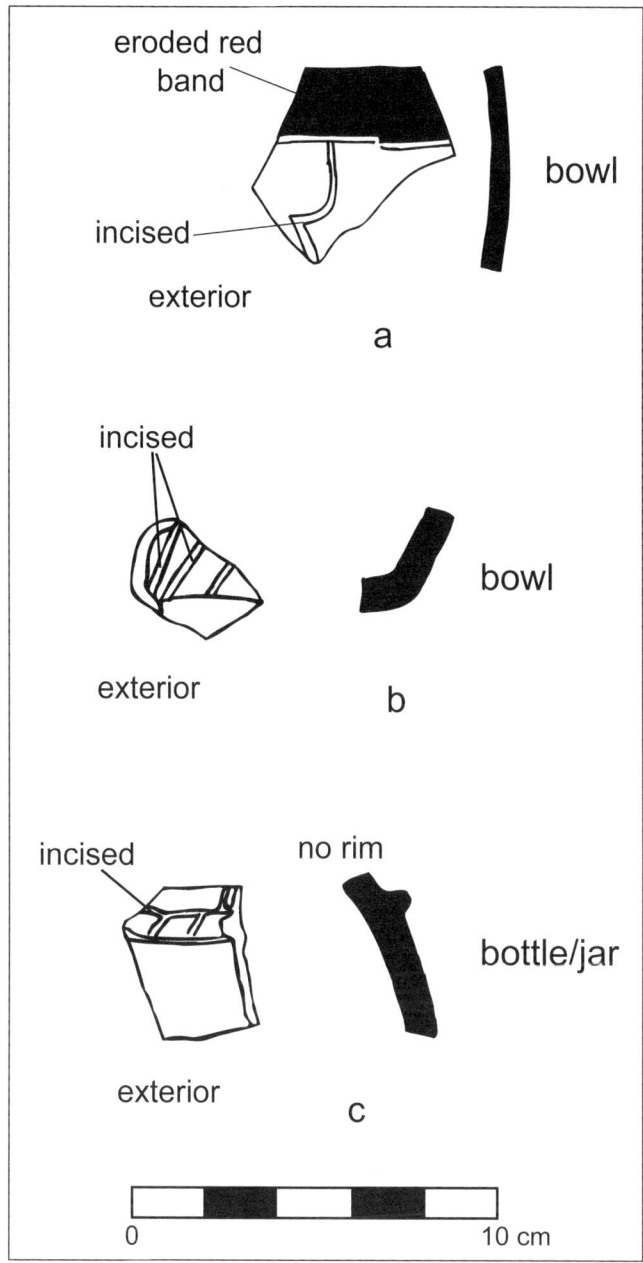

Figure A10. Examples of A.11 rim form and vessel decoration from Cerro Tilcajete.

Table A3. Diagnostic aspects of orange-paste ceramics.*

	Str. 1	Str. 3	Str. 4
As Percent of Paste			
undecorated	46.07%	52.86%	80.38%
A.9	44.94%	35.71%	21.05%
A.11	8.99%	11.43%	1.91%
Undecorated Rim Form	n = 27	n = 19	n = 48
1	1	0	0
4	1	1	13
6	1	3	8
12	0	0	2
19	0	0	1
34	0	0	1
31	2	1	0
46	1	1	0
71	0	0	2
72	0	0	1
73	0	1	0
A.9 Color/Design Location			
interior	50.00%	24.00%	61.36%
exterior	27.50%	56.00%	36.36%
both	15.00%	20.00%	2.27%
unclear	7.50%	0.00%	0.00%
A.9 Rim Form			
1	1	0	2
4	1	1	2
6	3	2	1
31	4	0	0
33	0	1	0
46	4	0	0
71	0	2	4
72	2	2	1
73	1	1	0
74	1	0	0
75	4	1	0
A.11 Rim Form			
31	1	0	0
73	1	0	0
94	0	0	1

*For rim forms, see Chapter 4, Figures 4.30-4.31.

(*Facing page*) Figure A9. Examples of A.9 rim form and vessel decoration from Cerro Tilcajete. *a*, vase; *b-c*, jars; *d-i*, bowls; *j-l*, bowl bases. Most bowls probably were flat-bottomed but some had hollow supports (illustrated in *k*).

Figure A11. K.17 vessels with incised motifs. Bottom right sherd is 4 cm.

Café Wares

Probably the most diverse group of ceramics are the café wares. Caso et al. (1967:49) noted that some of the cafés were tempered with sand, some with diorite, and about 15% of them were "strange" types with other textures. Many café vessels were utilitarian cooking wares that were probably made at every site, or even by every household, in the valley. Chapter 4 addressed the frequency of café wares and vessel forms in Structures 1 and 3 at Cerro Tilcajete, where it appears that some "finer" Monte Albán II café wares may have conveyed status information. A preliminary study of the trace elements of Monte Albán II café wares from Cerro Tilcajete shows that they are a compositionally diverse group (Sherman et al. 2004). There are a few decorated café wares that probably convey chronological and status information.

K.2. This is a thick-walled jar manufactured from sand-tempered paste. The exterior is roughly incised or scratched (in no particular pattern), as if to make the vessel "more rugged" (Caso et al. 1967:50). It occurs infrequently in Monte Albán I and II and becomes more frequent in Periods III, IV, and V—meaning that the K.2 does not function as a temporal diagnostic. Very few of these jars were found at Cerro Tilcajete.

K.3. This type is described by Caso et al. (1967:50-51) as having a reddish-colored, sand-tempered paste that can be burnished on the interior, and can be covered with a brown-red to bright red slip. At Monte Albán, there are two categories of vessel forms. The first is made up of large domestic jars and bowls, some with mat impressions on the base. The second is made up of small, well-burnished bowls. I found examples of only the second group at Cerro Tilcajete. These sherds occurred in low numbers (a total of 27 K.3 sherds were coded), but they occurred in all three structures (although most were found in Structure 1) and some of the bowls had very fancy rim forms (Fig. 4.30: rim forms 1, 4, 6, 20, 31, 39, 42, 46, 49, 65, 66).

K.7 and K.4. The K.7 first appears late in Monte Albán I, while the K.4 is a Monte Albán II ware; however, these two types are similar in several respects. K.7 ceramics have a range of paste composition, but usually have a dark brown paste and a dark gray burnished exterior (Caso et al. 1967:52-53). The vessel forms are outleaned-wall bowls that may have one or two incised lines on the interior rim (just like gray-paste G.12 vessels).

The K.4 also has a dark brown paste, but these vessels are treated with a dark "slip" that is then polished, often leaving horizontal "bands." K.4 vessel forms are outleaned-wall bowls that sometimes have one or two lines incised in the rim interior.

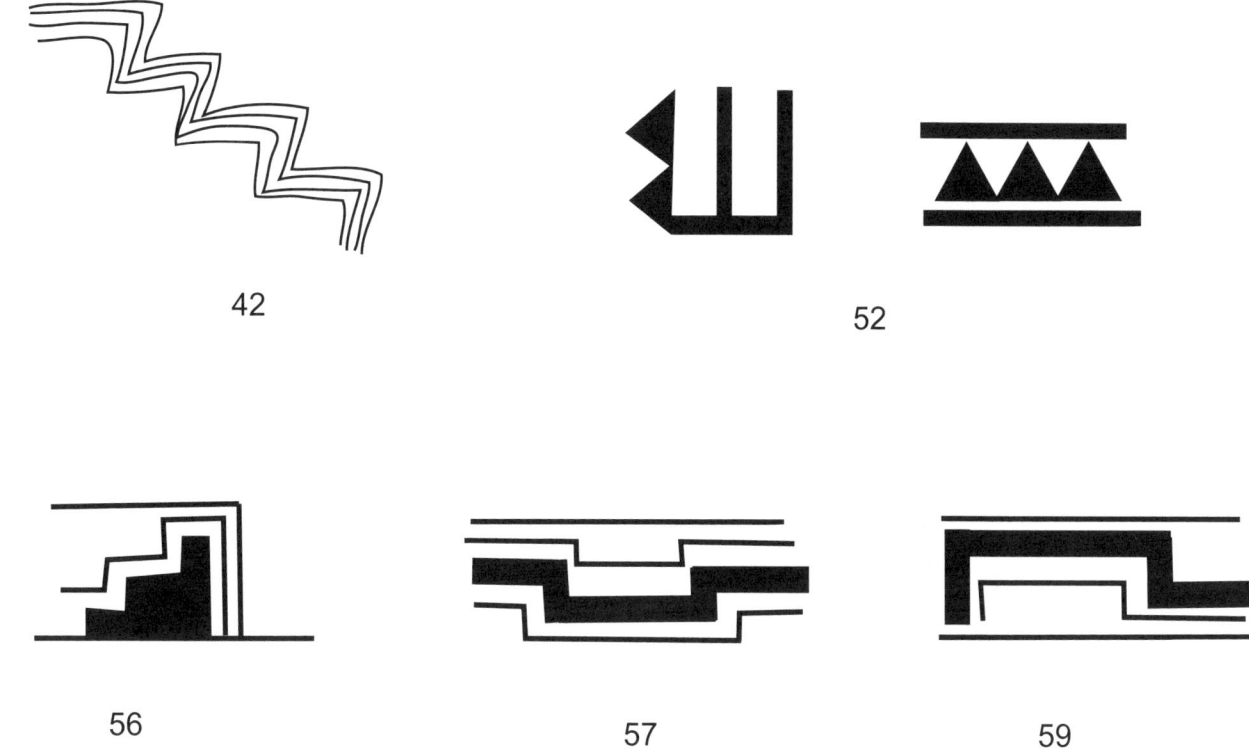

Figure A12. Motifs found on C.11, C.12, and K.17 vessels. Thin line incisions: *41*, exterior scratching visible as parallel lines (not shown); *42*, a step-fret; *43*, indeterminate (not shown). Deep, widely incised motifs: *52*, parallel lines and pennants; *56*, "steps"; *57, 59*, wide-line step-fret.

At Cerro Tilcajete, I coded vessels as K.4s because the bowls (and one example of a shallow cooking bowl) have lines incised at the rim interior. The vessels have a dark slip but do not necessarily have polished horizontal bands. K.4s appear most frequently in Structure 4 at Cerro Tilcajete (Figs. 4.30-4.31: rim forms 1, 4, 6, 15, 38, 45, 46, 51, 72).

K.17 (Fig. A11). Caso et al. (1967:53) considered this type "intrusive," perhaps because it has a finer paste type than most other café wares and because it was found in small quantities at Monte Albán, the capital. They suggested that the K.17 was a regional variant of the C.20 because the exteriors of the two types are almost the same. K.17 vessels have a dark brown paste; black, dark brown, or dark gray slip; and interior and exterior burnishing. At Monte Albán, vessel forms include outleaned, incurving, and straight-wall bowls.

At Cerro Tilcajete, K.17 vessels occur more frequently in the higher-status residences (Structures 1 and 3) than in the lower-status residence (Structure 4) (Table 4.7). These vessels occur as bowls with rim forms 1, 2, 4, 6, 7, 10, 17, 31, 35, 39, 40, 45, 49, 59, 62, 63, and 71; however, K.17s with incising occur only with rim forms 2, 6, and 63 (Fig. 4.30a). As shown in Figure A12, I found K.17 vessels with the following kinds of decorative incising: 41 ($n = 8$), 42 ($n = 7$), 56 ($n = 1$), 57 ($n = 1$), and 59 ($n = 1$). It is difficult to infer too much from these data.

In Structure 1 at Cerro Tilcajete, K.17 and C.20 vessels make up 12.93% of the diagnostics coded, suggesting a real preference for dark-colored serving vessels (Table 4.7). Only 7 of the 115 K.17 diagnostics coded (or 6%) have incised decoration, while 55 of the 220 (25%) diagnostics coded as black creams (C.11 and C.20) do.

It is possible that—like A.9 ceramics—K.17 ceramics were locally made, but conveyed less status than imported cream-paste vessels; however, much more work needs to be done to determine the production network for fancy café-paste vessels.

I would suggest that during Monte Albán II, there was a preference for dark-colored serving vessels (K.17, C.12, and C.20), at least at Cerro Tilcajete. For Monte Albán, Caso et al. (1967:68) also suggested that dark-colored cream-paste vessels were more popular during Monte Albán II than were red-painted cream-paste vessels.

Motifs found on C.11, C.12, and K.17 vessels include thin line incisions as well as deep and widely incised motifs (Fig. A12). Thin line incisions include exterior scratching visible as parallel lines and step-frets. Examples of deep and widely incised motifs include parallel lines and pennants, "steps," and step-frets.

Figure A13. Photo of C.7 and C.11 sherds found at Cerro Tilcajete. *top row*, C.11 sherds with zigzag or lightning motifs; *bottom row, left*, C.7 sherd; *bottom row, right*, C.11 sherd with a step-fret motif (sherd is 8.5 cm).

Cream Wares

Some of the most diagnostic Monte Albán II wares are made from cream paste. Caso et al. (1967:44-45) noted that there was "fundamentally only one kind of cream paste," which they divided into types based on decoration. In Chapter 4, I evaluated data showing that cream-paste wares were produced near Monte Albán and that their distribution to subregional centers such as Cerro Tilcajete was probably controlled by the capital. The distribution of cream-paste wares is one way to examine how regional elite participated in a production sphere defined by Monte Albán. Six cream-paste types are referred to in this text (also see Tables A4-A6).

C.5. These vessels, with a very fine white slip, really are a Monte Albán I type. Only one C.5 was coded in the Structure 1 excavations and that vessel could have been an heirloom.

C.6. This type is a thin- to medium-walled serving vessel with a clear to reddish coffee-color slip. Caso et al. (1967:46-47) state that the C.6 appears early in Monte Albán I and becomes much more frequent in Monte Albán II; the slip color becomes lighter over time.

C.7 (Figs. A13-A14). This type is a thin- to medium-walled vessel that has an orange-red slip over which red paint is applied. It can have cloudy black "spots" created during firing. C.7s appear in small quantities in Monte Albán I, but are much more typical of Monte Albán II (Caso et al. 1967:47). The red paint used on the vessels almost always contains hematite, easily noticeable because the paint's shiny flecks glisten in the light. Hematite sources have been identified in the Etla branch of the Valley of Oaxaca (Flannery and Marcus 1994:23).

C.20 (Fig. A15). This type is a cream-paste vessel with a polished dark brown or black slip. It appears in very small quantities in Monte Albán I, but becomes much more frequent and more finely made in Monte Albán II (Caso et al. 1967:47).

C.11 and C.12 (Figs. A13-15). Caso et al. defined the C.11 as a C.6 or C.7 with post-firing incising in a step-fret motif (*xicalcoliuhqui*). The C.12 is a C.20 vessel with the same kind

Table A4. All cream-paste rim forms coded in Structures 1, 3, and 4.

Rim Form*	Str. 1	Str. 3	Str. 4	Total Rims	Freq. Rims (%)
Bowl					
1	34	53	2	89	22.19
2	18	6	2	26	6.48
3	1	11	5	17	4.24
4	20	32	0	52	12.97
6	25	40	9	74	18.45
7	3	5	0	8	2.00
17	2	0	0	2	0.50
23	3	2	0	5	1.25
26	1	0	0	1	0.25
31	29	19	7	55	13.72
35	5	10	6	21	5.24
39	2	0	0	2	0.50
40	1	6	2	9	2.24
41	1	1	0	2	0.50
42	1	0	0	1	0.25
43	2	0	0	2	0.50
46	4	0	1	5	1.25
47	1	0	0	1	0.25
48	4	0	0	4	1.00
59	1	4	3	8	2.00
63	0	1	0	1	0.25
65	0	1	0	1	0.25
71	1	0	0	1	0.25
72	1	0	0	1	0.25
73	0	2	0	2	0.50
Tecomate					
49	3	0	0	3	0.75
Comal					
54	1	0	0	1	0.25
Jar					
57	1	0	0	1	0.25
58	0	0	1	1	0.25
Vase					
10	3	2	0	5	1.25
Total Rims	168	195	38	401	100.00

*See Chapter 4, Figures 4.30-4.31.

Table A5. Motifs on C.11 and C.12 vessels.*

Decoration	Str. 1	Str. 3	Str. 4	Total	Freq. Decoration (%)
41	36	33	21	90	46.88
42	37	15	8	60	31.25
43	13	15	6	34	17.71
52	2	1	0	3	1.56
56	3	0	0	3	1.56
57	1	1	0	2	1.04
Total	92	65	35	192	100.00

*See Figures A11-A12.

Table A6. The frequency of cream-paste types of all decorated cream vessels coded.

	Str. 1 (%)	Str. 3 (%)	Str. 4 (%)
C.5	0.18	0.00	0.00
C.6	21.92	29.28	26.95
C.7	30.80	35.24	38.32
C.11	7.25	6.45	19.76
C.12	9.96	9.43	1.80
C.20	29.89	19.60	13.17
Total	100.00	100.00	100.00

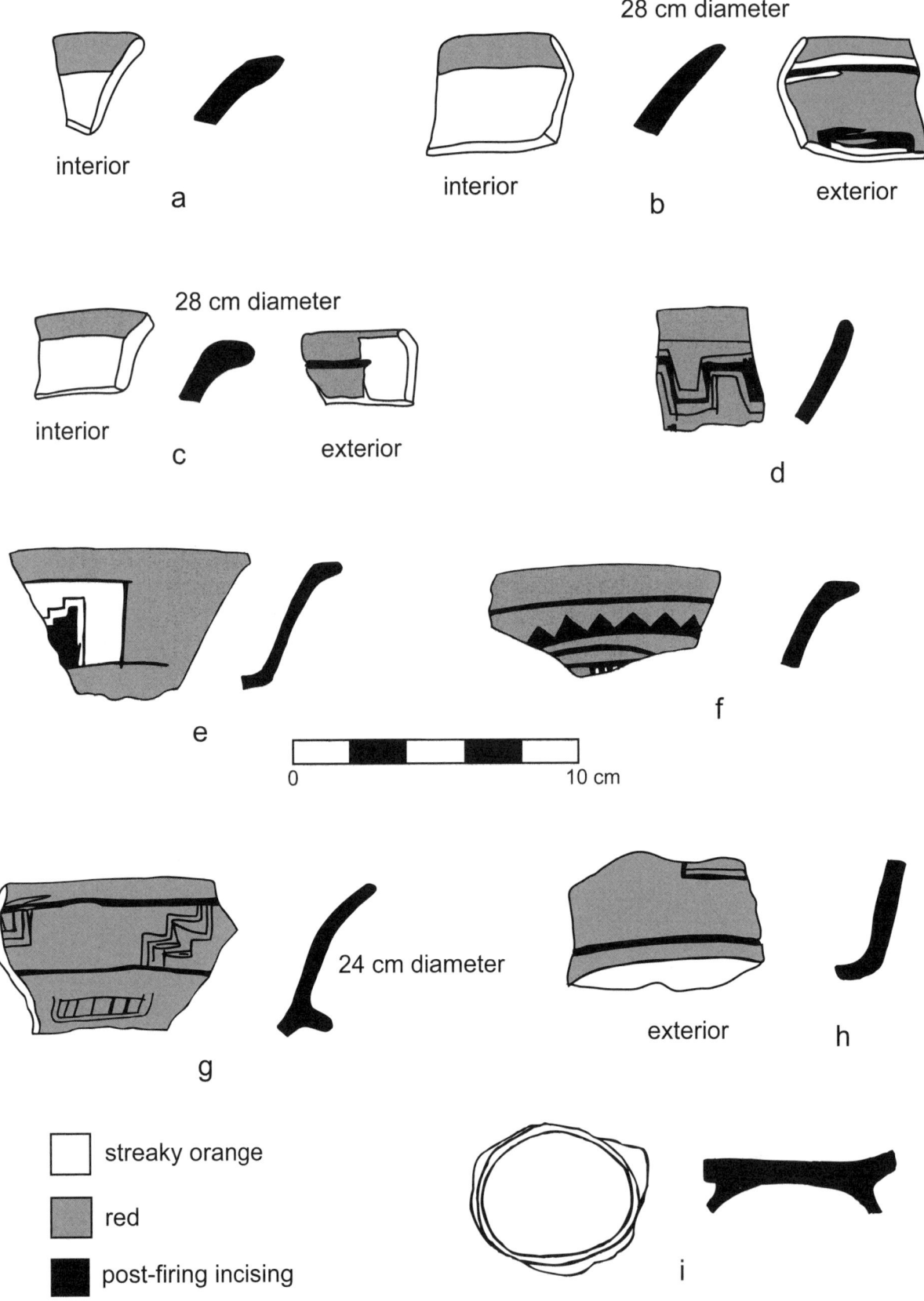

Figure A14. Examples of C.7 and C.11 rim form and vessel decoration. All vessels were found at Cerro Tilcajete. *a*, C.7; *b-h*, C.11; *i*, C.7 base.

Appendix A: Ceramic Terms, Analysis, and Illustrations 117

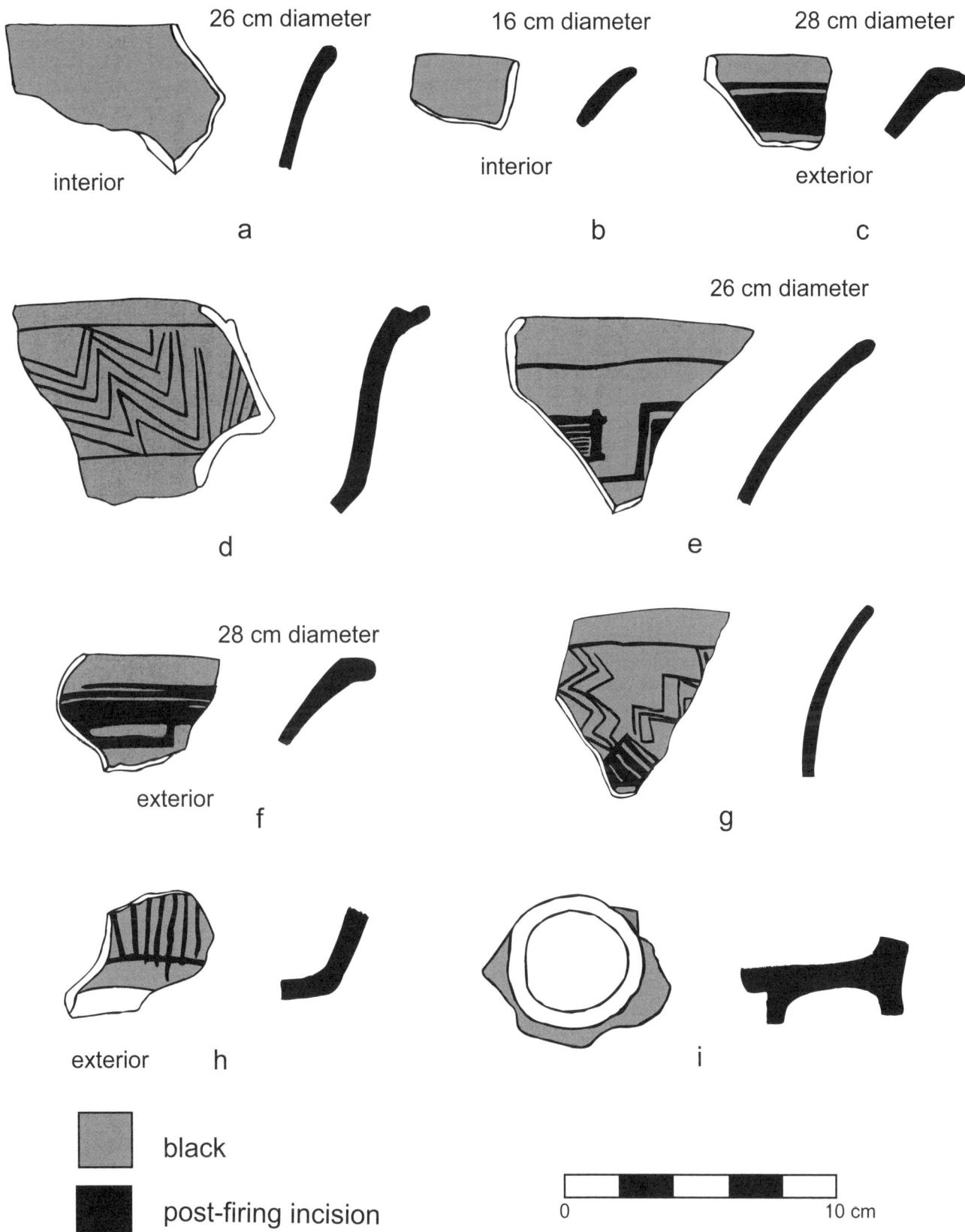

Figure A15. Examples of C.12 and C.20 rim form and vessel decoration. All vessels were found at Cerro Tilcajete. *a*, C.20; *b-h*, C.12; *i*, C.20 base.

of post-firing incising. In addition, C.12s often have vestiges of red pigment rubbed into the incisings. In both cases, the incising occurs in zones, so not every sherd from a C.11 or C.12 vessel would exhibit the design, and such undecorated sherds would be coded as a C.6, C.7, or C.20.

In tombs and burials at Monte Albán where whole vessels were available for study, Caso and his colleagues determined that while C.6, C.7, and C.20 vessels occurred as bowls and bowls with large hollow supports, C.11 and C.12 vessels occurred almost exclusively as bowls with large hollow supports (Caso et al. 1967: Table 7).

At Cerro Tilcajete, red (C.7 and C.11) and black (C.12 and C.20) cream-paste vessels occurred in all three residences. In Structures 1, 3, and 4, red cream-paste vessels account for 9.70%, 9.61%, and 6.39% of the diagnostic types coded, while black vessels account for 10.16%, 6.69%, and 1.65% of the diagnostic types coded, respectively (Table 4.7). While it is true that C.11 vessels occur roughly in the same proportion in all three structures, I suggest that overall, higher-status residents had greater access to cream wares. In Chapter 4, we noted that an incomplete C.11 vessel was recovered in a lower-status burial context in Structure 4 at Cerro Tilcajete. Nevertheless, there are differences in how cream-paste vessels were acquired and used. Table A6 gives the distribution of decorated cream types in the three structures. C.6 ceramics occur at about the same frequency in all three residences. Red-painted cream wares constitute a much greater percentage of cream wares in Structure 4, while black cream wares make up a much greater percentage of the ceramics in Structure 1. Overall, while high-ranking elites in Structure 1 obtained more C.11 and C.12 vessels, they also may have preferred black incised vessels over red incised vessels, or at least those black incised types were more available to them.

Only two cream-paste jar rims and one *comal* rim were coded in residential structures. As seen in Table A4, vases do occur, but only one of the five vase rims was a C.12—a vessel with exterior incised designs. Most vessels were bowls, and rim forms 1, 4, 6, and 31 made up 67.35% of the rims coded by form at the site (Fig. 4.30a, Table A4). Also, while twenty-five bowls, one jar, one *tecomate*, one *comal*, and two jar rim forms were coded for all cream-paste vessels, C.11 and C.12 vessels occurred with only twelve rim forms (rims 1, 2, 3, 4, 6, 7, 10, 31, 35, 40, 46, 59). Finally, decoration on most C.11 and C.12 vessels appears as thin, incised designs in the form of zigzags and step-frets. A few vessels have very wide and deeply incised step-frets on the body of the vessel (see Figs. A13 *bottom right*, A14*e*). In Chapter 2, and in a detailed study of cream-paste vessels from Monte Albán, Cerro Tilcajete, and Yaasuchi, Jason Sherman and I suggest zigzag and step-fret iconography is associated with *Cociyo*.

Summary

To conclude, A.9, G.29, G.34, C.11, and C.12 types are good Monte Albán II diagnostics. G.12 bowl bases occur both in Late Monte Albán I and in Monte Albán II. For Monte Albán II, I have suggested that more of these G.12 bowls are sloppily made and that their popularity diminished in favor of cream- and orange-paste decorated wares.

Data from Cerro Tilcajete allow me to suggest that a Monte Albán II ceramic assemblage from an elite context or from a site with close ties to Monte Albán will contain a relatively high frequency of cream-paste ceramics in relation to serving wares (locally) made in café, gray, and orange paste. Still, it should not be surprising to find a number of "local" ceramics that imitate, in decoration or form, cream-paste vessels; good examples are red-painted versions of the G.29 and black versions of the K.17.

In general, elite residences outside the capital of Monte Albán will contain a more limited range of cream-paste vessels and most of the forms and sherds coded will be bowl rims. However, cream vessels may tend to be the most highly decorated—C.11 and C.12 bowls with bulbous feet—because such vessels fulfilled particular roles in domestic ceremony.

More work needs to be done to determine the patterns in the production and distribution of G.29, A.9, and K.17 vessels during Monte Albán II, because this information surely will shed light on the local and valley-wide ceramic production and exchange networks.

Appendix B

Human Remains from Surface Collections and Features in Structures at Cerro Tilcajete

William N. Duncan

In 2006, I studied the human remains from Cerro Tilcajete, Oaxaca, Mexico. Most contexts at the site, especially test pits and middens, produced fragmentary remains of adults, children, and infants. Complete burials were recovered only in Structure 4.

LM 173 Collection Square

A surface collection located at the southwest corner of Plaza II produced a fragment of a child's T1-9 vertebra (left neural arch), a fragment of a rib body (a rib between rib numbers 3 and 12; too fragmentary to age), and a partial left maxilla (adult, under 40 years old). The maxilla is of great interest because it had been cut horizontally through the inferior aspect of the nasal aperture and was probably cut vertically at the posterior aspect of the mouth, but postmortem damage makes this uncertain. There were no fragments of the left palatine bone and only fragments of the tooth roots left in occlusion. The superior aspect of the bone, though, was clearly cut in antiquity. The superior surface of the bone is parallel to what would have been the roof of the mouth and is smooth. The absence of any cutmarks or scrapemarks suggests that the bones were either defleshed when the maxilla was extracted or that the flesh was removed in some way that did not involve cutting (for example, boiling). The sex of the individual is unknown but the anterior median palatine suture was unfused, indicating that the individual was not in advanced age (under 40).

LM 171 Collection Square

This collection square is on the same terrace where Structure 4 was excavated. The collection produced human bone fragments from at least three individuals: one child, 3-6 years of age; one child, 5-9 years of age; and fragmentary adult remains (femoral and metacarpal fragments).

Structure 1

The looters' pit produced three teeth: a left maxillary third premolar, a permanent left mandibular canine, and a left maxillary deciduous canine.

Test Pit C, dug into the platform supporting Structure 1, produced a permanent mandibular first right molar.

Test Pit D, dug into the platform supporting Structure 1, produced a fragment of a young adult's left parietal.

Test Pit F, dug into the platform supporting Structure 1, produced a permanent maxillary first right molar.

Structure 3

Two proveniences make up Feature 1, a midden located just east of Structure 3. Two additional proveniences are stratigraphically above the feature. These four contexts produced remains from at least three individuals: an infant, an older child (6-10 years of age), and an adult. The infant probably was a primary burial that eroded out at some point. The adult is unlikely to be a primary interment as it consists of only isolated fragments. It is not clear if the older child is an eroded burial or (like the adult) just partial remains mixed in the midden.

Test Pit 1 was dug 76 cm into the platform supporting Structure 3, until striking bedrock and sterile soil. The test pit contained trash and adobes used to build the platform. The fill produced fragments of human remains:

1 right tibia from an infant
1 permanent fragmentary mandibular left central incisor
1 permanent mandibular left third premolar
1 right rib fragment from an adult
1 left third metatarsal from an adult that was burned

Test Pit 4 was excavated 124 cm into the platform supporting Structure 3. This test pit contained trash and adobes used to build the platform. The fill produced part of a skull and one cervical vertebra of a ten- to fifteen-year-old. Some burned cortical fragments were also mixed in this context.

Structure 4

Human remains were buried in four discrete contexts in Structure 4.

Burial 1: A child, 4-8 years of age. An adult left hamate bone and a burned animal bone were included with the remains.

Burial 3: A child, 5-9 years of age. An animal bone was included with the remains.

Burial 4: A child, 3-6 years of age, partially destroyed by an intrusive hearth. The context also contained femoral and metacarpal fragments from an adult.

Appendix C

The Shell Assemblage from Cerro Tilcajete

Gary M. Feinman and Linda M. Nicholas

In March 2007, we studied the shell assemblage from Cerro Tilcajete, Oaxaca, Mexico. This brief preamble to the tables serves both to provide an analytical context for the shell identifications that we made and to present some basic observations regarding the assemblage examined. Shell from the site included ornaments as well as worked debris and unmodified fragments. The shell reported on here includes 31 examples from surface collections (Table C1) as well as 118 examples from four excavation areas with Monte Albán II structures (Tables C2-C5).

Our experience with prehispanic marine shell from southern Mexico stems from our investigations at Ejutla, Oaxaca, Mexico (Feinman and Nicholas 1993, 1995), a Classic-period site where we recorded high intensity marine shell ornament manufacture for exchange. At that site, we found and analyzed well over 20,000 pieces of shell. Our experience with shell is largely self-taught, gained through analytical experience and background research. Our efforts rely heavily on published works by trained malacologists (e.g., Keen 1958; Morris 1966). In addition to the prehispanic shell assemblage from Ejutla, we also have examined archaeological shell collections from Monte Albán (Feinman and Nicholas 2000), Sola de Vega (Nicholas and Feinman 2002), and other Oaxacan contexts. Because our background is heavily experiential, we are most familiar with the shell species that are found in abundance in the archaeological contexts that we have studied. As a consequence, we are more apt to be able to identify marine species than freshwater varieties of shell.

The Cerro Tilcajete shell assemblage stands out from that of Ejutla in several respects. Like the shell assemblage at Monte Albán (Feinman and Nicholas 2000), that at Cerro Tilcajete has a higher ratio of ornaments (over 50% of the total shell) to debris and worked pieces in comparison to Ejutla. In contrast, at Ejutla, the abundance of debris was great and the percentage of finished ornaments small (less than 1%). The high percentage of ornaments reflects the much lower intensity of production activities (sensu Costin 1991) at the studied contexts of Cerro Tilcajete and Monte Albán compared to examined proveniences at Ejutla. What shell working occurred at the investigated contexts of the two former sites likely was for more local and immediate use. The sizes (the number of pieces) of the assemblages also are in accord with this view.

Another interesting aspect of the Cerro Tilcajete shell assemblage is the high frequency of whole shell beads. The vast majority of the ornaments (finished and unfinished) were whole shells. We should note that all 46 shells from the Structure 4 terrace came from Burial 1, a child four to eight years old. The production of whole shell beads requires just the perforation of the wall of the shell and occasionally some slight trimming of the shell. Thus, the production of these whole shell ornaments requires less concentrated work and seemingly skill than, for example, the manufacture of a cut, highly modified mother of pearl (*Pinctada mazatlanica*) ornament. The abundance of the whole shell ornaments at Cerro Tilcajete would seem to indicate that marine shell was procured, minimally modified, and then used locally in burial and other contexts. Not surprisingly, given the high frequency of whole shell beads at Cerro Tilcajete, gastropod genera that were generally used prehispanically in this fashion (the making of whole shell beads for stringing) are well represented (e.g., *Marginella*, *Olivella*) in this assemblage.

Finally, we note that although the intensity of manufacture does not seem especially high compared to what we observed at Ejutla, there is the possibility that some more labor intensive, low intensity ornament manufacture did occur at Cerro Tilcajete

Table C1. Shell found in surface collection units at Cerro Tilcajete.

Surface Collection Unit	Quantity	Family	Scientific Name	Object, Class	Type
133	1	Gastropod	*Cassis coarctata*	ornament, finished	pendant
139	1	Gastropod	*Mitrella?* sp.	ornament, finished	bead
141	1	Pelecypod	*Pinctada mazatlanica*	production by-product	wall
145	1	Gastropod	*Olivella* sp.	ornament, finished	bead
145	1	Pelecypod	*Pinctada mazatlanica*	unworked fragment	hinge
146	1	Pelecypod	*Pinctada mazatlanica*	production by-product	wall
147	1	Pelecypod	*Pinctada mazatlanica*	production by-product	wall
147	1	Gastropod	unidentified	ornament, unfinished	blank
152	1	Pelecypod	*Pinctada mazatlanica*	ornament, finished	pendant
152	1	Pelecypod	*Pinctada mazatlanica*	production by-product	wall
152	4	Pelecypod	*Pinctada mazatlanica*	unworked fragment	wall
152	1	Gastropod	*Olivella* sp.	ornament, finished	bead
152	1	Pelecypod	*Spondylus* sp.	unworked fragment	wall
153	1	Pelecypod	*Pinctada mazatlanica*	unworked fragment	wall
153	1	Gastropod	*Malea ringens*	production by-product	spire
154	1	Pelecypod	nacreous, unidentified	unworked fragment	wall
156	1	Pelecypod	*Pitar?* sp.	ornament, finished	bead
157	1	Pelecypod	*Pinctada mazatlanica*	production by-product	wall
157	1	Pelecypod	*Pinctada mazatlanica*	unworked fragment	wall
165	1	Gastropod	unidentified	unworked fragment	body whorl
165	1	Pelecypod	*Pinctada mazatlanica*	production by-product	wall
166	1	Gastropod	unidentified	unworked fragment	wall
167	1	Pelecypod	*Pinctada mazatlanica*	unworked fragment	wall
167	1	unidentified	unidentified	unworked fragment	wall
167	1	Gastropod	*Oliva porphyria?*	ornament, finished	pendant
171	1	Pelecypod	*Pinctada mazatlanica*	ornament, finished	pendant
173	1	Pelecypod	*Pinctada mazatlanica*	ornament, finished	placa*
173	1	Pelecypod	*Pinctada mazatlanica*	ornament, finished	bead

*Placas are smooth and flat, possibly used for mosaic inlay or woven into clothing.

Appendix C: The Shell Assemblage from Cerro Tilcajete

Table C2. Shell in excavations by excavation area and genus.

Genus	Mound A	Mound B	Area C	Str. 4 Terrace	Total
Acmaea	1				1
Anadara	1				1
Jenneria			1		1
Marginella	1			46	47
Mitrella?	1				1
Oliva	2				2
Olivella	5				5
Olivella?	1				1
Pinctada	19	4	12		35
Pyrene	1				1
Spondylus	4				4
Turritella	1				1
unidentified	9		9		18
Total	46	4	22	46	118

Table C3. Shell in excavations by excavation area and ornament class.

Object, Class	Mound A	Mound B	Area C	Str. 4 Terrace	Total
ornament, finished	18		5	46	69
ornament, unfinished	6		1		7
production by-product	7		3		10
unworked fragment	13	4	13		30
worked piece	2				2
Total	46	4	22	46	118

Table C4. Shell in excavations at Cerro Tilcajete by object and genus.

Genus	Ornament, Finished	Ornament, Unfinished	Production By-Product	Unworked Fragment	Worked Piece	Total
Acmaea					1	1
Anadara				1		1
Jenneria	1					1
Marginella	47					47
Mitrella?	1					1
Oliva	1			1		2
Olivella	5					5
Olivella?	1					1
Pinctada	10	7	8	10		35
Pyrene	1					1
Spondylus				4		4
Turritella	1					1
unidentified	1		2	14	1	18
Total	69	7	10	30	2	118

Table C5. Shell in excavations at Cerro Tilcajete by ornament type and genus.

Genus	Bead	Pendant	Placa	Ring	Total
Jenneria	1				1
Marginella	47				47
Mitrella?	1				1
Olivella	5	1			6
Olivella?	1				1
Pinctada		2	14	1	17
Pyrene	1				1
Turritella	1				1
unidentified			1		1
Total	57	3	15	1	76

in the Mound A area associated with elite Structure 1 residence. Unfinished ornaments, shell debris, and the waste by-products of manufacture were found here. Five unfinished ornaments were recovered in Mound A compared to only one in Mound B (the location of a two-room temple) and Area C (the location of an elite residence). The species found in Mound A include those Pacific shell varieties (e.g., *Pinctada mazatlanica*, *Spondylus calcifer*) that are highly prominent in ornament manufacture in the Valley of Oaxaca during much of the prehispanic sequence.

References Cited

Costin, Cathy L.
1991 Craft specialization: issues in defining, documenting, and explaining the organization of production. *Archaeological Method and Theory* 3:1-56.

Feinman, Gary M., and Linda M. Nicholas
1993 Shell ornament production in Ejutla: implications for highland-coastal interaction in ancient Oaxaca. *Ancient Mesoamerica* 4:103-19.

1995 Household craft specialization and shell ornament manufacture in Ejutla, Mexico. *Expedition* 37(2):14-25.

2000 High-intensity household-scale production in ancient Mesoamerica: a perspective from Ejutla, Oaxaca. In *Cultural Evolution: Contemporary Viewpoints*, edited by Gary M. Feinman and Linda Manzanilla, pp. 119-42. New York: Kluwer Academic/Plenum Publishers.

Keen, A. Myra
1958 *Shells of Tropical West America: Marine Mollusks from Lower California to Colombia*. Stanford: Stanford University Press.

Morris, Percy A.
1966 *Field Guide to Pacific Coast Shells*, 2nd ed. Boston: Houghton Mifflin Company.

Nicholas, Linda M., and Gary M. Feinman
2002 Shell from Sola de Vega. In *The Sola Valley and the Monte Albán State: A Study of Zapotec Imperial Expansion*, by Andrew K. Balkansky, pp. 123-24. Memoirs, no. 36. Museum of Anthropology, University of Michigan. Ann Arbor.

Appendix D

Resumen en Castellano

Christina Elson

El surgimiento del estado zapoteco culmina a principios del período Formativo Tardío, cerca del año 100 a.C. Para la fase Monte Albán II (100 a.C.–200 d.C.), existen varias indicaciones de organización política a nivel estatal que son evidenciadas por el registro arqueológico. En primer término, se observa un patrón de asentamiento jerárquico de cuatro niveles; Monte Albán, con una población cerca de 14,000 habitantes, era el sitio más grande y la capital del estado, mientras que otros sitios funcionaron como centros secundarios, dispersos y equidistantes de la capital. Cada centro secundario se encontraba, a su vez, rodeado por un anillo de centros terciarios. En segundo término, en la capital y los sitios secundarios, aparece arquitectura estatal como el templo de dos cuartos, el palacio, y el juego de pelota.

El Cerro Tilcajete se encuentra a unos 18.5 km al sureste de la capital sobre la cima de una cresta que alcanza los 300 m sobre el nivel del suelo del valle o hasta aproximadamente 1850 m sobre el nivel del mar. Su ubicación proporciona una vista del valle central y partes de la tierra de aluvión del Valle Grande/Ocotlán. El recorrido sistemático del Valle de Oaxaca identificó el Cerro Tilcajete (SMT-23) durante la fase Monte Albán II como el centro secundario de la zona del Valle Grande/Ocotlán.

Mapeo y recolecciones intensivas de la superficie

En 1993, Charles Spencer y Elsa Redmond llevaron a cabo un programa de mapeo y recolecciones intensivas de la superficie en el sitio. La autora analizó los datos de la superficie y llevó a cabo excavaciones y análisis entre 1999-2001. Los datos demuestran que el sitio fue ocupado casi exclusivamente en la fase Monte Albán II, a diferencia de Dainzú y San José Mogote, ambos sitios secundarios con secuencias largas de ocupación. Era probable que excavaciones en el Cerro Tilcajete pudieron aportar planos arquitectónicos pertenecientes a la fase Monte Albán II y otros datos para investigar si el Cerro Tilcajete funcionaba como un sitio de rango secundario y cual era la relación entre el Cerro Tilcajete y la capital de Monte Albán.

Las recolecciones intensivas de la superficie fueron realizadas en lugares del sitio que podrían dar muestras adecuadas de material, particularmente en áreas asociadas con montículos, terrazas y otros elementos. Para la fase Monte Albán II, habían cuatro tipos de cerámica con base en su pasta y entre ellos varios tipos de cerámica que servían como diagnósticos. La cerámica de las pastas gris, café, y amarillo pudieron haber sido producidas localmente. En cambio, la cerámica de pasta crema probablemente fue producida en masa en los alrededores de Monte Albán bajo algún grado de organización central.

Con base en su color exterior, se puede dividir la cerámica de pasta crema en tres tipos: café claro (C.6), rojo (C.7 y C.11) y negro (C.12 y C.20). Entre ellos, los tipos C.11 y C.12 llevan diseños de *xicalcoliuhquis* y de zigzags esgrafiados al exterior. El diseño de *xicalcoliuhquis* ha sido interpretado como un símbolo iconográfico de fuego-serpiente o rayo que se desarrolla de diseños conocidos desde la época Formativa Temprana (Flannery y Marcus 1994). El diseño de zigzag ha sido interpretado como el rayo de la lluvia. Así, los dos diseños tienen una asociación con *Cociyo*, un dios de gran importancia para la agricultura y la abundancia. La mayoría de las vasijas completas de los tipos de pasta crema C.11 y C.12 encontradas en tumbas y ofrendas en Monte Albán eran elaboradas con bordes elegantes y tres o cuatro soportes cilíndricos grandes y huecos. Estas vasijas seguramente requirieron mayor inversión de tiempo para su producción, además de ser difíciles para transportar. Generalmente, la cerámica de pasta crema es considerada como un tipo más elitista y su presencia en Cerro Tilcajete en las recolecciones intensivas de la superficie fue una manera de evaluar la presencia de zonas de residencias elites.

El mapeo localizó un camino prehispánico que asciende hacia el sitio desde el lado noroeste. En dos puntos, el camino pasa por nichos tallados en la cuesta. Los artefactos recuperados de los cuadros de recolección asociados con los nichos (cerámica, fragmentos de figurillas, concha, y fragmentos de urnas) indicaron que el camino fue utilizado en la fase Monte Albán II. Los nichos pudieron haber marcado puntos de entrada al sitio. Viajeros saliendo del sitio o entrando al mismo quizá se detenían aquí para realizar algunos rituales.

Dicho camino pasa por una plaza con tres plataformas pequeñas, Montículos M, N, y O, que se encuentran bien colocados para regular el acceso al centro ceremonial. Los cuadros de recolección en esta zona brindaron diagnósticos de la fase Monte Albán II y una frecuencia alta de cerámica de pasta crema. Los cuadros de recolección asociados con los montículos en el recinto ceremonial (Montículos de la Plaza I y la Plaza II) también brindaron mucha cerámica de pasta crema. En un cuadro de colección (Cuadro 173) en la zona suroeste de la Plaza II recuperamos parte de un maxilar humano. Este objeto fue parte de una tumba saqueada. Aparte del maxilar, el contexto contenía cerámica de pasta crema y concha. El maxilar fue trabajado (tallado) y se interpreta su función como un trofeo obtenido de un sacrificio humano.

Al descender hacia el oriente del sitio, el camino pasa por una zona de terrazas residenciales. Las recolecciones de la superficie de las terrazas al sur brindaron una alta frecuencia de diagnósticos de pasta gris, pero menos tiestos de pasta crema. En general, esta información sugiere que las residencias sobre el lado oriental de la pendiente fueron casas de status más bajo que aquellas situadas sobre la cima de la cordillera. Basado en el número de terrazas y en los restos de viviendas (*house mounds*) visible en la superficie, estimamos que la zona ceremonial tenía una población de entre 15-25 familias y que otras 143 familias vivieron afuera de la zona ceremonial. La población del sitio se puede calcular entre 790-1630 personas.

Los datos del mapeo y de las recolecciones intensivas en la Plaza I proporcionaron una cantidad de tiestos tipo G.35. Como describimos con más detalle adelante, los montículos de la Plaza I fueron sustancialmente modificados durante la fase Monte Albán IIIb-IV (circa 500 d.C.–1000 d.C.). Sin embargo, la distribución de la cerámica de la fase IIIb-IV en la superficie sugiere que la población que vivía en el sitio en esta época fue de unos cientos de personas.

En síntesis, el Cerro Tilcajete, con un total de 24.5 ha, fue ocupado principalmente durante la fase Monte Albán II. Los datos de la recolección indican que el sitio estuvo muy estrechamente vinculado al camino uniendo el valle central y el Valle Grande/Ocotlán. La arquitectura monumental del sitio estaba ubicada de tal manera para poder controlar el tráfico sobre el camino y mantener contacto visual entre la capital y el centro secundario. Cerro Tilcajete tenía diez edificios administrativos ubicados alrededor de tres plazas. A diferencia de Monte Albán o el sitio secundario de Etla, San José Mogote, Cerro Tilcajete no incluye un juego de pelota. Cerro Tilcajete fue abandonado al final de la fase Monte Albán II y fue ocupado de nuevo durante la fase Monte Albán IIIb-IV pero la reocupación fue restringida a la Plaza I.

Con el fin de investigar este centro secundario, y con base en los resultados del análisis de las recolecciones de la superficie, varias áreas del sitio fueron escogidas para un programa de excavación.

Las excavaciones de templos y edificios cívico-ceremoniales: fase Monte Albán II

El Montículo B de la Estructura 2 fue construido con muros de retención para nivelar la pendiente natural. El muro de retención del lado este tenía 1 m de grosor y al menos seis hiladas (70 cm) de alto. El muro oeste tenía al menos de 5 a 6 hiladas (1 metro) de alto. Los cimientos de los dos muros estaban sobre roca madre. La erosión destruyó los pisos de la Estructura 2 y la esquina noreste de la estructura fue afectada por saqueos; sin embargo, el plano del edificio era de un templo de dos cuartos con un total de 36.40 m² de espacio interior. Al igual que el Montículo A, el Montículo B aparentemente tenía una sola fase constructiva. Los pozos de prueba colocados en el relleno del montículo no recuperaron los restos de ninguna construcción anterior.

La excavación del Montículo E en la Plaza I determinó que la última fase de construcción data de después del 500 d.C. Debajo del edificio de la fase Monte Albán IIIb-IV, se hallaron restos de edificios de la fase Monte Albán II. Las estructuras de la fase II fueron examinadas con pozos de sondeo dirigidos a las áreas dañadas de la plataforma. El plano del edificio no está muy claro, pero las diferencias en la elevación de los lados oeste y este del montículo sugieren que era o una construcción de múltiples niveles o quizás varias estructuras separadas pero asociadas. En total, la estructura tenía alrededor de 100 m². Una muestra radiocarbónica (Beta-1654787) fue recuperada en el piso del Pozo 8 la cual rindió una fecha de 70 a 370 años d.C. (2 sigma calibrado), un poco más tardía que la fecha de 5 años a.C. a 300 d.C. obtenida del Montículo A. En general, la cerámica de los pozos consiste en tiestos vueltos a depositar, y no de buenos contextos primarios. No queda muy claro que tipo de edificio representa la estructura de la fase II del Montículo E; sin embargo, basado en la calidad de las construcciones—con pisos enyesados y muros de piedra cortada—es muy probable que haya sido una residencia elite o un edificio cívico-ceremonial. En cualquier caso, la estructura del Montículo E alcanza en tamaño a las estructuras descubiertas en los montículos alrededor de la Plaza II.

Las excavaciones de residencias: fase Monte Albán II

Las excavaciones sobre el Montículo A expusieron la Estructura 1 que mide 11 por 12 m (el lado occidental de la estructura fue parcialmente destruido por el arado y las dimensiones originales pudieron haber sido 12 por 12 m). No se conservó ningún piso de ocupación, pero las bases de los muros muestran que la estructura consistía de 4-6 cuartos distribuidos alrededor de un patio central. Los muros de la Estructura 1 estaban compuestos de grandes bloques de piedra bien labrada y adobe enyesado. Aunque un pozo de saqueadores invadió a la estructura y destruyó partes de los muros de contención, fue fácil limpiar el pozo que, junto con seis pozos de prueba colocados para sondear debajo de la superficie de las demás estancias de la Estructura 1, nos permitieron una vista del interior del Montículo A. Los resultados de estos pozos de prueba determinaron que no existían fases constructivas previas debajo de la Estructura 1 y aunque hay fragmentos de hueso humano, no había evidencia arquitectónica de una tumba. En Monte Albán las residencias elites de la fase II suelen tener tumbas y entierros en la misma estructura. Una muestra radiocarbónica (Beta-143356) tomada debajo de la base de la Estructura 1 brindó una fecha de 5 a.C. a 330 d.C. (2 sigma calibrado). Por la ubicación, el tamaño, y la calidad de la construcción, interpretamos la Estructura 1 como una residencia elite tipo palacio.

Los datos recuperados de la excavación de la Estructura 3 permiten sugerir que, semejante a la Estructura 1, la Estructura 3 funcionaba como una residencia elite. Allí las excavaciones expusieron una estructura de al menos 88.56 m² de espacio de vivienda y de patio. Para crear la terraza del Área C se requirió la construcción de muros de retención, en especial sobre la esquina sureste, donde determinamos que la terraza había sido respaldada al menos 1.23 m con varios niveles de piedra y adobe. Como los pisos no estaban del todo bien preservados, resulta un poco difícil determinar el plano original del edificio. La plataforma de la casa medía al menos 11 m por 8.5 m. Parte de la construcción inicial fue un muro central masivo de 1 m de ancho y 10 m de largo, hecho, en parte, de piedra bien labrada y en parte de grandes ladrillos de adobe. Algunos muros exteriores tenían un grosor de 80 cm y estaban hechos de piedra bien labrada. Proponemos que la Estructura 3 tenía entre 3 y 4 estancias alrededor de un patio abierto, y que la residencia tenía una planta en forma de C o de L. Los escombros de la casa contenían fragmentos de yeso y adobes enyesados. Algunos sondeos se hicieron en la terraza debajo de las estancias y probable área del patio. En estos pozos de prueba no se encontraron fases constructivas previas ni elementos como entierros u ofrendas. Justo al oriente (afuera) de la Estructura 3, encontramos el Elemento 1, un basurero sobre un nivel de tierra compacta y estéril.

La Estructura 4, ubicada 29 m sobre el descenso de la pendiente y 240 m al sur de la Plaza II, es un ejemplo de una residencia común. La terraza que soporta la Estructura 4 fue creada artificialmente, nivelando la pendiente natural que va de norte a sur. Esta estructura fue modificada en varias ocasiones, y en la última etapa llegó a tener una forma de L. Se encontraron varios elementos asociados con la estructura, los cuales brindaron datos de actividades domésticas. El Elemento 2, una estructura rectangular que contenía grandes trozos de utensilios, probablemente sirvió como área de bodega (no hay evidencia de trozos de carbón o piedra quemada). Las vasijas halladas dentro del elemento fueron principalmente cajetes y ollas utilitarias de pasta gris y café. El Elemento 4, un fogón casi rectangular alineado de piedra, fue rellenado de 7-9 cm de ceniza, carbón, hueso, y unos cuantos fragmentos de cerámica quemada incluyendo una sección de borde-a-base de un cajete gris tipo G.21.

Se encontraron cuatro entierros en la estructura. El Entierro 4, de un joven colocado en un pozo en el tepetate. Estaba acompañado de dos ofrendas: un cajete gris con un borde modelado colocado sobre la pelvis y una pequeña figurilla antropomórfica con rostro enmascarado, brazos y piernas extendidos que pudo haberse suspendido de un anillo en su espalda. La parte inferior de las piernas y los pies del Entierro 4 fueron destruidos por un fogón intruso. Los Entierros 1 (un niño) y 2 (un adulto) fueron colocados en una estancia que pudo haberse añadido para funcionar como una tumba. Sin embargo, no es una tumba formal. No tenía un techo de lápida y su muro oriental también funcionaba como parte del muro de retención de la terraza. El niño estaba acompañado de tres ofrendas: un sencillo cajete gris colocado al revés sobre el rostro, un silbato de pasta gris en forma de guajolote, y un cordón de 46 pequeñas conchas perforadas para suspenderse en un collar. El adulto estaba acompañado de dos ofrendas: un cajete tipo pasta amarilla con diseños pintados en rojo colocado al revés sobre la pelvis y una pendiente de piedra verde, hallada cerca del cráneo. El relleno produjo tres objetos de cerámica, un fragmento de metate y dos fragmentos de manos. El primer objeto es la cabeza y torso de un hombre que lleva un tocado elaborado. El segundo es un silbato en forma de hombre portando un tocado elaborado. El tercero es la mitad de una vasija de pasta crema tipo C.11 con los soportes rotos. El Entierro 3 era joven o niño colocado en una posición extendida en la esquina sureste del patio. Su cráneo estaba desgastado y destruido. En el entierro habían tres vasijas. La primera era un cajete tipo de pasta café bien bruñido de paredes delgadas con un motivo escalonado inciso. La segunda vasija era un cajete en pasta gris de fondo plano sin decoración y la tercera era una pequeña jarra en pasta gris.

El análisis de los artefactos: fase Monte Albán II

El análisis de las cerámicas y los demás artefactos de las residencias proporcionó datos para probar las indicaciones de las recolecciones intensivas de la superficie, para obtener datos de la economía del sitio, y para elaborar ideas de la vida ritual. El análisis de la cerámica fue enfocado en varios tipos:

1. La cerámica crema ya descrita: C.6 (color café-café claro); C.7 (rojo); C.11 (rojo con diseños incisos); C.20 (negro); C.12 (negro con diseños incisos). La cerámica de pasta crema ocurre más frecuentemente en las residencias elites (Estructuras 1 y 3) que en la residencia común (Estructura 4).

2. La cerámica tipo G.29, una cerámica de pasta gris, pudo haber sido hecha en el Valle Grande y Ocotlán para imitar las cremas tipos C.6 y C.7. Como es bastante escaso en Monte Albán, el G.29 pudo haber sido manufacturado localmente para satisfacer la demanda para la cerámica crema cuya disponibilidad fue regulada por la capital. La cerámica G.29 ocurre con más frecuencia en la residencia de gente común (Estructura 4) que en las residencias elites (Estructuras 1 y 3).

3. La cerámica K.17 es una cerámica de pasta café de origen desconocido. Es posible que algunas vasijas K.17 fueron producidas para imitar la cerámica C.20 y C.12. En Cerro Tilcajete, el tipo K.17 ocurre en cantidades pequeñas, pero es más frecuente en la Estructura 1. Como la cerámica C.12 y C.20 las vasijas de la cerámica K.17 pueden ser muy finamente fabricadas y toman la forma de cajetes con soportes y vasos con tapas.

4. La cerámica A.9 es una cerámica de pasta amarilla de origen desconocido. Las vasijas pueden ser cajetes sencillos o cajetes sencillos con soportes grandes y huecos. Las dos formas llevan diseños pintados en rojo que a veces son de *xicalcoliuhquis* pero también hay una variedad de diseños incluyendo flores, puntos, y líneas simples. Aunque se ha sugerido que la cerámica tipo A.9 fue fabricada en el Valle Grande-Ocotlán o Tlacolula, es menos frecuente (como una proporción de la cerámica diagnóstica) que la cerámica de pasta crema en las residencias elites. Estos datos nos sugieren que la cerámica A.9 fue menos codiciada como un símbolo elite.

5. La cerámica estucada y pintada aparece por primera vez en la fase Monte Albán II y se encuentra muy raramente en Monte Albán. Es considerado un signo de un contexto elite. En el Cerro Tilcajete, solamente encontramos cuatro tepalcates en la Estructura 1 y tres en la Estructura 3.

Otra manera de analizar la cerámica es por medio de su forma. Clasificamos los bordes por forma: olla, cajete, vaso, vaso con tapa, plato, apaxtle y comal. Después, hicimos una segunda división de la cerámica en dos grupos: servicio y utilitario. Este análisis nos proporciona datos similares a los del análisis por tipo: hay más cerámica de servicio en las residencias élites y menos (aunque de formas similares) en la residencia de gente común.

Finalmente, los datos del basurero de la Estructura 1 (Elemento 1) sugieren que las elites usaban una variedad de vasijas de servicio: al menos 108 vasijas diferentes (el número de vasijas con bordes, pasta y decoración casi exclusiva) estuvieron presentes en el basurero. Las formas de las vasijas incluyen cajetes, botellas, vasos cilíndricos, vasijas de silueta compuesta y platos, así como un fragmento de sahumador (quemador de incienso) de pasta café. En comparación, los datos del basurero de la Estructura 4 (Elemento 6) sugieren que los habitantes de la casa común usaban menos variedad en cuanto a las formas de las vasijas (49 formas distintas). En general, entre las residencias elites y comunes, no hay divisiones de blanco y negro sino más bien grados en la accesibilidad de tipos y formas de la cerámica.

Las figurillas, los fragmentos de urnas, y los artefactos de materiales no-cerámicos aportaron información sobre rituales hogareños. En general, los mismos tipos de figurillas se hallan en las residencias elites como en la común. La gran mayoría son figurillas sólidas hechas en pasta gris. Muchas de éstas tienen ojos en forma de almendra y la boca de "grano de café" típicos de la fase II y tienen tocados, joyas o incisiones corporales. Los tipos de figurillas humanas hallados en el Cerro Tilcajete sugieren que éstos fueron utilizados en rituales que involucraban antepasados difuntos, una continuación de los rituales domésticos del Formativo Temprano y Medio. Los fragmentos de urnas pertenecían a vasijas grandes y huecas con rasgos humanos. La mayoría de las urnas de la fase Monte Albán II en realidad son jarras con rostros de efigies. Muchas jarras con rostros de efigie de la fase Monte Albán II muestran al dios zapoteco Cociyo, otras pueden mostrar antepasados nobles difuntos o personas portando la máscara de Cociyo. Las verdaderas urnas zapotecas no aparecen hasta muy tarde en la fase Monte Albán II. Mientras comienzan a aparecer las urnas con mayor frecuencia, las figurillas pequeñas prácticamente desaparecen del registro. En el Cerro Tilcajete, los fragmentos de figurillas predominan aún sobre los fragmentos de urnas y se nota una tendencia de hallar más fragmentos de urnas en las residencias elites (Estructuras 1 y 3) que la residencia común (Estructura 4). La distribución puede indicar que mientras la mayoría de los habitantes conducía rituales domésticos tradicionales para venerar a sus antepasados, la elite fue involucrándose sobre todo en los rituales para invocar a antepasados nobles o a espíritus sobrenaturales como Cociyo.

En Monte Albán en la fase Monte Albán II, los sahumadores no son muy comunes y la mayoría de ellos se provienen de tumbas. Recuperamos dos fragmentos de dos sahumadores en la Estructura 1 y dos en la Estructura 3 que probablemente fueron usados en ritos domésticos.

La obsidiana del Cerro Tilcajete fue dividida en oscura y verde. La obsidiana oscura pudo haber provenido de varios lugares incluyendo Zaragosa (Puebla), el Pico de Orizaba (Veracruz) y Otumba (Estado de México). La obsidiana verde probablemente proviene de la fuente geológica de Pachuca en Hidalgo. En general, la obsidiana aparece como hojuelas pequeñas o navajas. Las navajas de obsidiana, en particular, predominan en las estructuras elites. Se ha sugerido que en la fase Monte Albán II el intercambio de la obsidiana fue dominado por Monte Albán y es probable que la mayoría de la obsidiana en Cerro Tilcajete haya sido obtenida como navajas. Al desgastar las navajas, fueron trabajadas para sacar hojuelas pequeñas.

Para resumir, las residencias elites en Cerro Tilcajete, como las residencias elites en Monte Albán, están compuestas de cimientos de piedra labrada con muros de adobe enyesado. A diferencia de las residencias elites de Monte Albán, donde se encuentran tumbas y entierros dentro de la misma estructura, ninguna de las residencias elites excavadas en el Cerro Tilcajete tiene tumba. La clase elite del Cerro Tilcajete tenía acceso a diferentes tipos de bienes de status. En particular, la elite deseaba y prefería la cerámica crema, especialmente los cajetes con pies grandes y huecos y diseños ligados con Cociyo. Es posible que dichas vasijas llegaran al sitio como regalos de los nobles de Monte Albán y fueron usadas en ritos comunales dirigidos por elites locales para pedir o agradecer dios Cociyo por la abundancia de la agricultura. También, el uso de las urnas puede indicar que las elites estuvieron involucradas en los rituales patrocinados por el estado.

Excavaciones de edificios de la fase Monte Albán IIIb-IV

Los artefactos nos permiten sugerir que la zona de la Plaza I volvió a ocuparse alrededor de 600/700 d.C. En este entonces, nuevos edificios fueron construidos en las cimas de montículos E, H, I, J, K, y L. El Montículo F fue construido por primera vez y una plataforma abierta fue construida en la Plaza I, asociada con el Montículo H. La excavación del adoratorio descubrió una plataforma de 5 × 5 m. En la cima a los lados recuperamos tepalcates tipo G.35. También recuperamos evidencia de uso del espacio como lugar de sacrificio: 28 navajas de obsidiana (25 verdes y 3 grises), un raspador de pedernal, una navaja de pedernal, una navaja bifacial de pedernal negro, y un fragmento de otra navaja bifacial de pedernal negro.

La Estructura 5 en la cima de Montículo E estaba bien conservada y se excavó completamente. La subida a la Estructura 5 fue por una escalinata desde la Plaza I. La estructura tiene forma de cuarto grande que mide 19.8 × 4.6 metros. Entre el recinto y la plaza había una plataforma abierta (a un nivel más bajo) de dos metros de ancho. La Estructura 5 funcionó como un espacio cívico o templo parecido a los que se han encontrado en Yagul y Mitla. En el Area G hicimos pozos de prueba pero no encontramos pisos ni restos de estructuras. El Montículo F tiene un espacio de solo 5 × 5 metros en su cima. Probablemente el montículo se construyó para contener una tumba, la cual encontramos saqueada. La tumba es cruciforme y sus paredes tienen tiestos de cerámica usados como relleno entre los bloques de piedra de los muros. Algunos tiestos, sacados de su lugar, fueron identificados como tipo G.35.

Cerro Tilcajete como centro secundario del estado zapoteco

Datos de Cerro Tilcajete brindan luz sobre cómo funcionaba la administración de Monte Albán sobre el Valle Grande/Ocotlán. A base de los datos de las excavaciones previas en los centros secundarios de Tlacolula (Dainzú) y Etla (San José Mogote), podemos comparar la administración del Valle Grande/Ocotlán con la administración de las otras subregiones. Por un lado, la comparación apoya la sugerencia que ya para la fase II los gobernantes de Monte Albán habían desarrollado una administración estatal. Por otro lado, la comparación brinda luz sobre como la administración estatal pudo haber variado y por qué no fue la misma en todas las subregiones.

Para empezar, los datos comparativos indican que el estado zapoteco emprendió un programa masivo de construcción tanto en Monte Albán como en los sitios secundarios. En la capital las construcciones masivas incluyeron la creación de la Plaza Principal y el agrandecimiento de la Plataforma Norte, una zona de templos y plazas, donde varios edificios fueron construidos o renovados. El conjunto de edificios en la Plataforma Norte ha sido interpretado como el punto más restringido del sitio y un lugar que posiblemente funcionaba como palacio gubernamental.

Dentro del Valle, el asentamiento de Cerro Tilcajete fue ubicado sobre terreno sin ocupación previa, requiriendo la construcción de montículos, terrazas, y edificios. En Tlacolula, el sitio de Dainzú creció de un tamaño de menos de 2 ha a un sitio que cubrió 45.6 ha. El informe de las investigaciones arqueológicas llevadas a cabo en Dainzú documenta una gran inversión en la construcción de terrazas, montículos, y edificios nuevos. Los datos de las excavaciones en San José Mogote indican que entre 500–100 a.C., la población del sitio disminuyó (quizá porque una porción de la población se trasladó a fundar a Monte Albán) pero después de 100 a.C., la población creció y nuevas estructuras fueron construidas encima de los montículos. En todo el Valle, vemos una gran inversión por parte del Estado para crear una infraestructura estatal de caminos, plazas, palacios y templos (y las terrazas y las plataformas para sostenerlos).

Los sitios secundarios demuestran algunas diferencias en los planes y en los tipos (y el número) de los edificios construidos. La Plaza Principal de San José Mogote imita en varios aspectos a la Plaza Principal de Monte Albán: es del mismo tamaño (300 m norte-sur por 200 m este-oeste), tiene un edificio que hubiera funcionado como palacio gubernamental encima del montículo norte, y es el único sitio secundario con un juego de pelota.

Mientras la renovación de San José Mogote seguía el mismo patrón de la capital, este no fue el caso en Dainzú y Cerro Tilcajete. En Dainzú, los montículos se ubican alrededor de unas terrazas con poco espacio abierto. Las excavaciones allí localizaron un templo de dos cuartos (de entre 50-60 m^2) encima del montículo oeste y los restos de un probable palacio (con tumbas y entierros) encima de las terrazas centrales del sitio. Aunque las excavaciones encontraron una galería con relieves de jugadores de pelota, no encontraron un juego de pelota asociado a la ocupación de la fase II.

No es claro porqué Dainzú y Cerro Tilcajete carecen de un juego de pelota. Es posible que en el Valle Grande/Ocotlán y en Tlacolula los juegos de pelota se construyeron en sitios no-secundarios. Para la fase II, el recorrido de la superficie ubicó un juego de pelota en el sitio de San Bartolo Coyotepec, a unos 5 km al norte de Cerro Tilcajete y otro en un sitio (Sitio 4-7-50) a unos 4 km noroeste de Dainzú. Se requieren excavaciones para determinar por seguro si estas canchas fueron usadas en la fase Monte Albán II. La práctica del juego de pelota podría estar relacionada con el poder militar, la resolución de conflictos entre diversas comunidades, o el castigo sancionado por el estado. La falta de canchas en estos dos sitios podría significar que los gobernantes del estado preferían mantener algunos aspectos del ejército, el castigo, o la resolución de conflictos fuera de las manos de las elites locales.

Los artefactos recuperados en los sitios secundarios demuestran que existía una cultura elite común. Las excavaciones en Monte Albán, San José Mogote, Dainzú, y Cerro Tilcajete documentan el uso de la cerámica crema y de los sahumadores en las zonas cívico-ceremoniales y residencias elites. Aunque no tenemos datos específicos de Dainzú, los datos de los otros sitios sugieren el desarrollo de un enlace fuerte entre las elites y rituales para invocar a antepasados nobles o a espíritus sobrenaturales como Cociyo. En general, los datos comparativos apoyan la sugerencia que la creación de una ideología enlazando los elites con Cociyo y la práctica de la religión estatal eran fundamentales en el desarrollo del poder de los gobernantes de Monte Albán.

Ha sido claramente documentado que Monte Albán encabezó campañas militares en el Formativo Medio y Tardío (500 a.C.–200 d.C.). Mientras las investigaciones llevadas a cabo en Etla sugieren que Monte Albán y el subvalle de Etla tenían una relación cercana, las investigaciones en El Palenque, el sitio Formativo Tardío más grande del Valle Grande/Ocotlán, sugieren que Monte Albán y la rama sur tenían una relación contenciosa. Aún no tenemos datos claros sobre la relación entre Tlacolula y Monte Albán antes de 100 a.C. La resolución del problema requiere excavaciones en el sitio más grande de Tlacolula en el Formativo Tardío, el sitio de Yegüih, que no fue abandonado en la fase Monte Albán II, aunque parece que la población del sitio disminuyó.

Se debe considerar que estas relaciones previas afectaron cómo los gobernantes de Monte Albán montaron la administración estatal. Los elementos materiales de la cultura elite aparecen en los tres sitios, pero el contexto, en donde se llevaron a cabo importantes actividades, varía. En San José Mogote, el contexto asemeja el de la capital. En el Valle Grande/Ocotlán y en Tlacolula, en vez de construir sitios secundarios que imitaban la capital, se construyeron centros secundarios con planes distintos que carecen de algunos tipos de edificios como el juego de pelota y el palacio gubernamental reconocidos en la capital.

Los datos de Cerro Tilcajete contribuyen a un mejor entendimiento del sistema dinámico de los estados prehispánicos. En el estado zapoteco, la trayectoria de una administración estatal siguió siglos de expansión irregular en donde las condiciones y las reacciones locales al crecimiento político de Monte Albán influyeron cómo los gobernantes del estado decidieron organizar e imponer localmente sus políticas. En la fase Monte Albán II, algunas de las políticas gubernamentales no eran regularizadas ni estandarizadas porque el sistema administrativo creció a base de las relaciones de cooperación y de conflicto que existían entre las elites de la capital y las elites en cada subregión del valle.

Bibliography

Acosta, Jorge R.
n.d. *Informes de la XII, XIV, XV, XVI, y XVII temporadas de exploraciones arqueológicas de Monte Albán de los años 1944 a 1949*. Manuscript in the archives of the Instituto Nacional de Antropología e Historia, México, D.F.
1958 Exploraciones arqueológicas en Monte Albán XVIII temporada. *Revista Mexicana de Estudios Antropológicos* 15:7-50.
1965 Preclassic and classic architecture of Oaxaca. In *Handbook of Middle American Indians*. Vol. 3, part 2, *Archaeology of Southern Mesoamerica*, edited by G.R. Willey, pp. 814-36. Austin: University of Texas Press.
1974 Informe de la XIV temporada de exploraciones en la zona arqueológica de Monte Albán, 1945-1946. *Cultura y Sociedad* 1(2):69-82.
1976 La XIII temporada de exploraciones arqueológicas en Monte Albán, 1944-1945. *Cultura y Sociedad* 3(4):14-26.

Akinjogbin, A.I.
1976 The expansion of Oyo and the rise of Dahomey 1600-1800. In *History of West Africa*. Vol. 1, edited by J.F.A. Ajayi and M. Crowder, pp. 374-412. New York: Columbia University Press.

Albrow, Martin
1990 *Max Weber's Construction of Social Theory*. London: St. Martin's Press, Inc.

Arendt, Hannah
1961 *Between Past and Future*. New York: Viking Press.

Balkansky, Andrew
1998 Origin and collapse of complex societies in Oaxaca (Mexico): evaluating the era from 1965 to the present. *Journal of World Prehistory* 12(4):451-93.
2002 *The Sola Valley and the Monte Albán State: A Study of Zapotec Imperial Expansion*. Memoirs, no. 36. Museum of Anthropology, University of Michigan. Ann Arbor.

Balsalobre, Gonzalo de
1656 Relación auténtica de las idolatrías, supersticiones, vanas observaciones de los indios del Obispado de Oaxaca. *Anales del Museo Nacional de México, Primera Epoca* 6:225-60. Reprinted, 1892.

Barker, Graeme, and Tom Rasmussen
2000 *The Etruscans*. London: Blackwell Publishers.

Beals, Ralph L.
1975 *The Peasant Marketing System of Oaxaca, Mexico*. Berkeley: University of California Press.

Bernal, Ignacio
1949 *La cerámica de Monte Albán IIIa*. PhD dissertation, Universidad Nacional Autónoma de México, México, D.F.
1967 Excavaciones en Dainzú. *Boletín del INAH*, Marzo, 27:7-13, México.
1968 The ball players of Dainzú. *Archaeology* 21(4):246-51.
1973 Stone reliefs in the Dainzú area. In *The Iconography of Middle American Sculpture*, pp. 13-23. New York: Metropolitan Museum of Art.
1981 The Dainzú pre-classic figurines. In *The Olmecs and Their Neighbors, Essays in Honor of M.W. Stirling*, pp. 223-29. Washington, D.C.: Dumbarton Oaks.

Bernal, Ignacio, and Lorenzo Gamio
1974 *Yagul, el palacio de los seis patios*. Instituto de Investigaciones Antropológicas, Serie Antropológica 16. México, D.F.: Universidad Nacional Autónoma de México.

Bernal, Ignacio, and Arturo Oliveros
1988 *Exploraciones Arqueológicas en Dainzú, Oaxaca*. México: INAH.

Blanton, Richard E.
1978 *Monte Albán: Settlement Patterns at the Ancient Zapotec Capital*. New York: Academic Press.
1983 Urban Monte Albán during Period III. In *The Cloud People: Divergent Evolution of the Zapotec and Mixtec Civilizations*, edited by K.V. Flannery and J. Marcus, pp. 128-31. New York: Academic Press.
1989 Continuity and change in public architecture: Periods I through IV of the Valley of Oaxaca, México. In *Monte Albán's Hinterland, Part II: Prehispanic Settlement Patterns in Tlacolula, Etla, and Ocotlán, the Valley of Oaxaca, México*, by S.A. Kowalewski, G.M. Feinman, L. Finsten, R.E. Blanton, and L.M. Nicholas. Memoirs, no. 23. Museum of Anthropology, University of Michigan. Ann Arbor.

Blanton, Richard E., Gary M. Feinman, Stephen A. Kowalewski, and Linda M. Nicholas
1999 *Ancient Oaxaca*. Cambridge: Cambridge University Press.

Blanton, Richard E., Jill Appel, Laura Finsten, Steve Kowalewski, Gary Feinman, and Eva Fisch
1979 Regional evolution in the Valley of Oaxaca, Mexico. *Journal of Field Archaeology* 6(4):369-90.

Blanton, Richard E., Stephen A. Kowalewski, Gary M. Feinman, and Jill Appel
1982 *Monte Albán's Hinterland, Part I: The Prehispanic Settlement Patterns of the Central and Southern Parts of the Valley of Oaxaca, México*. Memoirs, no. 15. Museum of Anthropology, University of Michigan. Ann Arbor.

Bossler, Beverly J.
1998 *Powerful Relations: Kinship Status and the State in Sung China (960-1279)*. Cambridge, MA: Harvard University Press.

Brumfiel, Elizabeth, and John W. Fox (editors)
1994 *Factional Competition and Political Development in the New World*. Cambridge: Cambridge University Press.

Burgoa, Francisco de
1670 *Palestra historial de virtudes y ejemplares apostólicos*. Publicaciones del Archivo General de la Nación 24. Talleres Gráficos de la Nación, México. Reprinted, 1934.
1674 *Geográfica descripción*. Publicaciones del Archivo General de la Nación 25-26. Talleres Gráficos de la Nación, México. Reprinted, 1934.

Carmagnani, Marcello
1988 *El Regreso de los Dioses*. Mexico: Fondo de Cultura Económica.

Carneiro, Robert
1970 A theory of the origin of the state. *Science* 169:733-38.
1981 The chiefdom: precursor of the state. In *The Transition to Statehood in the New World*, edited by G. Jones and R. Kautz, pp. 37-79. Cambridge: Cambridge University Press.

Caso, Alfonso
1928 *Las Estelas Zapotecas*. Mexico: Talleres Gráficos de la Nación.
1932 Las exploraciones en Monte Albán, temporada 1931-1932. *Instituto Panamericano de Geografía e Historia, Publicación 7*, México.
1933 Las tumbas de Monte Albán. *Anales del Museo Nacional de Arqueología, Historia y Etnografía, Tomo VIII*, pp. 641-47. México, D.F.
1935 Las exploraciones en Oaxaca, temporada 1934-1935. *Instituto Panamericano de Geografía e Historia, Publicación 18*, México.
1938 Las exploraciones en Monte Albán, quinta y sexta temporadas 1936-1937. *Instituto Panamericano de Geografía e Historia, Publicación 34*, México.
1942 Resumen del informe de las exploraciones en Oaxaca durante la 7a y 8a temporadas 1937-1938 y 1938-1939. *Actas del XXVII Congreso Internacional de Americanistas, 1939*, 2:159-87.
1947 Calendario y escritura en las antiguas culturas de Monte Albán. In *Obras Completas de Miguel Othón de Mendizábal*. Vol. 1, pp. 115-43. México.
1967 *El Tesoro de Monte Albán*. México: Memorias del Instituto Nacional de Antropología e Historia.

Caso, Alfonso, and Ignacio Bernal
1952 *Urnas de Oaxaca*. México: Memorias del Instituto Nacional de Antropología e Historia.
1965 The ceramics of Oaxaca. In *Handbook of Middle American Indians*. Vol. 3, part 2, *Archaeology of Southern Mesoamerica*, edited by G.R. Willey, pp. 871-95. Austin: University of Texas Press.

Caso, Alfonso, Ignacio Bernal, and Jorge Acosta
1967 *La Cerámica de Monte Albán*. Memorias del Instituto Nacional de Antropología e Historia, 13. Mexico: Instituto Nacional de Antropología e Historia.

Casparis, Luca
2005 *Early Classic Jalieza and the Monte Alban State*. Doctoral dissertation, University of Geneva.

Chance, John K.
1978 *Race and Class in Colonial Oaxaca*. Stanford, CA: Stanford University Press.
1989 *Conquest of the Sierra: Spaniards and Indians in Colonial Oaxaca*. Norman: University of Oklahoma Press.

Chase, Diane Z., and Arlen F. Chase (editors)
1992 *Mesoamerican Elites: An Archaeological Assessment*. Norman: University of Oklahoma Press.

Cohen, Abner
1981 *The Politics of Elite Culture*. Berkeley: University of California Press.

Córdova, Fray Juan de
1578a *Vocabulario en Lengua Zapoteca*. México: Pedro Charte y Antonio Ricardo.
1578b *Arte en lengua Zapoteca*. México: Pedro Balli.
1987 *Arte del idioma Zapoteco*. Reprint. México: Ediciones Toledo.

Covey, R. Alan
2006 *How the Incas Built Their Heartland: State Formation and the Innovation of Imperial Strategies in the Sacred Valley, Peru*. Ann Arbor: The University of Michigan Press.

Cyphers, Ann
1993 Women, ritual and social dynamics in ancient Chalcatzingo. *Latin American Antiquity* 4(3):209-24.

D'Altroy, Terence N.
2002 *The Incas*. London: Blackwell Publishers.

Drennan, Robert
1983 Appendix: radiocarbon dates from the Oaxaca region. In *The Cloud People: Divergent Evolution of the Zapotec and Mixtec Civilizations*, edited by K.V. Flannery and J. Marcus, pp. 361-70. New York: Academic Press.

Duncan, William, Christina Elson, Charles Spencer, and Elsa Redmond
2006 *A Human Maxilla Trophy from Oaxaca, Mexico*. Paper presented at the 33rd annual meeting of the Rochester Academy of Science, Rochester, NY.

Durkheim, Emile
1933 *The Division of Labor in Society*. London: Macmillan.

Eisenstadt, Shmuel N.
1963 *The Political Systems of Empires*. London [New York]: Free Press of Glencoe.
1969 *The Political Systems of Empires*. New York: Free Press of New York.
1995 Beyond collapse. In *The Collapse of Ancient States and Civilizations*, edited by N. Yoffee and G. Cowgill, pp. 236-43. Tucson: University of Arizona Press.

Elson, Christina
2006 Intermediate elite and the political landscape of the early Zapotec state. In *Intermediate Elites in Pre-Columbian States and Empires*, edited by C. Elson and R.A. Covey, pp. 44-67. Tucson, AZ: University of Arizona Press.

Elson, Christina, and Luca Casparis
2006 *Investigaciones en Santo Tomás Jalieza, Temporada 2006*. Informe Técnico para el Consejo de Arqueología del Instituto Nacional de Antropología e Historia.

Elson, Christina, and R. Jason Sherman
in press Crema ware and elite power at Monte Albán: ceramic production and iconography in the Oaxaca Valley, Mexico. *Journal of Field Archaeology*.

Esparza, M.
1994 *Relaciones Geográficas de Oaxaca, 1777-1778*. Oaxaca: CIESAS.

Evans, Susan
2004 *Ancient Mexico and Central America: Archaeology and Culture History*. London: Thames and Hudson.

Fash, William L.
1991 *Scribes, Warriors and Kings*. London: Thames and Hudson.

Feinman, Gary M.
1982 Patterns in ceramic production and distribution, periods Early I through V. In *Monte Albán's Hinterland, Part I: The Prehispanic Settlement Patterns of the Central and Southern Parts of the Valley of Oaxaca, Mexico*, pp. 181-206. Memoirs, no. 15. Museum of Anthropology, University of Michigan. Ann Arbor.
1986 Emergence of specialized ceramic production in Formative Oaxaca. *Research in Economic Anthropology*, supplement 2:347-73.
1998 Scale and social organization: perspectives on the archaic state. In *Archaic States*, edited by G.M. Feinman and J. Marcus, pp. 95-134. Santa Fe: School of American Research.
2006 The economic underpinnings of prehispanic Zapotec civilization. In *Agricultural Strategies*, edited by J. Marcus and C. Stanish, pp. 255-80. Los Angeles: Cotsen Institute of Archaeology.

Feinman, Gary M., and Linda M. Nicholas
1990 At the margins of the Monte Albán state: settlement patterns in the Ejutla Valley, Oaxaca, Mexico. *Latin American Antiquity* 1:216-46.
1999 Rethinking our assumptions: economic specialization at the household scale in ancient Ejutla, Oaxaca, Mexico. In *Pottery and People: Dynamic Interactions*, edited by James M. Skibo and Gary Feinman, pp. 81-98. Salt Lake City: University of Utah Press.

Finsten, Laura
1995 *Jalieza, Oaxaca: Activity Specialization at a Hilltop Center*. Vanderbilt University Publications in Anthropology, no. 48. Nashville, TN: Vanderbilt University.

Flannery, Kent V.
1972 The cultural evolution of civilizations. *Annual Review of Ecology and Systematics* 3:399-426.
1983a The development of Monte Albán's main plaza in Period II. In *The Cloud People: Divergent Evolution of the Zapotec and Mixtec Civilizations*, edited by K.V. Flannery and J. Marcus, pp. 102-4. New York: Academic Press.
1983b The legacy of the early urban period: an ethnohistoric approach to Monte Albán's temples, residences, and royal tombs. In *The Cloud People: Divergent Evolution of the Zapotec and Mixtec Civilizations*, edited by K.V. Flannery and J. Marcus, pp. 132-36. New York: Academic Press.
1983c Major Monte Albán V sites: Zaachila, Xoxocotlán, Cuilapan, Yagul, and Abasolo. In *The Cloud People: Divergent Evolution of the Zapotec and Mixtec Civilizations*, edited by K.V. Flannery and J. Marcus, pp. 290-95. New York: Academic Press.
1983d Zapotec warfare: archaeological evidence for the battles of Huitzo and Guiengola. In *The Cloud People: Divergent Evolution of the Zapotec and Mixtec Civilizations*, edited by K.V. Flannery and J. Marcus, pp. 318-22. New York: Academic Press.
1995 Prehistoric social evolution. In *Research Frontiers in Anthropology*, edited by C. Ember and M. Ember, pp. 1-26. Englewood Cliffs, New Jersey: Prentice-Hall.
1998 The ground plans of archaic states. In *Archaic States*, edited by G.M. Feinman and J. Marcus, pp. 15-58. Santa Fe: School of American Research.
1999 Process and agency in early state formation. *Cambridge Archaeological Journal* 9(1):3-21.

Flannery, Kent V., and Joyce Marcus
1976a Formative Oaxaca and the Zapotec cosmos. *American Scientist* 64:374-83.
1976b Evolution of the public building in Formative Oaxaca. In *Cultural Change and Continuity: Essays in Honor of James Bennett Griffin*, edited by C. Cleland, pp. 205-21. New York: Academic Press.
1983a San José Mogote in Monte Albán II: a secondary administrative center. In *The Cloud People: Divergent Evolution of the Zapotec and Mixtec Civilizations*, edited by K.V. Flannery and J. Marcus, pp. 111-13. New York: Academic Press.

1983b The growth of site hierarchies in the Valley of Oaxaca: part I. In *The Cloud People: Divergent Evolution of the Zapotec and Mixtec Civilizations*, edited by K.V. Flannery and J. Marcus, pp. 53-65. New York: Academic Press.
1983c Urban Mitla and its rural hinterland. In *The Cloud People: Divergent Evolution of the Zapotec and Mixtec Civilizations*, edited by K.V. Flannery and J. Marcus, pp. 295-301. New York: Academic Press.
1983d Monte Albán and Teotihuacan. In *The Cloud People: Divergent Evolution of the Zapotec and Mixtec Civilizations*, edited by K.V. Flannery and J. Marcus, pp. 161-66. New York: Academic Press.
1994 *Early Formative Pottery of the Oaxaca Valley, Mexico*. Memoirs, no. 27. Museum of Anthropology, University of Michigan. Ann Arbor.
2003 The origin of war: new ^{14}C dates from ancient Mexico. *Proceeding of the National Academy of Sciences* 100:11801-5.
2005 *Excavations at San José Mogote 1: The Household Archaeology*. Memoirs, no. 40. Museum of Anthropology, University of Michigan. Ann Arbor.

Flannery, Kent, Anne V.T. Kirkby, Michael J. Kirkby, and Aubrey W. Williams
1967 Farming systems and political growth in ancient Oaxaca. *Science* 158:445-53.

Freidel, David A., Linda Schele, and Joy Parker
1993 *Maya Cosmos: Three Thousand Years on the Shaman's Path*. New York: William Morris.

Ghindelli, Azzo
1971 The alimentation of the Maya. *Ethnos* 36:23-31.

Giddens, Anthony
1984 *The Constitution of Society*. Berkeley: University of California Press.

González, Roberto J.
2001 *Zapotec Science*. Austin: University of Texas Press.

Hansen, Edward C., and Timothy C. Parish
1983 Elites vs. the state. In *Elites: Ethnographic Issues*, edited by G. Marcus, pp. 257-77. Santa Fe: School of American Research Press.

Herskovits, Melville J.
1938 *Dahomey: An Ancient West African Kingdom*. 2 vols. New York City: J.J. Augustin.

Hodge, Mary
1996 Political organization of the central provinces. In *Aztec Imperial Strategies*, edited by F.F. Berdan, R.E. Blanton, E.H. Boone, M.G. Hodge, M.E. Smith, and E. Umberger, pp. 17-46. Washington, D.C.: Dumbarton Oaks.

Houston, Stephen, and David Stuart
1996 Of gods, glyphs, and kings: divinity and rulership among the Maya. *Antiquity* 70:289-312.

Hsu, Cho-yun
1995 The roles of the literati and of regionalism in the fall of the Han dynasty. In *The Collapse of Ancient States and Civilizations*, edited by N. Yoffee and G. Cowgill, pp. 176-95. Tucson: University of Arizona Press.

Joyce, Arthur A., and Marcus Winter
1996 Ideology, power and urban society in prehispanic Oaxaca. *Current Anthropology* 37:33-47.

Kaufman, Herbert
1995 The collapse of ancient states and civilizations as an organizational problem. In *The Collapse of Ancient States and Civilizations*, edited by N. Yoffee and G. Cowgill, pp. 219-35. Tucson: University of Arizona Press.

Kowalewski, Stephen A., Gary M. Feinman, Laura Finsten, and Richard E. Blanton
1991 Pre-hispanic ballcourts from the Valley of Oaxaca, Mexico. In *The Mesoamerican Ballgame*, edited by V.L. Scarborough and D.R. Wilcox, pp. 25-44. Tucson: University of Arizona Press.

Kowalewski, Stephen A., Gary M. Feinman, Laura Finsten, Richard E. Blanton, and Linda M. Nicholas
1989 *Monte Albán's Hinterland, Part II: Prehispanic Settlement Patterns in Tlacolula, Etla, and Ocotlán, the Valley of Oaxaca, Mexico*. Memoirs, no. 23. Museum of Anthropology, University of Michigan. Ann Arbor.

Kottak, Conrad P.
1980 *The Past in the Present: History, Ecology and Cultural Variation in Highland Madagascar*. Ann Arbor: University of Michigan Press.

Leslie, Charles
1960 *Now We Are Civilized: A Study of the World-View of the Zapotec Indians of Mitla, Oaxaca*. Detroit: Wayne State University Press.

Lesure, Richard
1997 Figurines and social identities in early sedentary societies of coastal Chiapas, Mexico, 1550-800 BC. In *Women in Prehistory*, edited by C. Claassen and R. Joyce, pp. 227-48. Philadelphia, PA: University of Pennsylvania Press.

Lipp, Frank J.
1991 *The Mixe of Oaxaca: Religion, Ritual, and Healing*. Austin: University of Texas Press.

Lockhart, James
1992 *The Nahuas After the Conquest*. Palo Alto, CA: Stanford University Press.

Lombard, J.
1967 The kingdom of Dahomey. In *West African Kingdoms in the Nineteenth Century*, edited by D. Forde and P.M. Kaberry, pp. 70-92. London: Oxford University Press.

López Austin, Alfredo, and Leonardo López Luján
2001 *Mexico's Indigenous Past*. Norman: University of Oklahoma Press.

López Luján, Leonardo, Laura Filloy Nadal, Barbara W. Fash, William L. Fash, and Pilar Hernández
2006 The destruction of images in Teotihuacán. *Res* 49/50:14-39.

Luttwak, Edward N.
1976 *The Grand Strategy of the Roman Empire from the First Century A.D. to the Third.* Baltimore, MD: Johns Hopkins University Press.

Marcus, George
1983 Elites as a concept, theory and research tradition. In *Elites: Ethnographic Issues*, edited by G. Marcus, pp. 7-28. Albuquerque: University of New Mexico Press.
1992 The concern with elites in archaeological reconstructions: Mesoamerican materials. In *Mesoamerican Elites: An Archaeological Assessment*, edited by D.Z. Chase and A.F. Chase, pp. 292-302. Norman: University of Oklahoma Press.

Marcus, Joyce
1976a The origins of Mesoamerican writing. *Annual Review of Anthropology* 5:35-67.
1976b The iconography of militarism at Monte Albán and neighboring sites in the Valley of Oaxaca. In *The Origins of Religious Art and Iconography in Preclassic Mesoamerica*, edited by H.B. Nicholson, pp. 123-39. Los Angeles: University of California-Los Angeles Latin American Center Publications.
1983a Monte Albán in the Macuilxochitl area. In *The Cloud People: Divergent Evolution of the Zapotec and Mixtec Civilizations*, edited by K.V. Flannery and J. Marcus, pp. 113-15. New York: Academic Press.
1983b The reconstructed chronology of the later Zapotec rulers. In *The Cloud People: Divergent Evolution of the Zapotec and Mixtec Civilizations*, edited by K.V. Flannery and J. Marcus, pp. 301-8. New York: Academic Press.
1983c Aztec military campaigns against the Zapotec: the documentary evidence. In *The Cloud People: Divergent Evolution of the Zapotec and Mixtec Civilizations*, edited by K.V. Flannery and J. Marcus, pp. 314-18. New York: Academic Press.
1983d Zapotec religion. In *The Cloud People: Divergent Evolution of the Zapotec and Mixtec Civilizations*, edited by K.V. Flannery and J. Marcus, pp. 345-51. New York: Academic Press.
1983e The conquest slabs of Building J, Monte Albán. In *The Cloud People: Divergent Evolution of the Zapotec and Mixtec Civilizations*, edited by K.V. Flannery and J. Marcus, pp. 106-8. New York: Academic Press.
1983f Stone monuments and tomb murals of Monte Albán IIIa. In *The Cloud People: Divergent Evolution of the Zapotec and Mixtec Civilizations*, edited by K.V. Flannery and J. Marcus, pp. 137-44. New York: Academic Press.
1983g Rethinking the Zapotec urn. In *The Cloud People: Divergent Evolution of the Zapotec and Mixtec Civilizations*, edited by K.V. Flannery and J. Marcus, pp. 144-48. New York: Academic Press.
1989 Zapotec chiefdoms and the nature of Formative religion. In *Regional Perspectives on the Olmec*, edited by R.J. Sharer and D.C. Grove, pp. 148-97. Cambridge: Cambridge University Press.
1992a Dynamic cycles of Mesoamerican states: political fluctuations in Mesoamerica. *National Geographic Research and Exploration* 8(4):392-411.
1992b *Mesoamerican Writing Systems: Propaganda, Myth, and History in Four Ancient Civilizations.* Princeton, NJ: Princeton University Press.
1998 *Women's Ritual in Formative Oaxaca.* Memoirs, no. 33. Museum of Anthropology, University of Michigan. Ann Arbor.
2006a Identifying elites and their strategies. In *Intermediate Elites in Pre-Columbian States and Empires*, edited by Christina M. Elson and R. Alan Covey, pp. 212-46. Tucson: University of Arizona Press.
2006b The role of ritual and technology in Mesoamerican water management. In *Agricultural Strategies*, edited by J. Marcus and C. Stanish, pp. 221-54. Monograph 50 in the Cotsen Institute of Archaeology series, UCLA, Los Angeles.

Marcus, Joyce, and Kent V. Flannery
1983 The Postclassic Balkanization of Oaxaca. In *The Cloud People: Divergent Evolution of the Zapotec and Mixtec Civilizations*, edited by K.V. Flannery and J. Marcus, pp. 217-26. New York: Academic Press.
1990 Science and science fiction in postclassic Oaxaca. In *Debating Oaxaca Archaeology*, edited by J. Marcus, pp. 191-205. Anthropological Papers, no. 84. Museum of Anthropology, University of Michigan. Ann Arbor.
1994 Ancient Zapotec religion and ritual: an application of the direct historical approach. In *The Ancient Mind*, edited by C. Renfew and E. Zubrow, pp. 55-74. Cambridge: Cambridge University Press.
1996 *Zapotec Civilization: How Urban Society Evolved in Mexico's Oaxaca Valley.* London: Thames and Hudson.

Martínez López, Cira
1998 *Contextos Mortuarios en Unidades Habitacionales de Monte Albán, Oaxaca, de la Epoca II Temprana a la Epoca V.* Licenciatura Tesis, Escuela Nacional de Antropología e Historia, México.

Martínez López, Cira, and Robert Markens
2004 Análisis de la función político-económico del conjunto Plataforma Norte lado poniente de la Plaza Principal de Monte Albán. In *Estructuras Políticas en el Oaxaca Antiguo*, edited by N.M. Robles García, pp. 75-99. Oaxaca: Instituto Nacional de Antropología e Historia.

Martínez López, Cira, and Marcus Winter
1994 *Figurillas y Silbatos de Cerámica de Monte Albán.* Proyecto Especial Monte Albán 1992-1994, no. 5. Oaxaca: INAH.

Martínez López, Cira, Robert Markens, Marcus Winter, and Michael D. Lind
2000 *La cerámica de la fase Xoo (Epoca Monte Albán IIIB-IV) del Valle de Oaxaca.* Proyecto Especial Monte Albán 1992-1994, no. 8. Oaxaca: INAH.

Martínez López, Cira, Marcus Winter, and Pedro Antonio Juárez
1995 Entierros Humanos del Proyecto Especial de Monte Albán. In *Entierros Humanos de Monte Albán: Dos Estudios*, edited by Marcus Winter, pp. 79-247. Proyecto Especial Monte Albán 1992-1994, no. 7. Oaxaca: INAH.

Marx, Karl, and Friedrich Engels
1848 [1969] *The Communist Manifesto.* Reprinted in *Marx/Engels Selected Works.* Vol. 1. Moscow, USSR: Progress Publishers.
1884 [1969] *The Origin of the Family, Private Property and the State.* Reprinted in *Marx/Engels Selected Works.* Vol. 3. Moscow, USSR: Progress Publishers.

McCall, John C.
1999 Structure, agency and the locus of the social: why poststructural theory is good for archaeology. In *Material Symbols: Culture and Economy in Prehistory*, edited by J.E. Robb, pp. 16-22. Occasional Papers, no. 26. Southern Illinois University. Carbondale.

McCaskie, Thomas C.
1995 *State and Society in Pre-Colonial Asante*. Cambridge: Cambridge University Press.

Miller, Arthur
1973 *The Mural Paintings of Teotihuacan*. Washington, D.C.: Dumbarton Oaks Research Library and Collection, Trustees for Harvard University.
1995 *The Painted Tombs of Oaxaca, Mexico*. Cambridge: Cambridge University Press.

Millon, René
1995 The last years of Teotihuacan dominance. In *The Collapse of Ancient States and Civilizations*, edited by N. Yoffee and G. Cowgill, pp. 102-64. Tucson: University of Arizona Press.

Mommsen, W.J.
1974 *The Age of Bureaucracy: Perspectives on the Political Sociology of Max Weber*. Oxford: Blackwell.
1989 *The Political and Social Theory of Max Weber: Collected Essays*. Chicago: University of Chicago Press.

Mosca, Gaetano
1939 *The Ruling Class*. New York: McGraw Hill.

Nicholas, Linda
1983 Land use in pre-hispanic Oaxaca. In *Monte Albán's Hinterland, Part II: Prehispanic Settlement Patterns in Tlacolula, Etla, and Ocotlán, the Valley of Oaxaca, Mexico*, by S.A. Kowalewski, G.M. Feinman, L. Finsten, R.E. Blanton, and L.M. Nicholas, pp. 449-506. Memoirs, no. 23. Museum of Anthropology, University of Michigan. Ann Arbor.

Obayemi, Ade
1976 The Yoruba and Edo-speaking peoples and their neighbors before 1600. In *History of West Africa*. Vol. 1, edited by J.F.A. Ajayi and Michael Crowder, pp. 196-263. New York: Columbia University Press.

Offner, Jerome A.
1983 *Law and Politics in Aztec Texcoco*. Cambridge: Cambridge University Press.

Ogburn, Dennis
2004 Dynamic display, propaganda, and the reinforcement of provincial power in the Inca empire. *Archeological Papers of the American Anthropological Association* 14(1):225-39.

Ortiz de Montellano, Bernard R.
1990 *Aztec Medicine, Health, and Nutrition*. New Brunswick: Rutgers University Press.

Oudijk, Michael
2000 *Historiography of the Bénizáa*. Netherlands: Universiteit Leiden.

Paddock, John
1955 The first three seasons at Yagul. *Mesoamerican Notes* 4:25-47.
1957 The 1956 season at Yagul. *Mesoamerican Notes* 5:13-35.
1960 Explorations in Yagul, Oaxaca. *Revista Mexicana de Estudios Antropológicos* 16:91-96.
1983 Lambityeco. In *The Cloud People: Divergent Evolution of the Zapotec and Mixtec Civilizations*, edited by K.V. Flannery and J. Marcus, pp. 197-204. New York: Academic Press.

Paddock, John (editor)
1966 *Ancient Oaxaca: Discoveries in Mexican Archeology and History*. Palo Alto, CA: Stanford University Press.

Paddock, John, Joseph R. Mogor, and Michael D. Lind
1968 Lambityeco Tomb 2: a preliminary report. *Boletín de Estudios Oaxaqueños* 25, Museo Frissell de Arte Zapoteca, Mitla, Oaxaca.

Paludan, Ann
1998 *Chronicle of the Chinese Emperors*. London: Thames and Hudson.

Pareto, Vilfredo
1935 *The Mind and Society*. New York: Harcourt, Brace and Company.
1950 *The Ruling Class in Italy Before 1900*. New York: S.F. Vanni.
1968 *The Rise and Fall of Elites: An Application of Theoretical Sociology*. Towota, NJ: Bedminster Press.

Parry, William J.
1987 *Chipped Stone Tools in Formative Oaxaca: Their Procurement, Production and Use*. Memoirs, no. 20. Museum of Anthropology, University of Michigan. Ann Arbor.

Parsons, Elsie Clews
1936 *Mitla: Town of the Souls and Other Zapoteco-Speaking Pueblos of Oaxaca*. Chicago: University of Chicago Press.

del Paso y Troncoso, Francisco
1905 *Papeles de Nueva España*. Vol. 4. Est. Tipográfico Sucesores de Rivadeneyra, Madrid.

Pollard, Helen P.
1993 *Taríacuri's Legacy: The Prehispanic Tarascan State*. Norman: University of Oklahoma Press.

Quezada, Sergio
1993 *Pueblos y Caciques Yucatecos, 1550-1580*. Mexico City: El Colegio de Mexico.

Rapoport, Amos
1993 On the nature of capitals and their physical expression. In *Capital Cities: International Perspectives*, edited by J. Taylor, J.G. Lengellé, and C. Andrews, pp. 31-67. Ottawa: Carlton University Press.

Redmond, Elsa M.
1983 *A Fuego y Sangre: Early Zapotec Imperialism in the Cuicatlán Cañada, Oaxaca*. Memoirs, no. 16. Museum of Anthropology, University of Michigan. Ann Arbor.

Redmond, Elsa M., and Charles S. Spencer
1982 Chiefdom and state in Formative Oaxaca. *Journal of the Steward Anthropological Society* 13:7-38.

Reilly, F. Kent, and James F. Garber
2003 The symbolic representation of warfare in Formative period Mesoamerica. In *Ancient Mesoamerican Warfare*, edited by M. Kathryn Brown and Travis W. Stanton, pp. 127-48. Walnut Creek, CA: AltaMira.

Restall, Matthew
1997 *The Maya World*. Stanford, CA: Stanford University Press.

Ritchie, William A.
1938 A perspective of northeastern archaeology. *American Antiquity* IV:94-112.

Robertson, Donald
1983a An analysis of Monte Albán II architecture. In *The Cloud People: Divergent Evolution of the Zapotec and Mixtec Civilizations*, edited by K.V. Flannery and J. Marcus, pp. 105-6. New York: Academic Press.
1983b Functional analysis of architecture at Monte Albán. In *The Cloud People: Divergent Evolution of the Zapotec and Mixtec Civilizations*, edited by K.V. Flannery and J. Marcus, p. 131. New York: Academic Press.

Roth, D.H., and C. Wittich (editors)
1968 *Economy and Society: An Outline of Interpretive Sociology*. 3 vols. New York: Bedminster Press.

Sanders, William T., and Barbara J. Price
1968 *Mesoamerica: The Evolution of a Civilization*. New York: Random House.

Scarborough, Vernon L., and David R. Wilcox (editors)
1991 *The Mesoamerican Ballgame*. Tucson: University of Arizona Press.

Scullard, Howard H.
1980 *A History of the Roman World 753 to 146 B.C.*, 4th ed. London: Methuen and Co.

Service, Elman R.
1975 *Origins of the State and Civilization*. New York: W.W. Norton and Company.

Shepard, Anna
1967 Preliminary notes on the paste composition of Monte Albán pottery. In *La Cerámica de Monte Albán*, by A. Caso, I. Bernal, and J. Acosta, pp. 477-84. Memorias del Instituto Nacional de Antropología e Historia, 13. Mexico: Instituto Nacional de Antropología e Historia.

Sherman, R. Jason
2005 *Settlement Heterogeneity in the Zapotec State: A View from Yaasuchi, Oaxaca, Mexico*. PhD dissertation, University of Michigan, Ann Arbor.

Sherman, R. Jason, Leah Minc, Christina M. Elson, Charles S. Spencer, and Elsa M. Redmond
2004 *The Preliminary Results of Trace-Element Analysis on Pottery from Periods Monte Albán I and Monte Albán II from the Sites of El Palenque, Cerro Tilcajete, and Yaasuchi (Oaxaca, Mexico)*. American Museum of Natural History, New York, http://anthro.amnh.org.

Sidky, H.
1996 *Irrigation and State Formation in Hunza: The Anthropology of a Hydraulic Kingdom*. Lanham, MD: University Press of America.

Smith, Michael E.
1987 Household possessions and wealth in agrarian states: implications for archaeology. *Journal of Anthropological Archaeology* 6:297-335.
1996 *The Aztecs*. Cambridge, MA: Blackwell Publishers, Inc.

Smith, Michael E., and Mary Hodge
1994 An introduction to Late Postclassic economies and polities. In *Economies and Polities in the Aztec Realm*, edited by M.G. Hodge and M.E. Smith, pp. 1-42. Albany: Institute for Mesoamerican Studies, State University of New York.

Smyth, Michael P.
1991 *Modern Maya Storage Behavior*. University of Pittsburgh Memoirs in Latin American Anthropology, no. 3. Pittsburgh, PA.

Spence, Michael W., Christine D. White, Fred J. Longstaffe, and Kimberley R. Law
2004 Victims of the victims: human trophies worn by sacrificed soldiers from the Feathered Serpent Pyramid, Teotihuacan. *Ancient Mesoamerica* 15:1-15.

Spencer, Charles S.
1982 *The Cuicatlán Cañada and Monte Albán: A Study of Primary State Formation*. New York: Academic Press.
1990 On the tempo and mode of state formation: neoevolutionism reconsidered. *Journal of Anthropological Archaeology* 9:1-30.
1998 A mathematical model of primary state formation. *Cultural Dynamics* 10(1):5-20.
1999 Palatial digs. *Natural History* 108(2):94-95.

Spencer, Charles S., and Elsa M. Redmond
1997 *Archaeology of the Cañada de Cuicatlán, Oaxaca*. American Museum of Natural History Anthropology Papers 80. New York.
2000 Lightning and jaguars: iconography, ideology, and politics in Formative Cuicatlán Cañada. In *Cultural Evolution: Contemporary Viewpoints*, edited by G.M. Feinman and L. Manzanilla, pp. 145-75. New York: Academic Press.
2001a Multilevel selection and political evolution in the Valley of Oaxaca, Mexico. *Journal of Anthropological Archaeology* 20:195-229.
2001b The chronology of conquest: implications of new radiocarbon analysis from the Cañada de Cuicatlán, Oaxaca. *Latin American Antiquity* 12(2):182-202.
2004 Primary state formation in Mesoamerica. *Annual Review of Anthropology* 33:173-99.

Spores, Ronald
1965 The Zapotec and Mixtec at Spanish conquest. In *Handbook of Middle American Indians*. Vol. 3, part 2, *Archaeology of Southern Mesoamerica*, edited by G.R. Willey, pp. 962-87. Austin: University of Texas Press.

Spores, Ronald, and Kent V. Flannery
1983 Sixteenth-century kinship and social organization. In *The Cloud People: Divergent Evolution of the Zapotec and Mixtec Civilizations*, edited by K.V. Flannery and J. Marcus, pp. 339-42. New York: Academic Press.

Stanworth, Phillip, and Anthony Giddens (editors)
1974 *Elites and Power in British Societies*. Cambridge: Cambridge University Press.

Strong, William Duncan
1933 The Plains culture area in the light of archaeology. *American Anthropologist* 35:271-87.

Taylor, William B.
1972 *Landlord and Peasant in Colonial Oaxaca*. Palo Alto, CA: Stanford University Press.

Thieme, Mary
2001 Continuity of ceramic production: an examination and analysis of ceramic production from Santa María Atzompa. In *Procesos de Cambio y Conceptualización del Tiempo, Memoria de la Primera Mesa Redonda de Monte Albán*, edited by N.M. Robles García, pp. 339-49. Oaxaca: Instituto Nacional de Antropología e Historia.

Thompson, Philip C.
1999 *Tekanto, A Maya town in Colonial Yucatan*. Middle American Research Institute, Publication 67, Tulane University. New Orleans.

Trigger, Bruce G.
1990 Monumental architecture: a thermodynamic explanation of symbolic world behavior. *World Archaeology* 22(2):119-32.

Upham, S.
1987 A theoretical consideration of middle range societies. In *Chiefdoms in the Americas*, edited by R.D. Drennan and C.A. Uribe, pp. 345-68. Lanham, MD: University Press of America.

Weber, Max
1976 *Wirtschaft und Gesellschaft*, edited by J. Winckelmann. Tübingen.

Webster, David L.
2002 *The Fall of the Ancient Maya: Solving the Mystery of Maya Collapse*. London: Thames and Hudson.

Wedel, Waldo R.
1938 The direct-historical approach in Pawnee archaeology. *Smithsonian Miscellaneous Collections* 97(7). Washington, D.C.

Whalen, Michael E.
1981 *Excavations at Santo Domingo Tomaltepec: The Evolution of a Formative Community in the Valley of Oaxaca, Mexico*. Memoirs, no. 12. Museum of Anthropology, University of Michigan. Ann Arbor.

Whitecotton, Joseph W.
1977 *The Zapotecs: Princes, Priests, and Peasants*. Norman: University of Oklahoma Press.

Whitecotton, Joseph W., and Judith Bradley Whitecotton
1993 *Vocabulario zapoteco-castellano*. Vanderbilt University Publications in Anthropology, no. 45. Nashville, TN: Vanderbilt University.

Williams, Aubrey W.
1973 Dietary patterns in three Mexican villages. In *Man and his Foods: Studies in the Ethnobotany of Nutrition*, edited by C.E. Smith, pp. 51-73. Birmingham: University of Alabama Press.

Winter, Marcus
1974 Residential patterns at Monte Albán, Oaxaca, México. *Science* 186:981-87.
1986 Templo, patio, adoratorio: un conjunto arquitectónico no residencial en Oaxaca prehispánico. *Cuadernos de Arquitectura Mesoamericana* 7:51-59.
1989 La Obsidiana en Oaxaca Prehispánica. In *La Obsidiana en Mesoamérica*, edited by M. Gaxiola and J. Clark, pp. 345-61. Mexico: Instituto Nacional de Antropología e Historia (Col. Científica).
1994 El Proyecto Especial Monte Albán 1992-1994: antecedentes, intervenciones y perspectivas. In *Monte Albán, Estudios Recientes*, edited by Marcus Winter, pp. 1-24. Proyecto Especial Monte Albán 1992-1994, no. 2. Oaxaca: INAH.

Winter, Marcus (editor)
1994a *Monte Albán, Estudios Recientes*. Proyecto Especial Monte Albán 1992-1994, no. 2. Oaxaca: INAH.
1994b *Escritura Zapoteca Prehispánica*. Proyecto Especial Monte Albán 1992-1994, no. 4. Oaxaca: INAH.
1995 *Entierros Humanos de Monte Albán: Dos Estudios*. Proyecto Especial Monte Albán 1992-1994, no. 7. Oaxaca: INAH.

Winter, Marcus, William O. Autry, Jr., Richard G. Wilkinson, and Cira Martínez López
1995 Entierros Humanos en una area residencial de Monte Albán: Temporadas 1972-1973. In *Entierros Humanos de Monte Albán: Dos Estudios*, edited by Marcus Winter, pp. 11-78. Proyecto Especial Monte Albán 1992-1994, no. 7. Oaxaca: INAH.

Wright, Henry T.
1977 Recent research on the origin of the state. *Annual Review of Anthropology* 6:379-97.
1986 The evolution of civilizations. In *American Archaeology: Past and Future*, edited by D. Meltzer, D. Fowler, and J. Sabloff, pp. 323-65. Washington, D.C.: Smithsonian Institution Press.